THE WEEKEND
CONNOISSEUR

THE WEEKEND CONNOISSEUR

*The Antique Collector's
Guide to the Best in
Antiquing, Dining, Regional
Museums, and Just Plain
Lovely Things to Do
When Touring*

JOAN BRAGIN

*Dolphin Books
Doubleday & Company, Inc., Garden City, New York*
1979 .

Library of Congress Cataloging in Publication Data
Bragin, Joan.
The weekend connoisseur.
1. Antique dealers—New England—Directories.
2. Historic buildings—New England—Directories.
3. Museums—New England—Directories.   4. Restaurants,
lunch rooms, etc.—New England—Directories.   5. Antique
dealers—Middle Atlantic States—Directories.   6. Historic
buildings—Middle Atlantic States—Directories.
7. Museums—Middle Atlantic States—Directories.
8. Restaurants, lunch rooms, etc.—Middle Atlantic
States—Directories.   I. Title.
NK1127.B6   381'.45'745102574
ISBN: 0-385-13465-7
Library of Congress Catalog Card Number 78–1187

Maps by Rafael D. Palacios
Drawings by Mona Mark

CONTENTS

INTRODUCTION

This book is dedicated to all those adventurous spirits for whom antiquing is the essence of feeling alive. There is simply no joy to compare with the sense of expectation a collector feels when on the road looking for the next treasure. However, even the most intrepid antiquer has been done in by the information available in many travel-guide books. The reason is simple: They have not been organized for the collector's special needs. It is important not only to know where the best antique dealers are, but what are the good restaurants, inns, and museums in the immediate vicinity of a specific shop.

Only what I consider quality dealers are listed in this book. Some are very famous, others almost unknown except to a chosen few. All of them have certain attributes in common which are essential to a collector, namely, knowledge, taste, and reliability. The painful truth is, the vast majority of dealers in this country know next to nothing about what they are selling. What is even worse, most believe they have the necessary expertise to sell objects that now cost thousands of dollars. These dealers are rather like typhoid carriers, passing on spurious information and material, often quite innocently. Obviously, this is a subjective list based largely on my own experience as an antiquer, which has been very extensive. However, interestingly enough, when I cross-referenced my choices among a number of very knowledgeable people, both in and out of the trade, we all came up with almost exactly the same basic names. I enlarged the list to include some first-rate, but less-known picker-dealers and a few young dealers that I felt have a natural flair for the business.

The great dealers are an essential part of the collector's education. These are the dealers who handle the most important material, set the price trends, and whose expertise is unmatched. Not visiting a Sack, Walton, or Kindig is like touring the Metropolitan and not bothering to see the Rembrandts. There is no way a collector can learn to match wits with a dealer, namely, spot the bargain before it becomes the treasure, unless he knows what constitutes a treasure. There is no way to read this expertise. You've got to see it. You cannot touch in a museum, you can in a shop. There are endless varieties of eighteenth-century New England highboys. Can you tell the difference between a fair, good, excellent, or superb example? Only by seeing the very best that is available, can a collector begin to judge the relative value of the pieces being offered to him. The fear of the so-called fancy dealer is an old-fashioned prejudice that is long overdue for burial.

At least 70 per cent of the dealers listed would be classified as moderately priced. These are the dealers who sell the good-to-excellent material that constitutes the bulk of the antique business. Most of them sell as actively to other dealers as they do to private collectors. In that sense, all dealers are pickers. A picker is the term used in the trade to describe the people who find material for the dealers. I have classified a number of dealers as picker-dealers because they maintain shops that do supply private collectors, but their business is primarily geared to other dealers. The people I have listed as pickers do not keep a regular shop and 99 per cent of their business is trade. However, if they are in this book, a private collector is always welcome.

The young dealers I've selected obviously will not have the vast store of knowledge that only experience can give, but they all have an instinct for buying. If you know what you are doing, it is often among this group of dealers that the occasional treasure turns up, undiscovered.

A problem with the kinds of antique-shop listings that usually found is that they are too general in their information. What I have done is to be as specific as possible in my listings of what dealers specialize in. Nothing, for example, is noted simply as porcelain, which is a meaningless word to the collector. The book explains what kinds of porcelain, painting, silver, or furniture is available. Whenever possible I have selected particular objects to describe which are typical of the kind of material you will find at the dealer. The shop may not have that specific piece when you visit, but it will undoubtedly have something very similar to it.

Every antiquer has faced at one time or another an eccentric dealer. I have tried, when possible, to indicate something of the dealer's personality. Antiquing is a delicate dance at best, but it does help to know the steps.

Incidentally, even the most exclusive dealers can be negotiated with, as far as price is concerned. It will not be possible on everything but if you are serious about a piece, I've never known a dealer not to try to come to terms. Most dealers are perfectly willing to arrange a payment plan for a collector. For many of us it is the only way we can afford to buy what we love. Ninety per cent of the collectors today are middle income. They support all the dealers including the expensive ones. The people who jam the auction houses all over the country are not the Rockefellers. They are the people who listen to educational television, stand on endless lines at the museums, pack esoteric concerts. They are the appreciators. They are the people for whom this book is written. To me the word connoisseur means an appreciator—someone who values the special pleasures of living.

I have also listed the local museums and interesting historic houses in the vicinity of dealers. Museums and historic houses are an essential part of a collector's life. They, in combination with the good dealers, help you round out your own point of view by developing your ability to evaluate what you are being offered. As prices continue to rise, it becomes more and more important to know exactly what you are buying and if it is the best quality available that you can afford. When a museum has what I feel is something very special in its collection, I do suggest you see it. If there is a beautiful walk to take, I mention that also.

I have organized the book around the dealers or, in a few instances where I felt there was no interesting antiquing, fine historic houses and museums. The restaurants and inns have been chosen not only for their quality, but their proximity to a particular dealer. In a few instances, I have had to settle for just food, rather than fine dining, because there wasn't a restaurant of distinction relatively near the dealer, and eating is essential, even to a passionate antiquer. I much prefer small inns to the anonymous motel chains. However, in some cases, there was nothing in the locality except a Holiday Inn or Howard Johnson to recommend. Unhappily, for those of you who love to travel without a definite destination in mind, reservations are essential at inns and restaurants.

What I hope this guide will do is create a total experience of such pleasure that even if you buy nothing, you will have a marvelous time.

THE WEEKEND
CONNOISSEUR

I

Land of Milk and Honey

Connecticut and Rhode Island are the chosen land: the verdant hills of Litchfield, dotted with villages unblemished by time, whose greens lack only the presence of a stray sheep or cow to recreate a Constable landscape; the harbor towns of Essex and Stonington, whose sailboats, safely tucked away at their moorings, move swanlike in gentle harmony with the ocean breezes. Travel up the old coast road to Providence, a well-named city, whose beautiful eighteenth-century past has been tastefully restored with the transformation of Benefit Street from a sad relic of another century into a vividly alive element of the city's life. Finally, returning again to the sea, there is Newport, that fascinating combination of eighteenth-century architectural restraint and the ultimate opulence of the great summer cottages, built as seasonal divertissements by the Vanderbilts and their friends. Connecticut and Rhode Island are, indeed, a land of milk and honey.

EASTERN CONNECTICUT

Antique Dealers

Robert Spencer
Spencer & Judd
Essex Square
Essex, Conn. 06426
(203) 767-8655

Appointment advisable

The town of Essex, Connecticut, possesses in miniature everything collectors hope to find, but rarely do, in their travels—a beautiful sailing harbor, fine restaurants, a tiny village square that isn't particularly square, and a talented antique dealer named Robert Spencer. For some reason I can't fathom, perhaps it's due to the gentleness of this dealer's personality, it is easy to underestimate the quality of his stock at first glance; so be sure to bear this in mind when going through the shop. Though Bob Spencer deals primarily in eighteenth-century New England furniture, he has a marvelous feeling for scrimshaw and eighteenth-century American and English silver. The single French example he had was a most extraordinary teapot, *circa* 1797, made for the English ambassador to France, who was a Scotsman. The teapot's decoration was marvelously extravagant with its eagle-head spout and swan finial on the cover. An English eighteenth-century silver coffee pot by Wickes, *circa* 1739–40, was a strange combination of very rococco embellishments on a simple Georgian pot, which was probably the result of the silversmith's client choosing an existing pot but wanting it done up in the latest fashion. This happened quite frequently and the results are sometimes delightfully unexpected. The only caution a silver collector must remember is that a piece with later decoration, even if done in the eighteenth century, is not as valuable. In the case of the Wickes pot, the decoration was original. Eighteenth-century American silver moves very rapidly in this shop as the prices are definitely not top of the market.

Robert Spencer exhibits at most of the major antique shows around the country and the merchandise reflects different regional points of view. The decorative accessories include small American genre paintings, English eighteenth-century Staffordshire, China Export, and bits of brass such as candlesticks, tea and tobacco boxes, and andirons. The most interesting of the decorative items were a number of Chinese port-scene paintings that were really very charming. A wonderful carrousel horse, made by C. W. F. Dare of Greenpoint, Brooklyn, was a terrific piece of folk art.

Though the shop's total inventory is small, the eighteenth-century American furniture is of excellent quality. A well-proportioned Connecticut cherry oxbow chest had blocked drawers, an unusual refinement, and good strong ogee feet. The Chippendale mahogany chest with ball-and-claw feet is a classic Boston/Salem piece. The surprise in the shop was a fine English Chippendale commode of a quality you seldom see outside of New York City. The pleasant part of buying an English chest from an American furniture dealer is, of course, the price, which is lower than a comparable American chest. Reflecting back to an earlier period is the inlaid border detail on the drawer fronts of a Rhode Island maple chest-on-chest. This particular herringbone pattern was very popular in William and Mary and Queen Anne English furniture. This overlapping of styles is a consistent feature of American furniture. In addition to small side tables, there is always at least one fine dining table in stock. A good Willard clock (and Bob Spencer loves clocks) was overshadowed by a beautiful English grandfather clock in red japanned lacquer by James Jordan, *circa* 1709. Absolutely gorgeous clock.

Robert Spencer, a lovely dealer, and the town of Essex provide a delightful antiquing experience.

F. Bealey
35 Main Street
Essex, Conn. 06426
(203) 767-0220

Sundays (all year) 2–4. April–November: Wednesday–Saturday 11–4
December–March: Friday, Saturday 11–4
Call before, if traveling any distance

This is as tiny a shop as you are likely to find in your travels. Its size obviously limits the amount of stock but what there is, is real. Mr. Bealey specializes in what he likes to call good American eighteenth- and nineteenth-century fireplace furniture. The andirons range from simple Federal pairs that can be bought for under $400 to signed eighteenth-century Boston makers that cost over $7,000. The shop is especially proud of having furnished all the fireplace equipment to the first floor of Boscobel.

The American eighteenth-century furniture is predominately country in feeling, with rush-seated ladder-back chairs, small simple tables, blanket chests, and an occasional side table. The folk art, which is nineteenth-century American, includes quilts, weather vanes, pottery. There is always a group of early American kitchen fireplace objects in both iron and brass. Oriental rugs are bought whenever possible as are nineteenth- and twentieth-century American genre painting. There are just bits of porcelains and glass.

What is nice about this dealer, aside from being a very pleasant gentleman, is the consistency of taste. He buys what he loves, even though the shop is the size of a dime. The prices are fair, and if you are knowledgeable, this is the kind of dealer who can turn up a very pleasant surprise on occasion.

Hastings House
Village Square
Essex, Conn. 06426
(203) 767-8217

Summer: June 15–September 15
Monday–Saturday 10–5
All other times, appointment advisable

This delightfully eclectic shop has a selection of tastefully chosen antiques, but its basic point of view is to provide decorative accessories, be they new or old, for the home. Their unique specialty is seventeenth- to nineteenth-century Japanese screens known as Byobu, which translates as wind screens. These exquisite pieces, which were painted on commission, functioned on two levels. The utilitarian purpose was as a room divider; the aesthetic, to create a pleasing environment. The decoration is based on Chinese painting. Sumi is a school of screen painting where the drawing is done in pen and ink on beige paper, making for a monochromatic look. This style first appeared in the fifteenth century. Two other well-known schools of screen painting are Kanō and Tosa which developed late in the sixteenth century. Kanō screens usually illustrate nature themes while the Tosa style depict figural scenes of daily life, both in colorful detail. There is almost nothing more attractive than these beautifully painted gold-ground paper screens with their brocaded borders.

The antique furniture available is generally seventeenth-, eighteenth-, and nineteenth-century English and French country oak chests and tables. These are usually oversized and meant to be treated more as pieces of sculpture than furniture.

The African art consists of small wood figures and artifacts. An exceptional African piece, when I was there, was an Ashanti throne chair shown in all its glory. A large assortment of North American Indian items such as pottery, basketry, jewelry, textiles, and a group of oriental lacquer and cloissoné were also to be seen. Among the wall decorations were American signs, carved-wood flowers, decoys, and modern painting. For the ornithologist, a huge antique English birdcage was a charming fantasy.

If you are interested in unusual but not necessarily antique decorative pieces, this shop has some marvelous things. Even the most serious antiquer will enjoy the gallery's flair.

Jane Wilson
One Hammock Street
Old Saybrook, Conn.
(203) 388-9547

Call before arriving
Always open when home

The fear of stumbling into a den of cutesyness has always kept me out of those little annexes that sit behind houses like a hiccup. Though Jane Wilson's shop bears a physical resemblance to those of ladies who keep bits of glass, her stock is another world. Mrs. Wilson, a fine old dealer, is famous for specializing in the blue and white China Export patterns, Canton and Nanking. I doubt if there is anyone else who regularly keeps as large an inventory of it as she does. Plates, platters, tureens of every size are available. Cups and saucers, also in various sizes, are found by the dozen. At one time or another, she has had every form that was ever produced in the Canton ware. The rarer items are now very costly. It is amusing to remember that this china was mainly used as ship ballast during the nineteenth century and ended up as kitchen pottery in most homes. Now, every museum must have its example! Mrs. Wilson has written three books on Canton ware. If you are interested in either starting or enlarging your collection, this is a dealer you'll enjoy meeting.

The shop also has pieces of Rose Medallion porcelain and various brass forms including candlesticks. There is a small amount of eighteenth-century American furniture. It is difficult to know what you may come across in furniture at this dealer's because she does almost all her buying locally out of private homes.

There are not too many dealers like Mrs. Wilson left in the business and it is always a pleasure to meet what I call an old-time trader. They really are a special breed. The shop is open seven days a week except for the three times a year when Mrs. Wilson packs up for the Boston, Washington, and Philadelphia antique shows.

Marguerite Riordan
8 Pearl Street
Stonington, Conn. 06378
(203) 535-2511

By appointment only

One of the most dramatic antiquing experiences I've ever had was provided for me by the weather and Marguerite Riordan. The day I visited Mrs. Riordan's marvelous house in Stonington, one of nature's wilder fall storms hit with incredible fury. Standing at the rain-lashed windows of the second-floor gallery overlooking the harbor, I had the eerie sensation of being at a ship's prow rather than in an antique shop. I suspect that, when Marguerite Riordan designed her second floor, this was precisely the effect she wanted to achieve. The steely-gray light heightened the pleasure of looking at her superb collection of American primitive painting and fine eighteenth-century New England furniture. I have always found Joseph Stock an interesting artist but imagine seeing his portrait of the child Martha Randall illuminated by lightning. The painting looked fantastic. Sadly, so was its price. Marguerite Riordan, a very straightforward, pleasant lady, is one of the major dealers in folk art and New England furniture in the country today. Aside from the essential requisites of knowledge, taste, and a gambler's instinct, she has a natural flair for the unusual. When this dealer buys a nest of Chinese Canton platters, they are the largest size anyone has ever seen, quite capable of feeding fifty. Considering the price of Canton today, it is difficult to remember this was considered kitchenware in the nineteenth century.

This is a dealer who doesn't simply buy pretty pictures: Her taste in art is first rate and covers most of the prominent primitives such as Prior, Field, Ammi Phillips, Stock, Samuel Gerry, and Blount, the velvet painter. These pictures are now uniformly expensive, but for the collector buying at that level, these artists command the price and Mrs. Riordan's selection is excellent. The young collector is by no means priced out of the art market at this dealer's. Fine quality embroidered painting is still available at reasonable prices. Many of these silk and water-color embroidery pictures, *circa* 1790–1810, were done by young ladies at finishing school. A delightful example was one signed by Louise Bellows, who attended Miss Patton's School in Hartford. The shop always has a large collection of great samplers, which, if not at preinflation prices, are still good values for the quality offered.

Quality is the key word for this dealer. At whatever level you are buying, from the simplest candlestand to a great Connecticut highboy, Mrs. Riordan offers the finest examples of the particular category she can find. Her stock of folk art—quilts; weather vanes in such unusual forms as dogs, roosters, and cocks; wood carvings; decoys; weaving material; hooked rugs; baskets—are all chosen with a great sense of form and color. If there are large burl bowls to be had, the shop tries to have the biggest and most exciting examples. Technically, it may not belong with the folk art but there is always a selection of children's furniture.

Marguerite Riordan is not a block-front dealer. She prefers the

quiet elegance of the simpler New England forms, best exemplified by an untouched eighteenth-century Queen Anne
cherry highboy from Glastonbury, Connecticut, covered with two
hundred years of smoke and dirt and unpolished brasses. This
piece has a wonderful look as does a slant-front Chippendale
cherry desk, from either Massachusetts or Rhode Island, with
bracket feet and with its original finish. A more formal point of
view were a pair of Hepplewhite card tables by Lloyd, from
Springfield, Massachusetts. This dealer specializes in windsors
and always has a large selection in addition to simpler Connecticut Chippendale chairs. The tables range from Queen Anne to
Hepplewhite in all sizes and shapes. There is always a stock of
chests, corner cupboards, beds, and even a charming country sofa
or two.

Mrs. Riordan is an extremely active dealer and the stock
changes constantly. Don't be surprised to find some European
pieces in the shop. Stonington was an old seaport and its ships
traveled everywhere. English chairs were not unexpected, but a·
magnificent Scandinavian trestle table, *circa* 1750, was a real treasure. The porcelains include English Staffordshire, American pottery, and occasionally China Export. This dealer will buy anything of quality, no matter what its country of origin, provided it
looks as if it belongs with the American pieces in the shop. There
are even some very amusing nineteenth-century Victorian and
Gothic furniture.

If I've described a large and varied stock, that is exactly what
the gallery contains. It is a fascinating place for every level of collector, including the novice, and in all probability you will find
something you can't live without.

Jerome Blum
Willow Corner
Ross Hill Road
Lisbon, Conn. 06351 (Jewett City)
(203) 376-0300

Appointment preferred

The advantage of the knowledgeable collector turned dealer

is the unusually developed sense of personal taste they bring to their selection of material. This element of taste is what particularly distinguishes Jerome Blum as a dealer in eighteenth-century New England country furniture and eighteenth- and nineteenth-century accessories. He has loved furniture and porcelains all his life, and his selectivity is evident in his delightful shop. The furniture is country, the taste elegant. The stock is not large but nothing is a throwaway. You cannot escape feeling that even the smallest piece of English eighteenth-century Staffordshire has been carefully chosen for the particular qualities that please Jerry Blum's eye. Mr. Blum is a reserved man until he starts discussing something he loves, then the constraints happily seem to disappear. He is especially interested in young collectors, having traveled that road himself years ago. The other advantage to collector-dealers is they never stop buying what fascinates them, even if the possibilities of selling it are nil. The result is an excellent chance of finding a completely unexpected object. The day I visited the shop there was a magnificent late eighteenth-century Chinese embroidered silk coverlet, in the European manner, made for the export market. Exquisite, fragile, perfect for a restoration museum. Jerry Blum couldn't resist buying it, and it took great self-control on my part to keep from walking out with it tucked under my arm.

The predominantly New England furniture is simple, not primitive, with very fine lines. A Massachusetts Queen Anne cherry highboy with maple sides best exemplified this elegant simplicity as did a daintily proportioned Connecticut Queen Anne cherry desk on frame with cabriole legs and pad feet. This particular piece was made even more delightful by its being a little bandy-legged. For me, the most charming element of country copies of city pieces of this period are their imperfections. I love furniture that has humor even when it's inadvertent. An eighteenth-century tripod table has been japanned during the Victorian era, turning it into a very stylish, if not entirely legitimate, piece for the purist. Six country Queen Anne Spanish-foot spoon-back chairs were lovely examples as were a set of six bow-backed windsors. I still find myself shocked at the price of bow backs today. Most of us remember them as the lowliest of kitchen chairs and it takes some adjusting when sets bring thousands of dollars. I feel the young collector would be much better off putting that kind of money into a major piece such as a chest, desk, or even a highboy. There were a number of ladder- and banister-back chairs, a variety of small tables, including tavern and gateleg, and as always at least one fine Queen Anne dining table.

The assortment of accessories is not large, but I found marvelous examples of primitive paintings (mainly portraits), small English and Dutch brass tobacco boxes, including a brass honor box for tobacco used in a tavern. The name is self-explanatory. The iron kitchen and fireplace ware, which is always available, are pieces of sculpture, one of the rarest being a signed 1820 rotisserie. The shop's folk art collection is terrific. There are cow, horse, rooster, eagle weather vanes, whirligigs, and a wonderful, decorative carved wood-horse sign. Jerome Blum is a solidly priced dealer, but I found his folk art very reasonable for its quality. The early quilts are usually sold to dealers. As a matter of fact, a great deal of this shop's folk art and paintings do end up at other dealers who rely on Mr. Blum's fine eye for decorative art.

I've left for last the shop's collection of porcelain which is predominantly eighteenth-century Staffordshire with classic examples of Whieldon, Leeds, Bow, and Mocha ware. The selection is limited but choice. The pleasures of visiting this dealer are many, including the charm of the shop itself, and if you find your taste in antiques similar to Jerry Blum's, the visit will prove to be only the first of many.

John Walton Antiques
Crary Road
Griswold, Conn.
Mailing address: Box 307, Jewett City, Conn. 06351
(203) 376-0862

By appointment only

There is a storybook quality to the setting of John Walton Antiques. The eighteenth-century red house with its huge red barn and adjoining ice house are situated at the junction of a beautiful, winding country road. Nothing could be more idyllic as you travel back to that earlier period except perhaps Mr. Walton's personality which, even in that unique world of great American antique dealers famous for their idiosyncrasies, is outstanding. He is tough, brusque, ornery, and marvelous. Along with Sack and Kindig, Mr. Walton belongs to that legendary group of dealer experts. Dealers agree about almost nothing except their respect for these giants of the American antique world. The collector who buys from Mr. Walton is considered special indeed.

When the shop was located in New York City the firm sold both the very finest formal and country American furniture; now that Mr. Walton has returned to rural Connecticut, he prefers dealing primarily in country pieces. This is not the so-called primitive country furniture but rather the most superb examples of, primarily, New England eighteenth-century craftsmanship available. The barn is a huge cavern filled with the simpler furniture. I found in the pecking order of buildings that each has its treasures. The barn does contain many country tables of all descriptions from pine-topped tavern tables to dining tables to tray-top center-pedestal ones. A few of the tables and a magnificent pencil-post bed had what Mr. Walton calls original paint. He cautions that probably 95 per cent of the pieces claiming to have the original paint, do not. The expertise necessary to make this determination is something that takes many years of experience. I was fascinated to learn that one of the original ingredients of eighteenth-century paint was buttermilk. Generally, the best way to determine paint age is by scraping down to the wood, invariably these pieces have been painted again and again. Don't believe a single coat or two, simple logic would tell you that after two hundred years of wear nothing could be left of the color. Incidentally, paint dating from as late as 1860 is perfectly acceptable.

The beautifully detailed corner cupboards or a fine camel-back sofa in the frame are hardly my idea of simple country furniture. The many blanket chests, windsors, and banister-back chairs certainly do fit into this category, as did a particularly delightful three-drawer chest painted to simulate wood graining. New England tables, chests, and even desks abound, but I was especially taken with a small drop-front Queen Anne desk that had the most primitive shell on the lid. Unquestionably, the country cousin of a city piece, it couldn't have been more charmingly ungainly. Mr. Walton loves miniature pieces and buys them whenever they are absolutely right. I must repeat this is his criterion for all his furniture no matter what the price. This dealer handles some of the most valuable and expensive furniture on the market. When John Walton finds a great piece he must have, price is no object. Like Sack, he has set records in the antique world. A word more about miniature furniture: most of them are children's pieces and toys rather than cabinetmakers' samples. There is a great casualness about the way furniture is displayed in the barn. I managed to trip over a drake-foot Queen Anne chair right into a fine Connecticut highboy. Fortunately, we all ended up intact.

The Ice House is a small building packed with gorgeous furniture. A Goddard Townsend mahogany Chippendale desk in pristine condition had all its original brass, including side handles and ogee feet. Another Newport piece, a mahogany tea table of extremely fine quality, was marred by the sad condition of its original top. Mr. Walton's attitude toward repairs is to do the least amount necessary. His feelings are, with this quality table, to leave the top alone except for wax and a little filler. The degree of restoration determines the value of an important piece. A lowboy with a new top is worth a fraction of its original value, a new leg would reduce the value by about half, but repairs or patches to the pads would only make a nominal difference. In addition, the Ice House contained a number of great chests, a fan-back windsor with its original writing arm, and the first piece of New London country furniture I was aware of seeing. It was a cherry chest-on-chest with the distinctive style of shell decoration that identifies the furniture from this area of Connecticut. I was quite pleased with myself the next day when I spotted this style shell in the Wadsworth Atheneum and was able to identify it before looking at the label. One of life's little triumphs.

The only way to describe the main house is as organized chaos. Among the specialities of this dealer are Spanish- and drake-foot chairs. Most dealers are justifiably proud to own a few of these rare eighteenth-century examples. John Walton has them by the dozen. A front room is filled with every variety of them from elegant Queen Anne to the simplest rush seat. There is furniture everywhere, and if there is an interior order to its arrangement I couldn't distinguish it. The front parlor, which houses most of the seat furniture, including a magnificent banister-back armchair very similar to one in Wethersfield, also had a number of period mirrors and a beautiful William and Mary veneered slant-front desk very much in the English manner, but, of course, American. The other parlor had a set of ten matched Queen Anne side chairs in addition to various lowboys, a porringer-top table, and a highboy or two. Upstairs in a bedroom is one of only seven original eighteenth-century japanned pieces Mr. Walton has ever owned. It is a magnificent William and Mary chest of drawers that I would have loved to own. The interesting thing about fine dealers is that there is always a good buy to be found if you can recognize it. This chest was it! The other pieces in this technique have all ended up in museums.

John Walton is not a dealer for the rank amateur. He is interested in young collectors who are seriously studying American furniture. With these people, he has all the patience in the world and frequently insists that they just look at his stock and return to buy only when they really understand the difference in the quality of material he is offering. John Walton is an acquired taste like fresh caviar. Once experienced, antiquing is never quite the same.

Nathan Liverant & Son
South Main Street
Colchester, Conn. 06415
(203) 537-2409

Monday–Saturday 10–5

The challenge offered by a major picker-dealer resounds like the call of the wild to a collector. Nathan Liverant Antiques is a perfect example of this genre of dealer. "Zeke" Liverant and his son Arthur will buy anything that can be sold. The result is a stock that runs from the sublime to the ridiculous. The range in material is as astonishing as the variations in quality. On a regular basis, superb eighteenth-century New England furniture passes through this shop. It then usually travels on to one of the famous dealers to be sold at its ultimate price, but don't bother rushing off to Colchester in hopes of some clever horse trading. The Liverants know exactly what their fine furniture is worth and nothing is given away. However, because they deal so actively, the lesser material is rationally priced, and it is at this level the young collector can do very well. If you have dreamed of owning a Queen Anne lowboy but can't afford it, this dealer offers interesting alternatives, namely a good New England lowboy with a new top or the so-called poor man's lowboy—the bottom of a highboy. These pieces are much less expensive and can eventually be used to trade up. There is nothing wrong with restorations as long as you are told exactly what has been done and the piece is priced accordingly. Zeke Liverant is an extremely knowledgeable dealer and knows precisely the condition of his furniture. The great problem faced by collectors is the number of perfectly nice dealers who think they know a great deal more than they actually do.

A collector must start somewhere and a shop like this offers many opportunities. Though of primary interest is their eighteenth-century American pieces such as Chippendale chests, Queen Anne and Chippendale chairs, Queen Anne highboys, Chippendale slant-front desks, and tables that range from the simplest country pine to a beautiful walnut Queen Anne dining table, there is, in addition, a large inventory of nineteenth-century American and English furniture of every conceivable style.

The shop, which is located in what was a lovely old white church, is literally filled to the rafters with mainly nineteenth-century paintings from everywhere in the world. They are for the most part quite ordinary and inexpensive. The exceptions again, in this case some marvelous eighteenth- and nineteenth-century American primitives and nineteenth-century ship paintings, are as fine and expensive as this dealer's great furniture. For the painting collector with a gambler's instinct, there was an early eighteenth-century portrait in terrible condition that had real possibilities. The problem is that since good restoration is very high, even a fine painting may not end up a bargain after all the costs are taken into consideration.

The stock of decorative accessories seems endless. There are nineteenth-century American and English pewter in a good selection of forms. I won't even start to list the different kinds of porcelains, glass, and silver except to say it is American, English, and European in origin and generally nineteenth century. There are also oriental rugs, American and Continental mirrors, clocks, and objets d'art for the most catholic taste.

The real excitement of the dealer who buys everything is discovering the objects you may know more about than he does. No dealer knows everything; there is simply too much material on the market. The Liverants are experts in eighteenth- and nineteenth-century American furniture and artifacts, but if you understand, for example, French silver or European clocks, you may find a great buy because these items are considered just so much merchandise. One of the joys of antiquing is the dealer who has a shopful of surprises.

Museums and Historical Houses

Yale Center for British Art
1080 Chapel Street
New Haven, Conn. 06520
(203) 432-4594

Tuesday–Saturday 10–5
Sunday 2–5
Closed Monday, January 1, July 4, Thanksgiving, December 25

If there were a rating system for museums, the Yale Center for British Art would be nothing less than a four-star entry. Filled with superb paintings of English life from the Elizabethan to the mid-nineteenth century, it succeeds in providing not only a marvelous aesthetic experience but a very interesting cultural one. After seeing the Elizabethan portraits in the museum, especially those of Robert Dudley, 1st Earl of Leicester, by Steven Van Der Meulen, and Lady Clopton of Kentwell Hall attributed to Marcus Gheeraerts the Younger, with their sense of power, their arrogance, and their almost primitive splendor, the great eighteenth-century Royal Academy likenesses paled by comparison. Curiously, the only paintings of the eighteenth century that seem to have a comparable vitality to the Elizabethans were the extraordinary George Stubbs animal paintings, which were my favorite pictures in the museum. I came away feeling the Elizabethans loved themselves and the Georgians loved their animals.

The great artists are well represented—Van Dyke, Gainsborough, Romney, West, a gallery of Turners and, if possible, an even more interesting room containing Constable cloud studies. Another aspect of eighteenth-century English life is covered by the delightful Francis Wheatley paintings of the country gentry. These pictures are the equivalent of strolling through a Fielding or Jane Austen novel. A most charming surprise is the Canaletto views of London. "The Lord Mayor's Procession at Westminster Bridge" could not be more Italianate. It has all the pageantry and color of a Renaissance painting. The Center also has a large collection of British manuscripts, drawings, prints, and sculpture.

The pleasures of this museum are enormously enhanced by the structure that houses it. It is that rare entity—a truly successful museum building, contemporary, spacious and intimate.

Yale University Art Gallery
1111 Chapel Street
New Haven, Conn. 06520
(203) 436-0574

Tuesday–Saturday 10–5
Thursday evening 6–9
Sunday 2–5
Closed Monday

Whether the Yale University Art Gallery would agree or not, the keystone of their collection is the Mabel Brady Garvan Galleries. Entitled the American Arts and the American Experience, it is one of the most effective exhibitions of Americana to be seen anywhere in the country. The examples of seventeenth-, eighteenth-, and nineteenth-century furniture, painting, silver, and pottery are not only superb in their own right but have been so creatively displayed as to make them totally accessible to the viewer. Chairs are dismantled to emphasize construction techniques of the period; style changes from Cromwell to Federal are marvelously arranged to show their sequential development. The manner of display is original, delightful, and illuminating. After seeing this exhibit you'll understand whether a peg is a functional part of the piece or decoration on a fake. It will also become quite apparent, from studying the decorative motifs, that a William and Mary chest shouldn't have late eighteenth-century detailing on it. This kind of knowledge offers some protection against casual faking. A fine fake is a problem beyond most collectors' ability to handle.

The painting collection of the museum spans the early Renaissance to contemporary art. It is a small collection with excellent examples. I felt their strong point was the contemporary art collection. This is not surprising as Yale University is an important teaching center for the arts.

The museum's Oriental, pre-Columbian, and African art collections are beautifully displayed. Unquestionably, the Yale University Gallery's great distinction is its Garvan collection which puts it in another category entirely from the usual college museum.

Peabody Museum
170 Whitney Avenue at Sachem Street
New Haven, Conn. 06511

Monday–Friday 9–5
Sunday and holidays 1–5
Closed January 1, July 4, Thanksgiving, December 25

This is a famous natural history museum.

Goodspeed Opera House
East Haddam, Conn. 06423
Reservations: (203) 873-8664

Early May–October
Tuesday–Friday 8 P.M.
Saturday 5 and 9 P.M.
Wednesday matinee 2:30 P.M., Sunday 5 P.M.

Musicals. Restored nineteenth-century opera house that is as charming as its musical productions.

Inns and Restaurants

Griswold Inn
Main Street
Essex, Conn. 06426
(203) 767-1812
Open all year. Closed December 24–25.

   Lunch and dinner. Lodging available.

Copper Beech Inn
Ivoryton
Essex, Conn. 06442
(203) 767-0330
Open all year. Closed Monday.

   Lunch and dinner. Reservations necessary. Lodging available.

Old Lyme Inn
Old Lyme, Conn. 06371
(203) 434-2600
Open all year. Closed Monday.

   Lunch and dinner. Lodging available.

Bee & Thistle Inn
Old Lyme, Conn. 06371
(203) 434-7861
Open all year.

   Breakfast, lunch, and dinner. Advance reservation for dinner.
No bar—bring own liquor. Lodging available.

The Gull, on the Marina
Essex, Conn. 06426
(203) 767-0916

   Breakfast, lunch, dinner.

Chart House
West Main Street
Essex, Conn. 06426
(203) 526-9898

Dinner only.

The Copper Beech Inn has a very fine reputation for food. The other inns are also considered excellent for dining.

Ye Olde Tavern
345 Bank Street
New London, Conn. 06320
(203) 442-0353

Closed Sunday, holidays, and February.

Dinner only.

Harbour View
60 Water Street
Stonington, Conn. 06378
(203) 535-2720

Open all year. Closed Tuesday and December 25.

Lunch and dinner.

Use inns in the Essex/Old Lyme area. It is not more than one hour away from Colchester.

CENTRAL CONNECTICUT

Antique Dealers

Lillian Blankly Cogan
22 High Street
Farmington, Conn. 06032
(203) 677-9259

Appointment advised

Lillian Blankly Cogan is a study in contradictions. Bearing more than a passing resemblance to the classic sweet grandmother in a romantic Victorian novel, complete with piles of soft white hair and bright china-blue eyes, she is in reality one of the two most important dealers in the United States in prerevolutionary American furniture, the starkest and most primitive of all furniture styles. Her physical appearance and personal charm completely belie the rigid austerity of her seventeenth- and early eighteenth-century house. No frills here, except perhaps in her home's name, Hearts and Crowns, a description of the primary decorative motif in furniture of this period.

Having only seen these pieces in museums and restorations, it was interesting for me to find a home completely furnished with them. In all honesty, I never realized how warm and beautiful a background they provide. Suddenly these simple objects were no longer abstract pieces of sculpture, which was how I had perceived them. I must admit, as a result of seeing Mrs. Cogan's home, I have developed a new appreciation of this early furniture. The house serves in part as a shop, in addition to the other buildings on the property. Do not miss seeing the "Shakespeare" herb garden. The herbs when ready for drying are hung in a small building which houses additional material. Everything is authentic right down to the fragrance.

The furniture is mainly New England with perhaps three quarters of it coming from Connecticut. The accessories are all of the same period and appropriate to the Pilgrim setting. The pewter, glass, Delft, and salt glaze are imported from England and Holland. The paintings are by both American and English artists. Small, beautiful seventeenth-century brass-lantern clocks are English as are the seventeenth-century mirrors with their stump-work borders. Because mirror glass was very costly at this early date, most of the mirrors are quite small, as in an English Queen Anne, *circa* 1710, with chinoiserie decoration.

The chairs are predominately banister- or ladder-backed. Many of the banister backs have reeded banisters. There are both side and armchairs in addition to a number of seventeenth-century Carver chairs with the spindles in the back. Some have the Heart and Crown crest, others the Connecticut Rose decoration. None are particularly comfortable. A group of small candlesticks were charming, especially one with its own fire shield, which is quite rare to find. There are many small William and Mary trestle tables, tavern tables, and chests with the original paint. A most unusual table is the large maple drop-leaf butterfly, *circa* 1700–20, that is illustrated in Wallace Nutting's *Furniture Treasury*. Mrs. Cogan has loaned her pieces to museums for special exhibitions. This includes pewter and pottery, as well as furniture. Many of the pieces have beautiful turnings, which, incidentally, refers to the way the wood was worked, namely, turned on a lathe by a turner.

There are all sorts of early lighting fixtures made of tin, brass, iron, and horn, including those charming round sconces with the pewter discs on tin backgrounds. The large assortment of early fireplace equipment is all made of iron.

Mrs. Cogan's proudest possessions, when I visited her, were a matching Connecticut Queen Anne highboy and dining table. Matched pieces are almost never found. These two will probably end up in a museum. Her other treasure, something she never thought she would own, is a Lorenzo Lotti carpet, which is, of course, the seventeenth-century Turkish rug used by this artist in so many of his paintings.

Pilgrim furniture was not an acquired taste for this dealer. It has been her passion since she was a girl. Perhaps this is the reason it gives her particular pleasure to share her interest with young collectors. It is a lovely way to relive one's youth.

Museums and Historical Houses

Wadsworth Atheneum
600 Main Street
Hartford, Conn. 06103
(203) 278-2670

Tuesday–Friday 11–3
Saturday and Sunday 11–5
Closed Monday and holidays

It may surprise you to learn that Hartford consists of more than just insurance companies and a terrifying highway system. It has a

museum that held the world premiere, in 1934, of Gertrude
Stein's opera *Four Saints in Three Acts*. The Wadsworth Atheneum looks like a fortress. Composed of five interconnected buildings, the last of which, the Goodwin, was constructed in 1967. The
Wadsworth, an 1842 Gothic Revival bit of fantasy, was the
original museum and has just been beautifully renovated. This
is my favorite kind of museum—it rambles all over the place and
is filled with lovely surprises. It is famous for seventeenth- and
eighteenth-century American furniture from the Wallace Nutting
collection, seventeenth- and eighteenth-century American and
English silver, nineteenth- and twentieth-century American paintings, superb examples of eighteenth-century Staffordshire, Meissen,
and Sèvres porcelains, classical bronzes, and a large collection of
Baroque paintings of questionable quality.

The first-floor galleries of the Wadsworth are usually reserved
for special exhibitions that change on a regular basis. As you walk
through the museum you are quite unaware that it is made up of
separate structures. However, I must warn you not to leave the
Morgan for the last as I did on my first visit. There is absolutely
marvelous material to see in its galleries, and I nearly died of ex-
haustion in the attempt. This building, donated by J. P. Morgan,
houses the nineteenth-century American painters including the
magnificent Trumbull paintings of the Revolutionary War. The
classic names are there—Kensett, Church, Cole, Cropsey, Eakins,
Inness, among the nineteenth-century contingent, with Glackens,
Bellows, Luks, Hartley, a small sampling of the twentieth century.
The fine Meissen and Sèvres porcelains donated by J. P. Morgan
have many unentcliché examples including a terrific Meissen garni-
ture set, *circa* 1725–40, which is a copy of the Chinese K'ang Hsi
porcelains. It is huge and fabulous. The museum's Baroque collection is also housed in the Morgan wing. There are certainly some
very fine paintings such as the Caravaggio, which is one of only
four in the United States, and a great Zurbarán.

Do notice the handling of the cream-colored robe in this picture; it has wonderful density. For myself, I found the majority of
the Baroque paintings quite second-rate, and what was worse, I

couldn't help wondering if the angel in the Caravaggio didn't have a nineteenth-century face. Among the more unusual objects donated by J. P. Morgan is a group of Renaissance cups, mainly German, shaped in marvelous animal forms. These pieces were not only utilitarian, but elegant and witty. The tiny rooms in this wing, housing the Greek and Roman bronzes from the Morgan collection, have a stillness that is perfect for the full enjoyment of these delicate treasures.

The most exciting part of the Wadsworth is the seventeenth- and eighteenth-century American-furniture galleries. The furniture is superb and displayed with great originality and feeling. The space of the large double-height gallery is broken into different levels with the furniture treated as pieces of sculpture. Each piece is totally accessible in-the-round to the viewer. It is unbeatable, for study purposes, to see these pieces in juxtaposition to each other. There are stylistic differences in areas that are just a few miles apart. A New London piece had distinctly different detailing from a Colchester piece. Incidentally, once you have seen the elegant proportions and carving of a Chapin highboy from East Windsor, Connecticut, you are not likely to be mislead in recognizing it again. Three Chippendale chairs, one New York, one by Affleck of Philadelphia, one Connecticut by Chapin, all with open center splats and ball-and-claw feet, are distinctly different in detailing and feeling. Shown next to each other they epitomize their regional differences. I cannot recommend this gallery too highly.

The seventeenth- and eighteenth-century American silver from the famous Philip H. Hammerslough collection contains fine examples of colonial silverwork. But my favorite exhibition is hidden in a small, dark-walled vault where the seventeenth- and eighteenth-century English silver glitters like gem stones. It is the most effective mounting of silver I've ever seen. The eighteenth-century English glass and ceramics are equally well displayed. The collection is small, but I don't remember ever being more charmed by a group of early Staffordshire teapots. What humor, what delight! The Wadsworth Atheneum proves again it isn't quantity, but creative taste, that counts in a museum.

The small group of French Impressionists are very interesting, especially the charming Monet "Beach at Trouville" which captures so completely the spontaneity of a windy afternoon at sea. There is a breathtaking double portrait of two cousins by Degas. Dark, moody, it is a fascinating contrast to his ballet and horse pictures. Look for a wonderful quick sketch of a boat by Monet called "Beach at Berck." Everything is done by suggestion; it is a greige painting.

The Goodwin wing of the museum houses the contemporary American paintings and there are first-rate examples of Rothko, DeKooning, Kline, Newman, Pollock, and Still. It is a very solid collection.

My overwhelming impression of this fine institution is that it is one of the most welcoming places I have visited. It is an open, informal museum worth all the time and attention you are willing to bring it. You will be well rewarded for your efforts.

Connecticut Historical Society Museum
1 Elizabeth Street
Hartford, Conn. 06105

Monday–Saturday 1–5
Closed Saturday, June–Labor Day

Smashing is the word for the Connecticut Historical Society. Barely a ten-minute drive from the new Civic Center, located right off Asylum Avenue, it should not be missed. The Barbour Collection of Connecticut eighteenth-century furniture is worth a visit from Alaska. Acquired specifically for the Society, the lowboys, highboys, chests-on-chests, desks, secretaries, chairs, bedsteads are classic examples of "carriage trade" cabinet work. Each of the fifty-odd pieces is a superb illustration of what makes Connecticut furniture unique. Look for the Colchester highboys, the decoration is extremely original; and on the main floor a highboy attributed to Chapin has exactly the same scrolled open fretwork on the pediment as one in the Wadsworth Atheneum. In addition to the furniture there are eighteenth-century silver, clocks, glass, great textiles such as embroideries, quilts, and a marvelous group of needlework mourning pictures. A whole section devoted to prerevolutionary artifacts, including such diverse items as swords, buttons, lighting fixtures, tomahawks and canteens, is really fascinating. An extremely effective exhibit is the Revolutionary War officer's hut that was used during encampments. Staged simply but dramatically, the hut is shockingly stark, lacking any creature comforts. The horror of those winter campaigns is evoked with enormous force. The paintings include works by Ralph Earl, Jennys, Johnston, Erastus Salisbury Field, and my new favorite, John Durand. Should you visit anytime except Saturdays or the summer months, don't be surprised to find the place deserted. I had the singular pleasure of going through the entire museum all by myself. I loved it!

Farmington Museum
(Stanley-Whitman House 1660)
37 High Street
Farmington, Conn. 06032

April–November, daily except Monday 2–5
December–March, Friday–Sunday 2–5
Also Tuesday–Saturday, June–August 10 A.M.–noon

One of the earliest houses in Connecticut.

The Webb, Deane, Stevens Museum
203–215 Main Street
Wethersfield, Conn. 06109
(203) 529-0612

Tuesday–Saturday 10–4 year-round
Also open Sunday 1–4
Mid-May–mid-October

These three eighteenth-century houses are simply gorgeous. The furnishings, paintings, and gardens are among the finest you will see anywhere in New England. The tour guides are very sympathetic; if you are alone and prefer viewing in silence, just indicate this and they will quietly escort you about.

Bultolph-Williams House
Broad and March streets
Wethersfield, Conn. 06109

July–October 1–5 daily

A 1692 house completely and appropriately furnished. Fascinating house, but some of the tour guides have a set talk that can drive you crazy.

Wethersfield is the largest historic district in Connecticut. There are over 150 pre-1850 buildings, the great majority of which are eighteenth century and still occupied. Don't miss the Town Cove area!

A few minutes drive from Wethersfield are the towns of Glastonbury, Rocky Hill, and Newington. These towns were settled in the late seventeenth century, just as Wethersfield was, by colonists who left Massachusetts for a variety of religious, social, and economic reasons. They are well worth visiting, and each has a number of historic houses open to the public.

Inns and Restaurants

Sheraton-Hartford Hotel
Trumbull Street at Civic Center Plaza
Hartford, Conn. 06103
(203) 728-5151

Open all year

I prefer small country inns. However, if you decide to stay in Hartford, this hotel is comfortable, but beware of the food.

The Hearthstone Restaurant
678 Maple Avenue
Hartford, Conn. 06114
(203) 246-8814

Open all year.

Lunch and dinner.

Howard Johnson's
1499 Silas Deane Highway
Wethersfield, Conn. 06109
(203) 529-7446

Open all year

Large, clean, comfortable—no small inns in the vicinity.

The Clam Box
1291 Silas Deane Highway
Wethersfield, Conn. 06109
(203) 529-7761

Open all year. Closed January 1, Thanksgiving, December 25.

Lunch and dinner.

Corner House (Farmington Motor Inn)
827 Farmington Avenue
Hartford, Conn. 06119
(203) 677-2828

Open all year

Lunch and dinner.

Special Note: Wadsworth Atheneum has a delightful small restaurant that is open for lunch.

WESTERN CONNECTICUT

Antique Dealers

Avis & Rockwell Gardiner
60 Mill Road
Stamford, Conn. 06903
(203) 322-1129

By appointment only

Every once in a while you run into people with a verve for living that is irresistible. Combine this with a passion for collecting and you have Avis and Rockwell Gardiner. Mr. and Mrs. Gardiner met over thirty-five years ago at an antique show where they were both exhibitors. Wisely recognizing what could be a better basis for marriage than a shared interest in Americana, they were on their way. Today these marvelous people are among the best dealers in American painting, prints, books, manuscript material, including maps, diaries, logs, account books, et cetera. All their print material pertains to Americana either directly or indirectly. For the city dwellers who think rats are their special province, Mr. Gardiner has just uncovered what he describes as a Rat Account book from Wethersfield, Connecticut, *circa* 1780. It seems the problem of rodents was so serious that a bounty was paid to kill them. Of interest is not only how sizable the bounty was, but the different types of currency that were used as payment, ranging from English to Dutch to Spanish and colonial. Because of the books, prints, and even photographic material piled all over the floors, their house, which serves as the shop, bears more than a passing resemblance to a storage vault.

A small number of their fine painting collection is hung on the walls, which is certainly an appropriate place for a beautiful Belknap child or a Brewster, Jennys, or Erastus Salisbury Field, but an equally important child's portrait, by Ralph Earl, was casually stacked against some books as were a number of other marvelous primitives. At this dealer's you really have to be observant as the treasures are hidden in the oddest places. A grat Persian lion carpet was stuffed under a couch, and an equally superb blue-and-white Delft tankard with dated seventeenth-century English silver mounts was sitting in a cupboard with some late Japanese porcelains. Aside from the Delft, the Gardiners generally have a selection of Canton and the historic blue English Staffordshire. When they can find early pewter and silver that interests them, they buy it. Fireplace equipment has always been a specialty, and at one time the Gardiners were responsible for much of the equipment sold to Williamsburg.

These dealers do not think of themselves as furniture people, but in the last ten years they have handled some really first-rate material. Their pride and joy was in finding the earliest signed Philadelphia highboy made by Henry Clifton in 1753. The piece was sold to Williamsburg. Although non-furniture specialists, they have a good assortment of very superior furniture and fortunately it is too large to get lost in the jumble. Among the eighteenth-century New England pieces were two fine block-front mahogany chests, one from Connecticut, the other Massachusetts, a rare Chester County linen press, a good New England butterfly table, Queen Anne country chairs, and a charmingly small Pilgrim chest.

The range of stock I've described is really just the tip of the iceberg. These are dealers who love eighteenth-century odds and ends. They have everything from playing cards and games to a Queen Anne doll, complete with her own lady's maid. My feeling is that, no matter how esoteric your request, there is a good chance the Gardiners will have it. If they don't, they'll love looking for it, and you'll have the pleasure of dealing with them.

I. M. Wiese
Route N. 67
Roxbury, Conn. 06783
Mailing address: Main Street
    Southbury, Conn. 06488
(203) 354-8911
(203) 264-5309

Appointment preferred

This is no little old country dealer. Mr. Wiese has, what can best be described as, a gloriously cantankerous personality. He fumes, he frets, and he has some of the best eighteenth-century American furniture on the market. I enjoyed his crankiness. I think you will, too, if you don't take seriously the terrible things he says about other dealers. Fortunately, he does enjoy his collectors, especially the young ones. The shop, which is located in one of the most beautiful areas of Connecticut, consists of a series of old dilapidated buildings, each containing very special material.

The main building has the furniture, which is housed on two floors. The first floor has superb corner cupboards, many with fine architectural detailing, some with original paint and glass. Really fine wing chairs of the $30,000 variety are casually displayed. There is nothing Mr. Wiese enjoys more than flipping through Sack's book *Fine Points of American Furniture* and showing you an illustrated piece that he happens to own. The more formal pieces, such as a small Boston serpentine chest with great ogee feet made of Cuban mahogany in a flame pattern, a porringer-top cherry chest, again with the typical Connecticut ogee foot, possibly by Beekman, a walnut pad-foot Queen Anne tea table with piecrust top and center pedestal, are on this floor with many other examples of typical and atypical New England furniture. Certainly not common pieces to find are a Massachusetts cherry day bed and a Connecticut cherry linen press.

The country furniture is on the floor above. I mention this because if Mr. Wiese is not in the mood or you've not been properly appreciative of his stock, he may not offer to take you upstairs and that would definitely be your loss. I have never seen so many sets of windsor chairs in my life. I don't mean pairs or even sets of four. I'm talking about matched sets of six, eight, and ten chairs. There are fanbacked, bow-backed, birdcage windsors, and one set I can't even quite describe as other than a cross between all the various styles put together. Big weather vanes are spectacular examples of folk art as was a huge carved wood swan. This dealer is famous for his fine andirons, some of which are signed; primitive pottery; huge burl bowls; pipe boxes; and blanket chests. Mr. Wiese buys anything he finds rare and fascinating.

I don't know why all the New England highboys are upstairs with the country pieces, but with this dealer, you don't question his arrangements. Needless to say, the examples are extremely fine and varied as to formality. A large group of good tavern tables are logically on this level, as is a cherry shoefoot butcher table from the New York Mohawk Valley, which is completely untouched and is a superlative primitive piece. A New Hampshire pencil-post bed is in the original red paint. Yes, there is a lot of furniture of every description; yes, it is expensive, but the quality is there.

Would you like to build yourself an eighteenth-century house? This dealer can supply you with everything you'll ever need in eighteenth-century building materials. You name it, he has it.

One building is filled with nothing but mantles from the simplest form to the most elaborate MacIntire piece. Another building has the wide floorboards, paneling, chimney breasts, wainscoting, stairways, old moldings ad infinitum.

Mr. Wiese may not have anything particularly delightful to say about members of his trade, but he is a very special experience and antique lovers worth their salt should not miss him.

Peter Tillou
Prospect Street
Litchfield, Conn. 06759
(203) 567-5706

Appointment advised

Charm is a quality rarely found today in anyone, let alone antique dealers. Peter Tillou is a natural-born charmer and an excellent dealer. The combination synthesizes into a uniquely delightful antiquing experience. A passionate collector himself, he is famous in the antique world as the dealer most responsible for making American nineteenth-century primitive painting a real factor in the art market today. These paintings, long overlooked except by a small group of devotees, have finally begun to assume their true value as a legitimate art form. There has been no turning back since the enormous success of the Whitney Museum Folk Art Show, which Mr. Tillou helped to organize. After years of benign neglect, this market is flying and the prices are a reflection of the activity. The days of finding a good quality primitive for a few hundred dollars are a thing of the past. The paintings Mr. Tillou handles are the finest examples available. The only pictures in the gallery not for sale are from his private collection, which is generally used for special exhibitions at museums. If you love folk art as much as he does, he'll be delighted to show you his collection, which is hidden away, but I repeat, the only pictures that are ever sold from it are his duplicates.

There are a number of beautiful Ammi Phillips portraits for sale. I couldn't believe these were duplicates; they are, but only in the sense that Mr. Tillou already has eighteen Ammi Phillipses of his own. A superb Ralph Earl portrait of Captain John Pratt was historically interesting on two counts: First, the officer served

with Washington; secondly, he is wearing his Order of Cincin-
nati. This is the first time this painting has been out of the family. Along with the famous names available, such as Prior-
Hamblen, Bard, Stock, Bundy, Belknap, Jennys, there is always a
selection of those marvelous itinerant painters who frequently
left as distinctive a mark as any of their more famous colleagues.
In addition to the portraits of adults and children there are
many beautiful examples of Frakturs, including a number of
rare eighteenth-century military ones. Though primarily famous
for its primitives, the gallery also has Inman, Bierstadt, and Kensett, the Hudson Valley School painters, and fine academic portraits by Peale, Stuart, and Sully. The young collector is pretty
much priced out of the categories of paintings I've just listed, but
the gallery does carry some lovely, and much less expensive, seven-
teenth- and eighteenth-century Dutch, French, and English pictures by lesser-known artists. These serve as a starting point for the
young collector or the experienced one interested in these schools
of art.

   The surprise of this dealer is the range of other material he carries—coins, stamps, American glass, oriental rugs, American silver,
American pottery, folk art such as statuary, weather vanes, and
fine eighteenth-century New England furniture. There are beautiful examples of lowboys, chests of drawers, chairs, and tables. The
furniture is very expensive but the quality is distinctive.

   Peter Tillou buys everything that fascinates him, provided it is
a marvelous example. His taste is wonderful and the gallery, which
is in his beautiful home, makes for a most exciting visit.

Museums and Historical Houses

Litchfield Historical Society, on the Common
Litchfield, Conn. 06759
(203) 567-5862

May–November 11–5
April 2–4
Closed Sunday, Monday, and holidays
Rest of year, call for appointment

   Charming small museum, eighteenth- and nineteenth-century

furniture, silver, glass, textiles, paintings of local origin. Wonderful group of Ralph Earl portraits.

White Memorial Foundation

Largest nature center in Connecticut; Route 63 just south of Litchfield; twenty miles of woodlands, trails, ponds, brooks. The Fine Ponds area perfect for picnicking.

One of the loveliest drives in the area is Route 199 from Roxbury to Washington Depot. Take it either coming or going to Litchfield; it runs along a small river.

The entire area of Woodbury, Roxbury, and Litchfield is unbelievably beautiful. They are wealthy eighteenth-century towns, and if Litchfield is perhaps the most spectacular to wander about in, the others have great charm of their own.

Inns and Restaurants

Meeting House Inn
Litchfield, Conn. 06759
(203) 567-8744
Open all year

Lunch and dinner. Lodging available.

Kilravock Inn
Brush Hill Road
Litchfield, Conn. 06759
(203) 567-8100

Open all year, except November and December

Lunch and dinner. Dining room closed Wednesday. Lodging available.

Hopkins Inn
Lake Waramaug
New Preston, Conn. 06777
(203) 868-7295

Open May–October

Lunch and dinner. Dining room closed Monday. Lodging available.

L'Ermitage
Route 45
Warren, Conn. 06754
(203) 868-2355

Closed Monday and February

Lunch and dinner.

Le Bon Coin
New Preston, Conn. 06777
(203) 868-7763

Closed Tuesday and April

Lunch and dinner.

Woodbury is a beautiful eighteenth-century town that has a cheese store and a bakery. What more do you need other than a bottle of wine for a bit of lunch?

RHODE ISLAND

Museums and Historical Houses

PROVIDENCE

Museum of Art
Rhode Island School of Design
224 Benefit Street
Providence, R.I. 02903
(401) 331-3511

June and July: Tuesday–Saturday 11–4:30
Winter hours: Tuesday, Wednesday, Friday and Saturday 11–5
Thursday 1–7; Sunday 2–5
Closed Monday, holidays, and month of August
Admission $1.00

For those collectors and art enthusiasts who are intimidated by the sheer volume of material and noise of large municipal museums, may I heartily recommend a delightful antidote—the charming Museum of Art of the Rhode Island School of Design. In the hierarchy of museums it is rather like a fine miniature painting; every bit of detail is there but on a tiny scale. All of the collections are limited in size but certainly not quality. The only exception is Pendleton House, its large and extraordinary American seventeenth- and eighteenth-century furniture wing.

The museum was basically conceived as a learning institution for students of the School of Design. Textiles and jewelry were important industries in Rhode Island during the nineteenth century, and what could be more inspiring to future artists and designers than an intimate knowledge of past treasures? All of the objects, from the smallest piece of archaic gold jewelry to a huge tenth-century Japanese Buddha, are displayed with unique sensitivity. Accessibility is the key to this museum's thinking.

The classical art objects are interestingly shown. Many of the pieces are small, as in the early gold jewelry and Roman bronzes, but there is never a sense of monotony. Light and space are used to dramatize each object to its fullest capacity. Among the stone carvings in the Medieval gallery is a particularly effective French Apostle, *circa* 1110, with a huge Ben Shahn-like hand. These earlier figures lack the elegant sophistication of later Gothic art but do convey an enormous sense of piety. These are deeply felt religious statuary. A collection of fifteenth- and sixteenth-century Majolica is excellent.

There really is an advantage to seeing only a dozen fourteenth- and fifteenth-century Renaissance paintings rather than fifty; it is so much easier to absorb and appreciate them. Particularly lovely was a Mary Magdalen by the Sienese painter Lippo Memmi. The room containing the fifteenth- to sixteenth-century Flemish art has

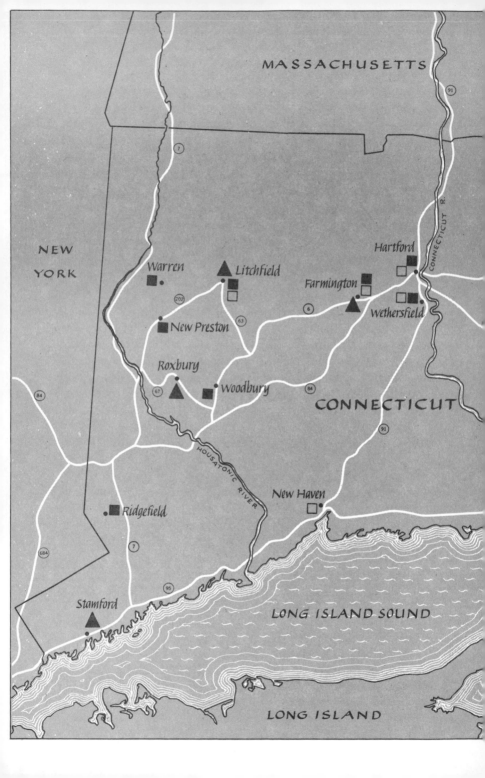

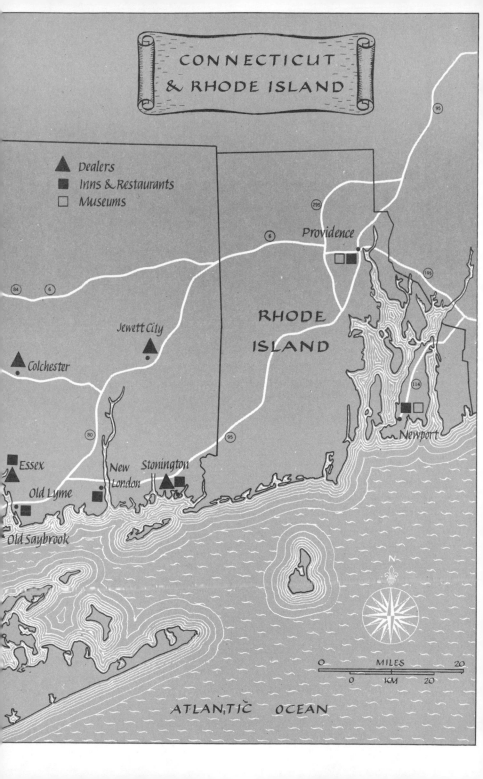

a small glass-enclosed wall display of the Annunciation made of a cameo shell with silver mounts and entitled "Pax"; it is an exquisite piece of workmanship. The funniest Baroque painting I've seen in years, called "Marriage of Peleus and Thetis" by Joachim Anthonisz Wtewael, *circa* 1610, is jam-packed with florid nudes done in bright pink flesh tones. I would suggest you not miss it, but on second thought I don't think you can. The French painting covers the seventeenth to twentieth centuries but in a very limited way. A wonderful Romney portrait is the star of the small eighteenth-century English group. Nineteenth-century American painting is well represented. There are beautiful examples of Winslow Homer and John Singer Sargent. Fitz Hugh Lane is best known for his ship paintings, but the museum owns his "View of Little Good Harbor Beach, Cape Ann." This peaceful, intimate painting is every tiny beach harbor you've ever loved. I found myself enjoying the nineteenth-century American landscape painters George Inness, Thomas Cole, Asher Durand, Thomas Doughty, and Albert Bierstadt much more than I usually do. I suspect it was because the paintings were small-sized rather than their usual wall monuments. There is also on exhibit a small selection of contemporary American art.

The second floor has for me the choicest objects in the museum except, of course, for the Pendleton furniture. This floor has Chinese and Japanese art objects, beautiful Persian miniatures, South American and Southeast Asian artifacts and finally a Benin bronze prince's head that is just super. Again, not many examples but really special ones. The tenth-century Japanese Buddha is sensational; it is nine feet eight inches tall and eight feet wide, and it is presented in a truly inspired manner. Placed in a small room, simulating a cave, the immense figure thrusts itself out at you like an apparition. It is incredibly dramatic. Chinese T'ang pottery figures are excellent examples of their period as are the fine group of K'ang Hsi *Famille Verte* porcelains. A group of Japanese prints by Hokusai, Harunobu, Koryusai, and Huoshige were given to the museum in memory of Abby Aldrich Rockefeller.

I have left for last what is known as the Pendleton House of the Museum of Art. It is a complete Georgian-style residence, attached to the museum, which was built in 1906 to Charles L.

Pendleton's specifications. Mr. Pendleton, one of the earliest collectors of fine eighteenth-century American furniture, wanted his
collection housed exactly as it was in his own home at 72 Waterman Street. This was the first time a museum had ever exhibited
furniture and accessories in this manner. Now, all the museums
do it; then, it was an extremely original concept. Mr. Pendleton and his friends Richard A. Caufield, Marsden J. Perry, and
Luke Vincent Lockwood, who catalogued the furniture for the
museum, were the collectors most responsible for the developing
interest in American furniture that occurred during the late nineteenth century. The house is a magnificent presentation of some
of the finest furniture ever made in this country. The paintings,
porcelains, glass, and other decorative accessories deftly round out
the sense of luxury these rooms contain.

This is an enchanting museum that is an essential part of the
whole experience of the Benefit Street area.

The John Brown House
The Rhode Island Historical Society
52 Power Street
Providence, R.I. 02906
(401) 331-8575

Tuesday–Friday 11–3
Saturday and Sunday 1–4
Closed Monday and holidays
Admission $1.50

There are mansions and mansions and mansions, but the John
Brown House, home of the Rhode Island Historical Society, is a
mansion and a half. John Quincy Adams, notorious for his un-
complimentary nature, called it "the most magnificent and elegant private mansion that I have ever seen on this continent." He
was simply stating a fact. The structure, built in 1786, was meant
to symbolize the power and wealth of this Providence merchant.
It did far more than that, for it became one of the finest examples
of colonial architecture in the United States. The Historical Society restored the house, duplicating original paint colors and wallpaper and filling it with the greatest examples of Rhode Island

furniture and American painting. The opulence of the house is especially surprising when you realize it is in Providence and not in a major center of wealth like Philadelphia or Boston.

If you do nothing else, be sure to see the staircase. It has a magnificent newel post and baluster turnings in mahogany. They are in pristine condition even after two hundred years of constant use. I have a feeling things used to be built a little differently than they are today. I will not detail the quality of the wallpaper, furniture, oriental rugs, accessories, because they are all glorious and must be seen. However, there is one piece of furniture that is really worth a trip from anywhere. It is John Brown's Chippendale mahogany block-front secretary desk complete with nine carved shells and a broken pediment arch. Unquestionably, one of the greatest pieces of American eighteenth-century furniture ever constructed. The formal rooms for entertaining are on the main floor, the master bedrooms on the second, and the children's rooms on the third, as was customary. What is most unusual about the third floor is that the rooms are as spacious and architecturally interesting as the lower ones. Children's rooms even in the wealthiest families were usually more like attics.

The Historical Society has a large and important collection of eighteenth- and nineteenth-century paintings, all, of course, pertaining to Rhode Island. These include portraits, landscapes, and ship paintings. Many famous artists, such as John Greenwood, Robert Feke, John Smibert, John Trumbull, came to paint the wealthy merchants. The Bard brothers painted their ships, and a wonderful Chinese artist known as Spoilum, who worked out of Canton, *circa* 1785–1800, painted the Providence sea captains when they visited the port city. The earliest portrait in the collection is attributed to Aetatis Sue Limner and is Mrs. Daniel Updike, probably done in 1722. This rarely found artist was both primitive and elegant, making for a very distinctive style. My favorite paintings, as usual, are by those amusing itinerants known as the Anonymous Artist. A delightful painting of Benjamin Franklin Greene and his family is complete with a cross-eyed daughter. The portrait of Washington, after the Gilbert Stuart painting, by an anonymous Chinese artist, is an exact replica except for the slightly oriental cast to George's eyes, which I think gives it a little something special. Many of these paintings are not on exhibit and can only be seen by appointment. You must call ahead if you want to see any particular group of paintings.

There is a pamphlet available at the Society called *Seeing Providence*. It is free and lists all the individual eighteenth-century houses on Benefit Street which is just down the block from the Brown House and a perfect place to start your walking tour of historic Providence.

Benefit Street Walk

PROVIDENCE, RHODE ISLAND

Benefit Street and the "College Hill" area of downtown Providence provide one of the most charming walks in New England. It has something for everyone. If you love beautiful eighteenth- and nineteenth-century houses, it has them by the dozens. If eighteenth-century cloistered halls enchant you, Brown University is right in the center of everything and so is the Rhode Island School of Design. And, finally, for the antiquer who feels no day is complete without a museum or two, there is the Museum of Art on Benefit Street and the John Brown House right off Benefit up the hill at 52 Power, which is the most aptly named street I've ever come across. When you see the size of the houses, you'll understand.

Start your walk at the base of Benefit, heading toward Power Street where the Rhode Island Historical Society is located in the John Brown House. Even if you don't wish to tour the house at this point, do pick up the free booklet already mentioned, called *Seeing Providence* that lists all the houses in the area and is marvelously helpful to have with you as you're walking. If you are looking for restaurants, turn left on Power to South Main Street, a beautiful restoration complex with an assortment of delightful eating places. Continuing on Benefit toward Waterman you'll notice the houses on the hill are rather magnificent compared to the modest-sized dwellings on Benefit. In every century, including the eighteenth, wealth tends to rise. Take the time to walk up these hill streets such as Charles Field and Benevolent. Make a right at Waterman—this is a very steep hill leading to Brown University and past the Rhode Island School of Design. If you stopped to visit the Museum of Art on Benefit Street, you saw the splendid Pendleton wing. The interiors of the house he was duplicating were in his home at 72 Waterman, which is a jewel even from the outside. Walk into Brown University, the diversity of architectural styles ranging from Georgian to Gothic to Victorian and finally modern is very pleasing. It is a wonderfully warm-looking university, not too bandbox pretty. If you want to sample the college atmosphere, the restaurants on Thayer Street will suit you perfectly. This area of Providence provides a solid day's looking, walking, and enjoying.

Restaurants

PROVIDENCE

Engine Co. 2
301 South Main Street

   Lunch and dinner daily.

Left Bank
220 South Water Street

   Lunch and dinner daily.

L' Elizabeth
South Main Street

   Pastries, fruit, and cheese. Irish coffee, plus bar. Perfect for afternoon tea. Noon–1 A.M. daily.

Spats Wine & Beer
Thayer Street near Angell Street
  Lunch and dinner daily.

Jake's Ice Cream Parlor
Thayer Street, corner of Angell Street

  Thayer is mainly a college shopping street.

Museums and Historical Houses

NEWPORT

The Elms
Bellevue Avenue

April, Saturday and Sunday 10–5
May 1–November 16, Daily 10–5
November–April, Saturday and Sunday 11–4
Thursday and Saturday 10–9, July–mid-September

  Symmetry and balance are the words used in a small booklet is-
sued by the Preservation Society of Newport County to describe
The Elms, the Edward J. Berwind mansion. They are key elements to this eighteenth-century French-style building. However,
there is a third word of equal descriptive importance that should
be added to complete the picture. The word is money, money,
and more money. Nothing else would have made this extraordinary structure possible. A fantasy of marble, limestone, and
space (the ballroom is forty-one by forty-nine feet, the ceiling
nineteen feet high), it was created as a summer cottage for the
new American royalty. Filled with fine furniture, paintings, and
objets d'art appropriate to the setting, it includes enough stone
statuary to fill a small European palace. Some of the objects are
period, others contemporary copies. The taste of the day usually
preferred ornate reproductions of eighteenth-century furniture to
the original. The furnishings are completely secondary to the opu-

lence of the architecture. Built to impress, it does so with great
authority. The Elms goes beyond the limitations of personal taste,
creating its own standards for acceptance.

The grounds are as impressive as the house. Beautifully landscaped, it is complete with sunken garden, marble gazebos, and a
glorious weeping beech tree. The Elms is marvelous fun to visit.

Rosecliff
Bellevue Avenue

April, Saturday and Sunday 10–5
May 1–November 16, Daily 10–5
Monday and Wednesday, July–mid-September 10–9

Rosecliff is justly famous as one of the most elegant mansions
in Newport. Facing the sea, surrounded by magnificent rose gardens, it was built for Mr. and Mrs. Hermann Oelrichs at the turn
of the century. Reflecting the extravagant taste of the period, it is
an adaptation of the Grand Trianon in Versailles. Constructed of
the palest terra cotta, seventeenth- and eighteenth-century architectural details were copied both in the interior and exterior
design. Mrs. Oelrichs, a woman of unbounded energy, gave legendary parties for as many as four hundred people in her
magnificent eighty-foot long ballroom which was the largest in
Newport. This mansion and its setting are quite unforgettable.

The Breakers
Ochre Point

April, Saturday and Sunday 10–5
May 1–November 16, Daily 10–5
Sunday 10–9, July–mid-September

Vanderbilt mansion with original furnishings.

Sanford-Covell House, c. 1869–70
72 Washington Street

June 1–September 30
Tuesday, Thursday, Sunday 1–5

Wonderful Victorian house, very period in feeling. Represents earlier wealthy taste before the great mansions were built in Newport.

Hunter House, *c.* 1748
Washington Street

Open during winter by appointment
Call (401) 847-7516

Furnished with great Newport Townsend and Goddard pieces, Newport silver and paintings.

There are more of the monster mansions to see if you have the energy. I've only listed a few favorites. Do not miss the newly restored eighteenth-century area near the waterfront or the Touro synagogue (first in America).

Inns and Restaurants

NEWPORT

The Inn at Castle Hill
Ocean Drive
Newport, R.I. 02840
(401) 847-1913

Open all year

Breakfast, lunch, dinner, end of May through beginning of October.
Lunch and dinner October–May; closed Monday. Lodging available.

II

Poets, Puritans, and Merchant Princes

BOSTON

What an interesting city this is. There are really two Bostons, a public and a private one. The private is Bulfinch—the Adam of Boston—restrained, elegantly proportioned red brick buildings with glorious fan lights and windows of lavender glass. A proper home for George Apley. The public Boston is the extraordinary result of the experiences of the nineteenth-century Boston traveler returning with his memories of "The Grand Tour." There is a unique sense of *déjà vu* in this city: the Gardner Museum, Venice; the Boston Public Library, Rome. Look at Copley Square on a hot summer day, even the light is Italian. Memories of Europe produced the Athenaeum, The Fine Arts, the Fogg, the hidden courtyards, the fountains. Try to hear a concert at the Gardner Museum. They are usually held in what was Mrs. Gardner's Tapestry Room. It is a charming experience. Louisburg Square is worth the trip itself. At the Ritz Hotel on the Common, the courtesy of the people reflects another age entirely. Take a picnic to the Charles River embankment and watch the sculls go by. I've spent whole afternoons doing just that, when I wasn't antiquing. And, finally, for me no trip to Boston is complete without an ice cream cone at Brigham's, a stop at Filene's basement, and a visit to the marvelous Quincy Market. No antiques, but what fun! Welcome to this wonderful, very human city.

Antique Dealers

Samuel L. Lowe, Jr., Antiques
80 Charles Street
Boston, Mass. 02114
(617) 742-0845

Weekdays 10:30–5
Saturday 10:30–4
Closed Saturday during summer

This shop is a must for anyone interested in American marine art and artifacts. It is filled with fascinating material that relates either directly or indirectly to the maritime trade of the nineteenth century. However, in good conscience I must issue a word of warning: Mr. Lowe, a lifelong collector before opening the shop in 1964, is really an expert in his field but does possess a somewhat quixotic temperament. I know he sees himself as "The Old Curmudgeon," straight out of Dickens, but to put it bluntly, if you visit him on one of his bad days, you've had it. He is quite capable of asking you to leave the shop if he doesn't like the question you've asked him. Just as he can carry rudeness to new heights, he is also perfectly capable of being charming, informative, and helpful. This is an important dealer and relationships with certain dealers can be difficult at times to establish. If you come at it easily, I am sure anyone who is interested in this field will enjoy knowing Mr. Lowe. It just takes patience.

Large as the visible stock is in marine paintings, books, carvings, scrimshaw, maps, porcelains, it is just the tip, according to Mr. Lowe who has enormous amounts of additional material in storage.

Aside from the usual unknown American, English, and Chinese artists, who did marvelous paintings of the old clipper ships, whaling vessels, port scenes, captain's portraits, there is an impressive selection of famous maritime artists such as Fitz Hugh Lane, Robert Salmon, James E. Buttersworth, William Bradford, Duncan McFarlane, and Charles Sidney Raleigh. There are also usually paintings by George Chinnery, a fascinating Englishman who lived and painted in China during the first half of the nineteenth century. The Chinese artists of his day were so taken with his port scenes and ship paintings that they began to copy his technique and became what is known as the Chinnery School.

The gallery has an excellent collection of scrimshaw, the native art of the whaling man. There are hundreds of pieces that range from carved whale's teeth to rare items such as half models, those dummy models used by a boat builder, instead of a modern blueprint, to construct a ship to scale. There are lap desks and all sorts of miniature furniture made for a beloved child. Remember, these voyages took two to three years at a time.

For the rare-book enthusiast, there are many out-of-print books such as *Whale Ships and Whaling, Sail Ships of New England*, and Salem Research Society Books, which is a set of volumes. Perhaps most fascinating of all are the old ship logs that tell the day-to-day story of a sailor's life in the time of the great sailing ships. Mr. Lowe has supplied many collectors and museums all over the world with these interesting documents.

In addition, there is usually on hand prints, water colors, marine instruments, China-trade porcelains, and ad infinitum provided it relates to ships.

As you can tell, I find this a fascinating shop. I know you will too.

Marika's Antiques
130 Charles Street
Boston, Mass. 02114
(617) 523-4520

Monday–Saturday 10–5
Closed Saturday during summer
(Also closes during August for three-week vacation)

A very interesting shop for both the sophisticated collector and the tentative beginner. It is a most delightful potpourri of objets d'art. Marika Raisz, a most unique lady, has a passion for jewelry, both antique and modern. It can range from bangles and beads to diamond tiaras. The selection is international in range.

The shop has an unusually large collection of nineteenth-century American portraits and ship paintings. I've seen some fine primitives there from time to time. Marika has sold at least seventeen paintings over the years to Mr. Maxim Karolik, a great part of whose collection is in the Museum of Fine Arts in Boston. The shop buys nineteenth-century European paintings, too. Russian eighteenth- and nineteenth-century objects of almost every variety, including icons, silver, porcelain and jewels, are also a specialty of this dealer.

While jewelry and paintings are her strong points, the shop does carry a large stock of English, Continental, and some China Export porcelains: you'll generally find English nineteenth-century Luster and transfer wares and a selection from the German and French factories of the nineteenth century. There is very little eighteenth-century pottery available now. An early nineteenth-century English transfer tea service the shop had owned went to Sturbridge. Also some China Export porcelain of theirs ended up in the China Trade Museum in Milton, Massachusetts.

There are vast amounts of early nineteenth-century French, Irish, and English glass, both clear and colored. You will also readily find Bohemian and American art glass.

The silver collection is mainly nineteenth century. The eighteenth-century pieces that come in are gone in a flash. They are primarily English, and American and some Chinese serving pieces, tea services, boxes, and flatware.

There are a few miscellaneous pieces of eighteenth- and early nineteenth-century English and American furniture.

Marika loves to buy and will buy anything interesting that is offered to her. It can range from gorgeous Fabergé to beautiful table linens with the kind of hand embroidery you haven't seen in forty years. If you are lucky enough to be in the shop when Marika is there, be sure to introduce yourself. She is a beautiful lady who makes age meaningless. In all my years of collecting, she is one of the most genuinely sophisticated and knowledgeable dealers I've ever met. Warning: There is no way to know what you will find at any given time. If, unfortunately, you come after a group of dealers has gone through, don't be disappointed, just come again.

Hyman Grossman
51 Charles Street
Boston, Mass. 02114
(617) 523-1879

Monday–Saturday 10–5
Closed Saturday during summer

This is the best-camouflaged shop in Boston. The owners do everything possible to be overlooked by the casual visitor. The dusty windows and tired old bits of china sitting on a seedy table of no particular interest, effectively hide one of the best American-furniture dealers in the New England area. Mr. Grossman, whose father was an antique dealer before him, has been in this exact location for fifty-three years, and the shop looks as if nothing has moved in fifty-five years.

This is a dealer for the serious collector of first-quality, and that does mean expensive, American furniture. You cannot browse or chat because Mr. and Mrs. Grossman do not encourage casual social amenities. They can be, and have been, rude. However, if you have wondered where many of America's most important dealers and collectors have bought, it is here. Mr. Grossman has sold some of the most important furniture to come out of the Boston area. We are talking about highboys, lowboys, tea tables, desks, block-front chests, beds. These are not exclusively New England pieces but also include Philadelphia and New York furniture, which may have arrived in the New England area via a marriage contracted some two hundred years ago: such are the curious travels of fine furniture. If you have expertise and money and are willing to pay a fair market price, there is a good possibility of finding the special piece you are looking for, provided the Grossmans are willing to show it to you.

Incidentally, they also have Chinese Export porcelain. Not a large selection, but you'll usually find a part dinner service, a tureen, and certainly some important-size serving plates.

The Grossmans are interesting dealers in the sense that they represent a traditional European dealer's point of view, which is that a great piece of furniture is far rarer than money and should be treasured. You are not particularly encouraged to buy, but if you do share a common feeling for a piece, I think you'll find this shop a very interesting experience.

George Gravert
122 Charles Street
Boston, Mass. 02114
(617) 227-1593

Monday–Saturday 10–5
Closed Saturday during summer

This is one of the few shops in Boston to handle Continental furniture. They have French country pieces and marvelous decorative accessories. If it's an old butcher's table or French baker's rack you may be looking for, there is a good probability of locating it here.

Mr. Gravert has beautiful taste and is a very active dealer. The stock of the shop constantly changes. I've found some excellent Chinese porcelains and pleasing objects for the walls like weather vanes, old tavern signs, and mad-looking mythological animals.

Nineteenth-century stone garden statuary is bought by Mr. Gravert whenever it can be found.

Chandeliers are an important part of the stock. There are usually rock crystal, brass, or iron ones available, both antique and reproduction.

What is most interesting about this shop, although a decorator's paradise because of the emphasis on accessories, is that if you look carefully you will find objects of real quality that frequently end up at expensive dealers. John Strathi, who manages the shop, is a delightful man and extremely helpful.

Alberts-Langdon, Inc.
126 Charles Street
Boston, Mass. 02114
(617) 523-5954

Monday–Saturday 10–5
Closed Saturday during summer

Oriental porcelains and art are the specialties of Alberts-Langdon. The stock originally consisted of porcelains and art objects Mrs. Langdon had collected during her years in the Orient. The shop is not primarily Chinese but covers a range of material from Japan, Korea, Thailand, the Philippines, and North Vietnam (Annam).

It is always fascinating with wares from Southeast Asia to compare the pottery that was exported from China during the T'ang dynasty and later, to the indigenous pieces produced during the same periods. There is a fascinating overlapping of styles and pottery techniques.

The shop has excellent examples from Thailand of Ban Chieng neolithic pottery which dates approximately 3000 B.C. Most of these are simple earthenware vessels that were used for cooking. The forms are the classic bowl and stem cup shapes with geometric red paint decoration that is very similar to Chinese neolithic pottery of the same period. There are also from Thailand fifteenth-century Sawankhalok ware which consists of blue-and-white covered boxes.

The Annamese pottery is considered Chinese, though the area is now North Vietnam. The shop has many examples of this charming underglaze blue-and-white ware in vases, dishes, ewers, and even a tiny teapot. The forms are classic Sung, Yuan, and early Ming in style.

There are some Chinese Ming porcelains but these are provincial ware.

Do not expect to find the material that appears at Tai in New York, C. T. Loo in Paris, or Eskanazi in London. Very few dealers have the capital needed to invest in important oriental pottery.

The shop does carry examples of later Chinese porcelains. I saw a lovely pair of eighteenth-century yellow bottles. There is usually a selection of both Peking enamel and glass objects.

The gallery carries a contemporary Japanese potter, named Hamada, of whom they think very highly.

Mr. Russel Alberts, who also manages the shop, is a pleasant, low-key person who is invariably patient and informative with his clients.

James Bakker Antiques Inc.
113 Charles Street
Boston, Mass. 02114
(617) 742-7467

Monday–Saturday 10:30–4:30

There is a magic ingredient present in every talented antique dealer. It is called instinct. For some dealers this special sense lies dormant for years; for others it is functioning like crazy by the time they are fourteen or fifteen years of age. James Bakker is one of the latter group. He is what I call a born trader. Actively dealing since he was a teen-ager, he is now, in his mid-twenties, a fully established young dealer with a fine reputation in New England as a coming major dealer. This is obvious when you meet him: He literally sparkles with pleasure and enthusiasm for the business. What is even more remarkable, he has already found his niche. Jim Bakker has almost singlehandedly created an active market in relatively unknown late nineteenth- and early twentieth-century American artists. This is art for young collectors who have literally been priced out of the art market. The gallery always has at least twenty-five to thirty paintings by lesser-known artists for under $500. These unknown painters represent just a small portion of the American painting stock. To solidify his position in this area, Mr. Bakker has bought the estates of Lee Lufkin Kaula, Bernard Lintott, and Gertrude Tousberg. Certainly not great names but genuinely talented artists and still very well priced. Additionally, he has a number of really first-class early nineteenth-century American primitives and a sizable group of paintings by some of the more important names in American art —Gertrude Fiske, Edmund Tarbell, Charles Hoffbauer, Frank

Benson, Willard L. Metcalf, Frederick C. Frieseke, Frank Boggs, John J. Enneking, and Seymour J. Guy. These works, of course, are much more expensive.

Mr. Bakker is an eccentric dealer as far as antiques are concerned. The shop is filled with a conglomeration of furniture and accessories. The furniture is mainly eighteenth-century country New England with a more formal piece or two to be seen. There are also examples of English, Italian, Dutch, and whatnot of various and sundry periods. This is a dealer who will buy anything he thinks is marvelous and decorative. A seventeenth-century English court cupboard had American quilts, coverlets, and baskets strewn about it. There were bits of China Export, English and Dutch Delft, and a better than average weather vane sat on a pile of oriental rugs.

Jim Bakker is the kind of dealer I cannot resist—open-minded, willing to buy anything with a bit of dash, still mainly selling to dealers: this is a likely place to find an underpriced little treasure.

James Moriarity
115 Charles Street
Boston, Mass. 02114
(617) 227-6113

April–September, Monday–Friday 10–4:30
October–March by appointment

Jim Moriarity is in this book because he is one of the nicest people you will ever meet in the business. He is neither an important dealer nor picker and has no aspirations to either position. He is not going to sell you the crown jewels of Arabia but if you want simple seventeenth-, eighteenth-, and nineteenth-century Italian country furniture, and mainly nineteenth-century European accessories such as lamps, sconces, mirrors, porcelains, he is a likely source who is quite inexpensive. He also deals in later Chinese, Japanese, and Korean porcelains, especially celadon and blanc de chine with occasional examples of earlier wares. There is generally a good supply of nineteenth-century Chinese vases converted into lamps. At one point in his career he was a

sure bet for eighteenth-century Russian silver and wonderful
China Export porcelain, but unfortunately that time is pretty
much passed.

Mr. Moriarity will sometimes turn up an American piece but
generally stays away from that market because of the costs involved. The European chairs, tables, and consoles he has are
highly decorative, if not particularly valuable. The collector with a
limited pocket book and a good eye will find this little shop an interesting place to see. Jim Moriarity knows where everything is,
and if he doesn't have it, he is always delighted to suggest who
might be able to help you.

Shreve, Crump & Low & Co.
330 Boylston Street
Boston, Mass. 02116
(617) 267-9100

Monday–Saturday 9:30–5:30
Closed Saturday during summer

It is almost impossible to imagine Boston without Shreve,
Crump & Low. Shreve's has been a Boston institution since 1800.
The roster of Shreve's clients reads like an index to the first
families of Boston. This great carriage-trade shop specializes in
magnificent jewels, contemporary porcelains, silver, crystal, and
many other fine gift selections. For the last hundred years they
have also had an antiques department which reflects not only the
current taste of Boston collectors, but of collectors throughout the
country who could not imagine an issue of *Antiques* magazine
without a Shreve advertisement on the back cover. A position it
has occupied since 1923.

Mr. Edgar M. Bingham has been director of this department
for over forty years. Mr. Bingham, a gentleman of great elegance
and charm, buys what he feels will fit in comfortably among the
antiques many of his clients already own. Though there are many
lovely pieces of eighteenth- and nineteenth-century English and
American furniture, it is the fine antique accessories that are really
the department's strong point. There is always an excellent choice
of English nineteenth-century tea and dessert services, large selec-

tions of paintings and prints, which are frequently more decorative than important but always in beautiful taste. Mr. Bingham is especially knowledgeable about silver, and there is usually a good assortment of eighteenth- and nineteenth-century English, Irish, and American pieces that are perfect to add to any collection or even give as a gift. It is one of the few antique shops that regularly carries a large selection of old fireplace equipment. In addition to the American and English milk glass, there is an unusual group of Spanish glass. This is one of those rare items that can go in and out in a moment. The English porcelain factories most often represented in the department are Coalport, Davenport, Derby, and various nineteenth-century ironstones. There are also Chinese wares available.

Shopping at Shreve, Crump & Low is an instantaneous trip to London's Bond Street. The sales help are intelligent and courteous. Shreve's is one of those civilized experiences that is a Boston trademark.

Firestone & Parsons
Ritz Carlton Hotel
Boston, Mass. 02117
(617) 266-1858

Monday–Saturday 9–5
Closed Saturday during summer

Firestone & Parsons are primarily fine jewelers. They have an international clientele as one would expect from the location. Their business is jewelry, but Mr. David Firestone does have a passion for very fine antique silver. There is always a selection of first-quality English, Irish, and American silver in this lovely but austere-looking shop. A silver collector is always welcome; however, this is not a bits-and-pieces gallery. Almost all of the seventeenth- and eighteenth-century silver is of museum quality and the prices reflect its rarity. Mr. Firestone is proud of having paid world record prices for pieces he has bought at auctions.

What is a surprise is the presence at any given time of three or four good paintings. The gallery has sold Renoir, Fantin-Latour, Modigliani. However, do not go expecting a painting collection.

They are so discreetly hung that they look like part of the furniture.

The jewelry the gallery has ranges from modern custom work to antique.

The great John Coney bowl that the Museum of Fine Arts owns was owned by Firestone & Parsons, as was also the museum's 1750 Irish Racing Punch Bowl. They have owned two of the three Liverpool jugs made by Paul Revere. The list can go on to include pieces that ended up in the New York Metropolitan, National Museum of Ireland, Los Angeles County Museum, and so on.

What is equally important is that Mr. Firestone and his son David are charming people.

Childs Gallery
169 Newbury Street
Boston, Mass. 02116
(617) 266-1108

9–5 Tuesday–Saturday
Closed Saturday during summer

Roger Howlett and Carl Crossman, the two young men who own this old, established Boston gallery, have brought great energy and intelligence to making this one of the most important painting galleries in the New England area.

Their personal taste has dictated the amazing range of art the gallery owns. Both the novice and seasoned collector will feel completely at home and be equally welcome.

The gallery is strong in American painting from the eighteenth to twentieth century, covering the academic painters of that period and the primitives or perhaps non-academic is a better term for painters like William Matthew Prior, Erastus Salisbury Field, Ammi Phillips, and William Jennys. The gallery has sold Peale, Sully, Stuart, Copley, Greenwood, and generally at least one of these important painters is available. It is not only portraits that interest the gallery, but also landscape, still life and genre painting. They have European paintings of the eighteenth–twentieth century also and these, too, show the same consistency of taste that makes everything the gallery buys interesting be it a Sargent, Burchfield, Luks, Severini, a Klee water color, or one of the very large selection of rare prints which they stock. The gallery has a most extensive collection of the great etching revival that started in England about 1850 with Whistler and Sir Francis Seymour Haden and in France with painters like Corot, Meryon, Jonkind (who is Belgian). They set off a great wave of etching that continued unabated until 1870. It then slowly died out (almost entirely by 1930), but it is interesting to realize that in the early 1920s the best Whistler and Zorn etchings were ten times more expensive than Rembrandt's. It is equally interesting to note how current taste can dictate price.

The gallery also specializes in Frank Benson bird prints, and their marine art collection ranges from such academic painters as Salmon, McFarlane, and Walters to those wonderful, unknown primitive painters who simply delight the eye with their instinctive feeling for color and design. The majority of the marine paintings relate to American subjects even when they are done by European or Chinese painters.

The policy of this gallery, as it is of any fine painting gallery, is to buy what they love, and their passion is quality painting.

Vose Gallery
238 Newbury Street
Boston, Mass. 02116
(617) 536-6176

Monday–Saturday 8:30–5:30

The Vose Gallery belongs to that special elite of painting dealers who combine exquisite taste and extraordinary knowledge with beautiful manners. The gallery exudes quality. Don't be intimidated by the photos in the entrance hall of famous paintings the Vose family has sold during five generations in the art business. The Rembrandts, Corots, Delacroixs, Millets, Stuarts, Copleys are very impressive, but Mr. Robert Vose, Jr., director of the gallery, whose two sons are now in the business, would be the first to assure you that they pride themselves on being able to start even young collectors of limited means on their way. It is not a large gallery by New York standards, but its stock would hold its own quite nicely on Madison Avenue.

The gallery is historically interesting as the primary force in introducing the Barbizon School of Corot, Millet, Delacroix, Tryon, Daubigny into the United States in the nineteenth century. They also sold the American followers of the school—Inness, Martin, and Alexander Wyant. Mr. Vose regrets that his father and grandfather were not particularly interested in the French Impressionists, but they were instrumental in selling the principal American Impressionists—John Henry Twacktman, William Hassen, Theodore Robinson, Willard Metcalf. The gallery handled the estates of Walter Griffin and Reynolds Beale.

The gallery is not likely to have a Rembrandt on hand anymore, though they do remember those they sold were from $300,000 to $400,000. How prices have changed!

The gallery prides itself on its collection of seventeenth-, eighteenth-, and nineteenth-century American portraits by the famous academic painters of that time—Blackburn, Stuart, Sully, Copley, Greenwood, Badger. There was a marvelous painting by William Yorke of the ship *David Tenney* hanging when I visited. There are always a number of marine paintings in stock.

The gallery has not overlooked the English painters and has sold portraits by Gainsborough, Reynolds, Romney, and Raeburn. They usually have at least one of these painters in stock.

Mr. Vose thinks there are still good buys to be found in nineteenth-century American academic portraits. However, he does warn about forgeries. Ralph Blakelock, he feels, is one of the most forged American painters.

There is no question that one leaves the Vose Gallery secure in the knowledge that any painting bought from the gallery has had enormous expertise brought to it. But Mr. Vose doesn't hesitate to admit they have made a few errors. Mr. Vose and his brother are now dedicated to finding any paintings that may have been sold by the family firm in the nineteenth century with mistaken attribution and are buying them back. These paintings are then donated to the Fogg Museum for study purposes. The mistakes were primarily made because information was so limited about the painters at that time. So far they have bought back a Daubigny, a Delacroix, and a Corot. It really is an act of courage by this gallery to face a family that thinks they have owned a Corot for seventy-five years and tell them it isn't one. Needless to say, many owners preferred not accepting the truth; considering the number of fakes on the market today, it is a comfort to deal with a gallery that guarantees practically into perpetuity everything they sell.

This gallery is well worth seeing, whether you buy or not. I am sure you will find your visit rewarding.

Gebelein Silversmiths
286 Newbury Street
Boston, Mass. 02115
(617) 523-3871

Monday–Friday 10–5
Preferably by appointment

After years of antiquing, it is still a special experience to meet a dealer like J. Herbert Gebelein of Gebelein Silversmiths. Mr. Gebelein is one of the great scholars in his field. His knowledge of antique silver, whether it be American, English, Irish, French, German, Russian, or even Chinese Export silver, seems limitless. There are a number of silver studies that owe a good deal of their expertise to Mr. Gebelein's assistance.

Mr. Gebelein's father, George C. Gebelein, started his own silversmith establishment, in 1909, where for practically the next fifty years craftsmen made silver by hand exactly as it had been done in the eighteenth century, using eighteenth-century tools and methods.

In addition to selling their own silver, they also sold very important antique silver and continue to do so. The family treasures among their collection of eighteenth-century smithery paraphernalia Paul Revere's own brass scale. Gebelein has, of course, its own hallmark, which when found means the very finest quality on a modern piece. Gebelein did not simply reproduce old American, English, and Irish silver but also created free adaptations of pieces which it felt captured the spirit of the original.

The shop on Newbury Street is a rather casual affair. The silver is primarily eighteenth-century American, English, Irish, although, whenever available, China Export silver is bought. There is also antique Sheffield. Much of the silver is neither particularly well displayed nor highly polished, which is a bit startling when you realize you may be looking at a Revere or John Coney piece. Many of the shop's pieces have found their way to museums throughout the world. I do not think this shop is for the novice silver collector. It is expensive as befits the quality of the silver offered. Mr. Gebelein does prefer dealing with a more knowledgeable collector. If you fall into that category or simply feel you want to start with the best, he is a man you should meet. There are a number of important silver collectors who would not dream of purchasing a piece from anyone without having Mr. Gebelein check it out.

Museums and Historical Houses

Boston Athenaeum
10½ Beacon Street
Boston, Mass. 02108

Monday–Friday 9–5:30
Saturday 9–4 (October–May)
Closed on legal holidays

The Boston Athenaeum, that marvelously impressive private library just up the street from the State House, had a rather informal beginning. A small group of Bostonians who loved books discovered they were duplicating each other's purchases in London. Being true Boston merchants, namely literate and frugal, it naturally occurred to them to share the books and use the money more expeditiously. Thus, this great institution came into being in 1807. Incidentally, many of the original books are still in circulation. Though the library is for the use of its 1,049 proprietary shareholders and their families, scholars do use its special research facilities. The general public is allowed into restricted areas of the building, which is quite beautiful. The original three-story structure was built in 1847; the two additional floors were added on, starting in 1913. They were designed by Henry Forbes Bigelow who greatly admired the original building. The additions are so contiguous to the original that I defy even the most astute architectural scholar to show where one begins and the other ends.

Aside from the beauty and brilliance of the design of the building, I was captivated by the idea that while reading a newspaper in the Long Room one can commune with Paul Revere or John Hancock or even Samuel Adams, all of whom are buried right next door in the Old Granary Burying Ground. The library has the unusual advantage of having all of its stock open. This means a member can wander freely through all five floors of eighteenth-, nineteenth-, and twentieth-century books.

The specialties of the collection do reflect a basic interest in art, history, and architecture. Possibly its most important single collection is of Confederate States imprints. It is fascinating to realize that a great portion of these documents was purchased within two months of Lee's surrender. There were trustees of the library who realized that, despite the anguish and bitterness of the times, these were terribly important historical documents and should be saved from destruction at all costs.

There are the books from George Washington's library at Mount Vernon. These were bought by the Athenaeum when it was discovered a bookseller was planning to send them off to London for auction.

The King's Chapel library was originally a gift from King William III of England to Boston's King's Chapel in 1698. Then, of all things, there is the important Groome Gypsy collection covering all facets of Romany life. The library also has a large portion of J. Q. Adams's personal books and family tracts.

The casual visitor is normally restricted to certain areas, but if you are a lover of architecture or history, you will probably be invited to see the entire building. The staff members at the Athenaeum love working there and enjoy sharing their pride in the library with a sympathetic visitor. It is a wonderful experience and well worth the time you give it.

Boston Public Library
Copley Square
Boston, Mass. 02116

Monday–Friday 9–9
Saturday 9–6
Sunday (October–May) 2–6
Closed on all legal holidays

There is an irresistible serenity about this elegant Renaissance building designed by Charles Follen McKim. Like a museum it is a building that must be repeatedly seen before it finally reveals all its hidden treasures. If you are interested in architecture or fine mural painting, this library should not be missed. It took me three visits to feel I had at least gotten some sense of the building. The Puvis de Chavannes mural paintings cover the entire upper portion of the main staircase and the second floor corridor, which is called the Chavannes Gallery. They are lovely, romantic tributes to the Muses and the Humanities. Remember, this building opened in 1895 and the art and decoration does reflect the taste of the period.

If you are a Civil War buff, do look at the great pair of lions by Louis Saint-Gaudens on the main staircase. They are memorials to two Massachusetts regiments, the 2nd and the 20th. Engraved on the statuary are listings of the battles these regiments fought; all were famous and bloody. It is chilling to see those names on this monument to reason and sanity.

The Abbey Room which is right off the Chavannes Gallery has a series of murals called "The Quest of the Holy Grail," painted by Edwin Austin Abbey. They are lushly realistic illustrations of this fascinating legend done with amazing technical facility, and they fit perfectly into their opulent architectural surroundings.

Finally, if you are diligent, you will find your way up a long dark staircase to a large third-floor gallery, with dark sandstone walls, that has the feeling of a cathedral. This feeling is quite appropriate, for the glorious murals that hang there are John Singer Sargent's "Judaism and Christianity." It is a superb mural painting; however, there is a real problem. Unless you possess fantastic eyesight, you will have trouble seeing them because of the poor lighting. I do understand the desire to create a mood for these paintings, but isn't it carrying it a bit far if you can't see them? I was very sorry I didn't have a flashlight with me.

If you are aggravated by the problems of the Sargent Gallery, take yourself to the courtyard and all will be forgiven. Henry James wrote that "in this place, a wealth of science and taste has gone to producing a service, when the afternoon light sadly slants, of one of the myriad gold-colored courts of the Vatican." The soft, dappled light and the play of its fountain make it one of the loveliest havens to be found in Boston.

Isabella Stewart Gardner Museum
280 The Fenway
Boston, Mass. 02115
(617) 734-1359

Tuesday 1–9:30
Wednesday–Sunday 1–5:30
No admission charge

Probably one of the most fascinating and delightful private memorials ever created is the Gardner Museum. At the turn of the century, Mrs. Gardner had this fifteenth-century Venetian palace built to her exact specifications. Functioning as a museum and home, it is filled with everything she collected over the years, aided by her close association with Bernard Berenson. There is an incredible combination of great treasures and some of the ugliest furniture and art objects ever made. It would be an understatement to call this collection eccentric. Whatever Mrs. Gardner loved and was interested in is reflected in the museum. The most exciting architectural element in the building is the huge inner court. It is filled with light and flowers. The flowers are replaced regularly to provide a refreshing reminder of the changing seasons. If you think the museum's Christmas flower display is spectacular, wait till you see the ones for spring and fall. Among the fragments of statuary placed in the garden are a stone chair and footstool. It delights me to imagine Mrs. Gardner sitting in it as she checks the placement of everything around her. You cannot help but be aware of the subtle arrangement of the various pieces of sculpture, be they a fine French Gothic madonna or a huge Roman torso. All have been placed by

Mrs. Gardner to please her eye and sense of drama. Everywhere light and shadow have been carried to their extreme.

Mrs. Gardner's primary interest was in the Renaissance, and the museum has a large selection of paintings and objets d'art from that period. Many are fantastic treasures; others have had their attributions changed so often one can hardly keep up. The problem for the director of the museum is that according to Mrs. Gardner's will absolutely nothing can be removed. For example, a painting was originally thought to be, let us say, a Raphael, but additional scholarship suggests perhaps school of Raphael, and even more study leads to its being simply labeled influenced by Raphael, with no date, name, or even country of origin. Very embarrassing indeed! But enough of the odd ones; there are so many fine paintings it is unfair to the museum to harp on its problems.

Among the Renaissance gems is the "Scarlet-turbaned Man" by Masaccio. An extremely important painter, he was one of the first if not the first artist to reflect the secularization of painting and the awakening of the Renaissance spirit in art. The "Hercules" by Piero della Francesca is also a unique painting for its time. The elegance of the Simone Martini "Madonna and Child with Four Saints" is dazzling. Another gem is the Bermejo painting, of "Saint Engracia." There is a painting by Da Rimini, dated 1307, of a Madonna and Child that must be seen just for the tender expressions on the saints' faces as they look at the Holy Child.

The Dutch Room contains a superb pair of portraits by Hans Holbein the Younger. The self-portrait by Rembrandt possesses that fantastic power he had for revealing the soul. Look up over the door next to the Rembrandt. There, a Bavarian sixteenth-century wood statue of St. Martin the Beggar riding a horse with a wildly expressive face, creates a curious contrast to the great painting.

Also in this room are other Rembrandts and a Vermeer called "The Concert." The extraordinary intimacy of Vermeer's painting was never really achieved again until the Impressionists, who were also totally involved with capturing the simplest moments of daily life.

There are many, many other paintings, including a number of Impressionists and some great Sargents.

Mrs. Gardner loved music and had regular concerts in her home. The museum continues this tradition by giving concerts twice a week on Thursdays and Sundays. They are held in the Tapestry Room and the effect could not be more pleasing. I know once you see this wonderful building, no trip to Boston will seem complete without a return visit.

The Boston Museum of Fine Arts
479 Huntington Avenue
Boston, Mass. 02115
(617) 267-9300

Tuesday 10 A.M.–9 P.M.
Wednesday–Sunday 10 A.M.–5 P.M.
Admission: Adults $1.50; children under sixteen free

This is an absolutely first-rate museum. Talk about quality, it is all there but on a human scale. There is no show business here, just beautiful art easily seen.

The Fine Arts is famous in its own quiet way for an extraordinary collection of eighteenth-century American furniture (mainly courtesy of the Garbisch family), American silver, and family portraits of the eighteenth and nineteenth centuries that are so revealing of our past. They have reorganized their American furniture galleries so that they no longer resemble warehouses. Frankly, I miss that old look, although the new rooms are lovely. It was enough to drive a collector to madness seeing one Queen Anne highboy after another, then its matching lowboy, and so much serpentine furniture you get seasick. They would also leave huge Export tureens sitting casually on pieces where anyone could handle them. I really loved this museum's American Wing.

Bostonians have always been interested in oriental artifacts. It harks back, of course, to their seafaring days on the China coast. The museum has an amazing collection of Chinese and Japanese art, especially early Chinese porcelains. There is a large gallery packed from floor to ceiling with pottery of the Han to Sung dynasties. Don't try to see it all on a single visit. I think the only way to approach a mass of material like this is on a one-to-one basis. Pick out a particular form or glaze that interests you and limit yourself to just looking at that and ignore everything else. You will be astonished at how much more you'll enjoy the experience and it will not be exhausting either physically or spiritually.

The museum has recently redone the wing that houses their Chinese sculpture collection. It would be difficult to find an ambiance more sympathetic to these great T'ang, Wei, and Sung pieces. The exquisite lighting, the subtle relationship of the sculpture to the scale of the room work to perfection. There is a heightened sense of drama but no theatrics. What beautiful taste went into planning this arrangement. I never miss the T'ang stone sculpture when I'm there. I have a great weakness for this art. It is a culmination point in Chinese sculpture and the finest pieces of this period combine a serenity and boldness that are very moving.

Grouped together in a smallish room is the Van Gogh portrait of the postman, a Cézanne portrait of his wife, and a little-known Bernard painting of his mother that is fantastic. This room literally bedazzles the senses as does the entire collection of Impressionists. However, no matter what period of painting interests you, don't leave the museum without seeing their great Gauguin "Where did we come from? What are we? Where are we going?" This huge painting is overwhelming. It is a modern version of a great religious tableau. You cannot believe its power until you see it for yourself.

The Fine Arts has in addition a superb Renaissance art collection. Their selection of Japanese and Chinese paintings is one of the most remarkable in the world. This list of treasurers could go on indefinitely. Give yourself plenty of time—have lunch or tea there. I could not imagine Boston without a visit to the Fine Arts.

Fogg Art Museum
28 Quincy Street
Cambridge, Mass. 02138
(617) 495-2387

Monday–Saturday 9–5
Sunday 2–5

The Fogg Art Museum is part of the Fine Arts Department of Harvard University. For a museum, that is definitely the equivalent of being in the right place at the right time. A number of Harvard graduates of great taste and wealth have endowed this institution with the treasures of their personal collections. Most university-connected museums are very modest affairs with an occasional choice painting here or there; not true of the Fogg. Housed in a building constructed to provide an example of sixteenth-century Italian architecture, the two lower floors are exact replicas in detail, materials, and proportions as those of the Canon's House at Montepulciano built in 1518. The center is an open court just shimmering with light. The museum also had the good fortune to have had an extraordinary director in Edward Waldo Forbes from 1909 to 1944 and his equally fine associate director Paul J. Sachs from 1923 to 1944. These two gentlemen were known as the exuberant mendicants. Despite having very little capital to purchase paintings, they managed to find the funds and donors to enlarge the museum's collection to nearly its present size.

The core of the Fogg's Chinese bronze, jade, and sculpture collection and French nineteenth-century paintings and drawings is from the Grenville L. Winthrop collection. There is a small chamber off the classic-sculpture room that has a group of Mr. Winthrop's paintings. It contains eight by Ingres and four by David. What is interesting is that the paintings are all small in size rather than the monumental scale one usually associates with these artists. Perhaps because of their modest proportion they have an amazing sense of intimacy. The David portrait of Napoleon in his coronation robes projects more vulnerability than majesty. The 1839 Ingres Odalisque is miraculously soft and sensual. This is an exquisite version of a subject vulgarized later in the century. Another beauty in the room is Ingres' (1814) "Raphael and the Fornarina."

The classic sculpture room has hidden in a corner a major Assyrian head of Divine Winged Figure from a palace at Nimrud which dates from 883 to 859 B.C. It is a superbly elegant piece, carved in pale gray stone with a marvelous stylized beard that looks like hundreds of tiny snails. There is also in the classic section a large pornographic red figure, Calyx Krater, *circa* 500 B.C. The pottery is beautifully drawn and very funny.

The museum has over 3,500 drawings. In addition to many by David, Géricault, Delacroix, Courbet, Degas, the Ingres drawings constitute the finest group of his work outside of France. Drawings are usually exhibited in a series of small alcove rooms that are perfect in scale for appreciating them. When I visited, there was a group of Piranesi being displayed.

The museum has a beautiful Renaissance art collection. The very early Italian primitives are hung in the Warburg Hall. The later Renaissance paintings are appropriately shown around the open galleria, overlooking the court. One of my two favorite pieces in this museum hangs at the foot of the stairs leading to these paintings. It is a very large austere eleventh-century Virgin from Tahull. This primitive sculpture from Spain is a religious experience even if you possess no religion.

When touring the museum it is but a few steps from a thirteenth-century Daddi to a Modigliani painting of a young girl. I love this juxtaposition of the Renaissance and the modern. The Fogg also has the Wertheim collection of Impressionists.

Although this is a modest-size museum, even its smaller collections, like the ceremonial silver of the seventeenth and eighteenth centuries, are all very choice.

The Fogg is extremely proud of its Chinese collection, and it has every reason to be. My other favorite piece in the museum is a Chinese prancing horse, which for me totally captures the spirit of the T'ang dynasty. It is neither large nor glazed. It is merely glorious. The Shang bronzes and the early jades are extremely fine. There is also an elegant Buddhist Trinity from a Six Dynasties stele. The three stone heads, with their finely carved eyebrows, couldn't be more aristocratic. Right next to these beauties are three great Apsaras, which are water sprites, from the same period.

Yes, I do love this museum. I never miss a chance to visit it when I'm in Boston. Take the subway; it couldn't be easier or pleasanter and is only an eight-minute ride from Back Bay.

Harrison Gray Otis House
141 Cambridge Street
Boston, Mass. 02114
(617) 227-3960

Monday–Friday 10–4

Home of the Society for the Preservation of New England Antiquities, this is the only remaining freestanding eighteenth-century house in Boston. It is amazingly beautiful. This is Charles Bulfinch's first house for Mr. Otis and marks the start of the development of Beacon Hill. Tastefully restored and furnished, it is an exquisite Federal mansion. I really don't think the later houses hold a candle to this building. Be sure you do not miss it.

Women's City Club of Boston
39-40 Beacon Street
Boston, Mass. 02114

Open Wednesday 10–4

This is a fine Greek Revival mansion and typical of those built on Beacon Street. It is appropriately furnished and will give you an excellent example of the interior taste and style of nineteenth-century Boston. It is quite opulent.

American Meteorological Society
45 Beacon Street
Boston, Mass. 02108

Monday–Friday 10–5

This is the third home built by Bulfinch for Harrison Gray Otis in 1806. It marks the final stage of the growth of Beacon Hill. The houses built on Beacon Street were for the wealthiest members of nineteenth-century Boston society. There are only bits and pieces of the original house left, but you do get a very good idea of the sumptuous way of life. The original attached stable has been restored and is a fascinating structure.

Beacon Hill Walking Tour

There are many different ways to walk Beacon Hill. Each devo-
tee has his or her favorite route. I prefer to divide it into two sections. The first walk starts at the Public Gardens and covers those
tiny streets west of Charles Street and bordering the embankment. It is a charming and easy walk.

Come in at Brimmer and Beacon. Do not overlook the little
streets and alleyways to your left. Return to Byron Street and
head east to River Street and again be sure to see all the side
streets between Byron and Mount Vernon. At Mount Vernon go
to Charles Street and walk two blocks down Charles to Cambridge Street. Turn right at Charles and Cambridge and then one
block to West Cedar Street. This is where Beacon Hill begins
in every sense. The first modest houses were built off Cambridge
and you can trace the economic ascent of the hill from this
point. Incidentally, the property that became Beacon Hill
belonged to the painter John Singleton Copley who sold it to the
developers. If you are a solid walker, continue along Cambridge
until you reach South Russell. By looking up each street you pass,
you will get a good sense of this portion of the hill. At this point I
would go to 141 Cambridge Street, the New England Preservation
Society and Bulfinch's earliest house for Harrison Gray Otis, one
of the developers of Beacon Hill. The house was built there to
encourage prominent people to buy houses on the land. It is one
of the most beautiful homes in New England. I find it aesthetically
more interesting than any of the later, grander mansions he built
for Mr. Otis. It would be a good idea to stop for lunch or coffee at
this point because you are going to do some solid climbing. I think
West Cedar is the loveliest of the small streets cross-secting the hill
from north to south. Take West Cedar to Pinckney and walk to
Joy. One block up Pinckney is Louisburg Square, which really does
look like a stage set with its beautiful Greek Revival houses. Turn
right on Joy to Mount Vernon. You will notice the houses on
Mount Vernon are much grander than those on Pinckney which
was home to the literary artistic circles of that time. Each house
on Mount Vernon is more beautiful than the next. Turn left

on West Cedar and stroll up Chestnut, an equally splendid street. Turn right on Walnut and continue to Beacon Street. From the State House look down on the Common and Beacon Street. For the wealthy nineteenth-century Bostonian, this was the summit of living and he was absolutely right.

Allow a minimum of one hour for this walk; it usually takes at least two, depending on how many stops you make.

Inns and Restaurants

Ritz-Carlton
15 Arlington Street
Boston, Mass. 02117
(617) 536-5700

This is one of the most pleasant and comfortable hotels I've ever stayed in. It is the only non-commercial hotel in Boston, and it is expensive. Reservations must be made in advance as there are only 265 rooms. Primarily a family hotel, many people consider the Ritz an annex to Harvard. Be sure not to plan a weekend in Boston during the Harvard-Yale football game. Reservations are made two years in advance for that particular weekend. The hotel is reasonable about animals. If you have a quiet, well-behaved dog, it is welcome. The management did have to say no to a client who tried to sneak in a kangaroo by reserving their rooms simply as Mr. and Mrs. and party. Some primal hotelkeeper's instinct made the Ritz ask who was in the party. They felt bad; she was a charming kangaroo but you have to draw the line somewhere.

Copley Plaza
Copley Square
Boston, Mass. 02116
Toll Free (800) 225-7654

This is as good a commercial hotel as is available in Boston. It has recently been redone in rather opulent bad taste; the rooms are filled with terrible French-style furniture. It is expensive, well located, and comfortable.

Word of warning: Reservations are not particularly well handled. You do not necessarily get what you reserve; the rooms on Copley Square are the only decent, relatively quiet ones in the hotel. Make a fuss if they put you anywhere else.

Holiday Inn
5 Blossom Street
Boston, Mass. 02114
Toll Free (800) 238-5510

I recommend Holiday Inns because my experience with them has been good. They are reasonably priced, clean, comfortable, and well run. The staffs usually couldn't be nicer. This one is very convenient to Charles Street and Beacon Hill. They do take well-behaved animals.

I am convinced there really is a Boston cuisine. It does not matter whether you dine on French, Chinese, Italian, or even fish, the food tastes pretty much the same, rather dull and uninteresting. However, there are redeeming factors: Most restaurants are relatively inexpensive and the service pleasant. Don't be surprised to find many places have a rather tea-roomy atmosphere which isn't bad for lunch or tea. The following restaurants are attractive, fashionable for Boston, with pleasant food:

Ritz-Carlton Dining Room (Ambiance very grand)
15 Arlington Street
Boston, Mass. 02117
(617) 536-5700
Reservations necessary

Luncheon, dinner

Cafe at Ritz-Carlton

Open for breakfast, lunch.
Dinner

Informal small dining room. Have marvelous blueberry muffins for breakfast.

Cafe Plaza
Copley Plaza Hotel
Copley Square
Boston, Mass. 02116
(617) 267-5300

Lunch 12–2:30 P.M.
Dinner 6–10 P.M.

A really beautiful rather Edwardian dining room. It is more atmosphere than food, but well worth a visit.

Copley Court
Copley Plaza
Boston, Mass. 02116

Breakfast, lunch, tea.

One of my favorite places for lunch or tea. Located in main lobby of hotel. Informal, good English-style tea: unfortunately they do use tea bags. Have great sandwiches that are not listed on menu.

Cafe L'Ananos
281A Newbury Street
Boston, Mass. 02116
(617) 353-0176

Reservations necessary
Lunch 12–2:30 P.M.
Dinner 6–11 P.M.

Lovely, elegant restaurant. Continental cuisine. Lunch, dinner.

There are a number of new little restaurants opening on Cambridge Street. I didn't list them because I don't know how long they will last. This street is very convenient if walking Beacon Hill.

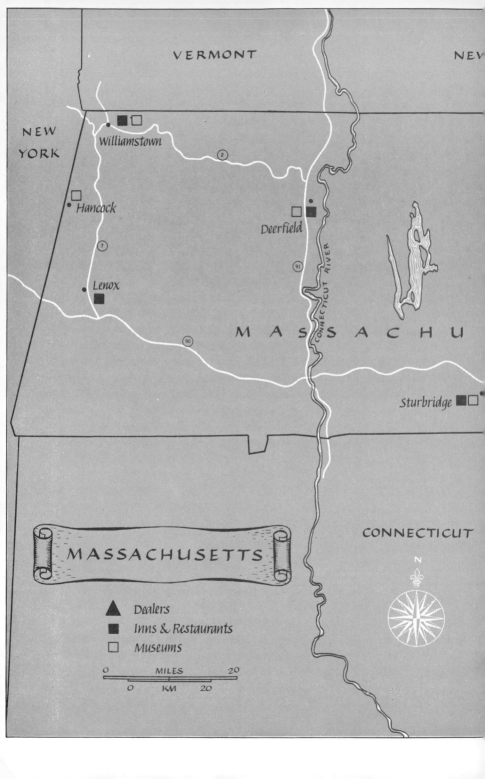

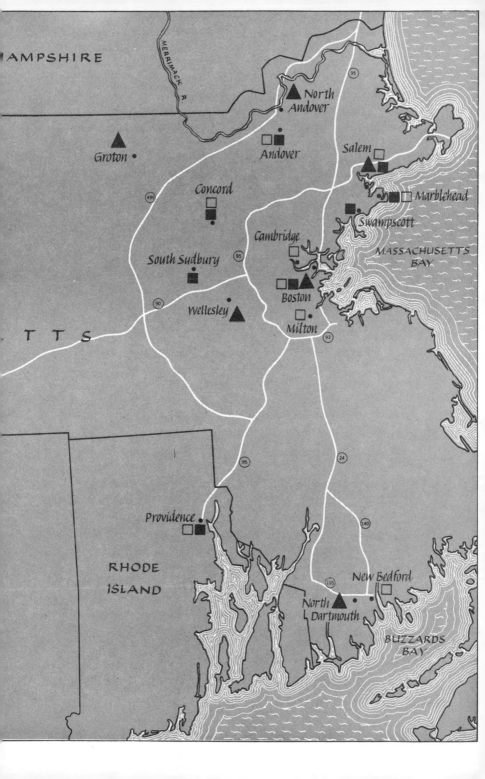

EASTERN MASSACHUSETTS

Antique Dealers

George Considine
Faunce Corner Road
North Dartmouth, Mass. 02747
(617) 995-9425
Monday–Saturday 9–4:30

George Considine, with a wicked gleam in his eye, loves to call himself a little old country dealer—that is about as accurate as describing Cartier's as a store that sells watches. A master of understatement, Mr. Considine has a delightfully perverse sense of humor. He is fully capable of describing a magnificent bonnet-top highboy as a nice piece of old wood. This marvelous gentleman is for me and many, many other people a very special dealer. He is a dealer's dealer, a collector's dealer, and a connoisseur's delight. There are other shops with more eighteenth-century New England furniture and larger selections of American, English, and Chinese porcelains, more American paintings, glass, folk art, and even oriental rugs, but none has objects that have been chosen with a more discriminating eye. Mr. Considine's taste is legendary in the trade, and after twenty years of consistent buying from this dealer, I am still astonished by the quality and uniqueness of many of the objects he has handled.

Basically, he is a fine Americana dealer whose prices could not be fairer. The barn serves as the main shop with a large inventory of good eighteenth-century country pieces that range from the simplest pine chest or table to a beautiful New Hampshire chest-on-chest. The chairs are mainly windsors and ladder backs, with an occasional fancy Sheraton or even country Queen Anne to be found. There are always camphor chests in both wood and leather. A lovely New England blanket chest still had its original blue paint. Tables are available in every size and description. I have never found the shop with less than two or three good New England dropfront desks. All of the objects, from a pair of Bristol wine washers to the finest lowboy, have been chosen with the same consideration. Nothing is a throwaway at George Considine's.

Don't be surprised to find examples of English and Continental furniture. As a matter of fact, one of the pleasures of this dealer is never quite knowing what he will turn up next. One example was a fabulous Japanese Export punch bowl, made for the Dutch market, which I bought from Mr. Considine years ago and is now once more in Japan. The American porcelains are later nineteenth century, with earlier pottery available. The English Worcester, Derby, Bloor Derby, and an especially attractive Gaudy Dutch Tea Service are all pre-1830. The Dutch and English Delft pieces are eighteenth century. Mirrors are eighteenth-century English and American. The accessories such as tobacco boxes, candlesticks, tea caddies, and every sort of eighteenth- and nineteenth-century glass are English and Dutch.

The finest material is always kept in the house. It is in this jewel of an eighteenth-century setting that the Queen Anne lowboys, highboys, drop-leaf tables, side and corner chairs are to be seen. The latest acquisitions of China Export are always very casually displayed on the dining-room table. These are now the blue-and-white Nanking, Fitzburgh, and Canton. Mr. Considine and I have a favorite game which consists of remembering rare pieces of porcelain he has had and I didn't buy. The crowning example for me was a part dinner service of the cherry pickers design with its soup tureen. I have as much difficulty understanding why I didn't buy that service as well as the Modigliani water color offered me at $1,200. These, of course, are stories all collectors love to tell on themselves.

The important ship paintings and American primitive portraits are also in the house. Not infrequently, Mr. Considine finds himself unable to part with a particularly delightful object such as a Fraktur or a fine weather vane. If it happens to you, just forget about the piece, because he will invariably give it to a favorite museum. The selection of whaling material may not be large but the examples are marvelous.

I do not want to mislead you as to the amount of stock available in the house. There may only be a painting or two for sale, one porringer table, though I do remember seeing four fine lowboys for sale at one time, or possibly just one Export bowl, but the chances are that single pieces will be as lovely an example as any to be found and the price below the going value.

If you should arrive on a day when the stock seems picked clean, which can happen, especially just before the major antique shows, there is still a great treat in store for you. The gardens surrounding the house are George Considine's passion, and there isn't a season of the year when something spectacularly beautiful isn't happening somewhere in them. I envy you your first visit to this very special dealer.

Den of Antiquity
552 Washington Street
Wellesley, Mass. 02181
(617) 235-3240

Monday–Saturday 9–5
Closed Saturday July and August

One of life's smaller mysteries is the names antique dealers find to christen their establishments. Mr. Leslie Slavid, a Scot to his fingertips and as knowledgeable an English-porcelain dealer as you will find, has chosen a name which conjures up images of an old rummage shop—Den of Antiquity! I grant you this name is not nearly as odd as the talented Renaissance dealer in New York who calls himself Metro Antiques, which sounds like a subway arcade. I am only complaining because Mr. Slavid is a good solid dealer and a very pleasant man to do business with.

The Slavids, father and sons, are primarily trade and decorator dealers who, in addition to carrying a small stock of English eighteenth- and early nineteenth-century oak furniture, are one of the major sources for antique Wedgwood in the country. Their reputation in this field is so fine that almost 50 per cent of their Wedgwood sales are conducted by mail. The shop can supply you with photos and prices of their large stock on request, but you must be specific as to the type of Wedgwood you collect. There are an astonishing variety of forms, colors, and glazes available in this very elegant pottery. Even such rarities as moonlight luster, caneware, rosso antico, agate, and the mulberry jasper ware are regularly in stock. Age does not necessarily determine cost so far as Wedgwood is concerned. Mulberry, produced in limited quantities during the twentieth century, is far more expensive than many earlier examples of jasper ware in the usual green, or blue, combinations.

Though Mr. Slavid's special interest is the Wedgwood, the shop also has a good selection of eighteenth- and early nineteenth-century English Worcester, Staffordshire (large collection of animal forms), and Derby. The modest collection of Export is in the Canton, Fitzburgh, and Rose Medallion patterns. Chinese and Japanese vases and bowls are late nineteenth century and mainly used as lamp bases.

The furniture, until recently just small English oak tables and chests, has been augmented by American eighteenth-century country pieces that reflect the shop's growing interest in Americana. The decorative accessories are now both English and American.

What Den of Antiquity may lack in the spectacular is more than compensated for in good quality merchandise that is very fairly priced. These are dealers not particularly interested in making a killing.

Marine Arts Gallery
127 Essex Street
Salem, Mass. 01970
(617) 745-5000

Monday–Saturday 9–4

As the world becomes a more and more mechanized place, the romance of the sailing ship takes on an entirely different meaning. Beyond the pleasure of their visual grace, they offer the collector a means of escape from the rigidity of today's world. They are a vestigial remnant of a time when man's skill was the essential factor in his own survival. Even the non-collector of marine art can-

not escape its primordial lure. The strange dichotomy of my collecting experience is that I have never bought a marine painting,
but I love looking at them. Perhaps I'm storing knowledge for my
next reincarnation when I come back a full-fledged ship aficionado.
I know my first port of call will be Marine Arts Gallery. Don
Kiernan and his brother Russ provide a first-class voyage all the
way.

The buying is Russ Kiernan's responsibility, with Don Kiernan
maintaining the gallery. These two quiet, unpretentious gentlemen
have one of the most important specialized painting inventories
in the entire country. Though nineteenth-century American ship
painting is their primary interest, there are marvelous examples of
English and Continental ships and any peripheral material that
they feel relates directly to their field, American ships. The great
English nautical painters Fitz Hugh Lane, Salmon, James Buttersworth, Walters, and McFarlane are well represented in the gallery's stock. As with much specialized subject matter, the price
varies greatly even when painted by the same important artist. A
Salmon or McFarlane ship with an American flag is worth perhaps 40 per cent more than one with a European flag. This offers
a perfect opportunity for the collector, who loves these painters
simply as great marine artists, to own one at a considerably lower
cost, provided they are not American purists. The gallery has a
pair of Boston Harbor views by Robert Salmon that are the only
ones of this subject on the market today. It is very interesting to
observe the influence Chinese painting exerted on this artist. The
handling of the shadows on the sails and the color of both the
sails and water are particularly Chinese in feeling, in the painting
of a ship in Liverpool Harbor, 1824. And, of course, there is always the classic Salmon touch of the bit of red on his figures.

It is their selection of rarities which gives Marine Arts its particular position in the art market. "Departure of Jenny Lind" a portrait of the singer, seen waving her white handkerchief, is one of
the most important paintings ever done by Samuel Walters. A
large beautiful double portrait by George Durrie of two midship-
man brothers and a superb Dutch seventeenth-century whaling
scene by Abraham Storck are just two examples of a very long list
that includes paintings by Prendergast, not nautical, just lovely,

William Marsh's primitive sailing ship, William Bradford's arctic views to say nothing of works by Yorke, Norton, De Haas, and finally the great American primitive James Bard. As most collectors know, there are almost no Bards available and when they come on the market their prices are quite romantic. At the other end of the price spectrum from Bard are the enchanting little primitive ship paintings by the ubiquitous anonymous artist that can be bought for just a few hundred dollars, making the pleasure of ownership possible for even the novice collector.

The sense of quality that permeates this unpretentious gallery is one of its most attractive assets. Marine Arts exclusively represents a number of contemporary artists who work in the classical mode of the eighteenth- and nineteenth-century painters. The best of them is the Englishman Ray Cross, who is absolutely marvelous. He is truly a painter possessed by another time. His paintings hang in many museums and private collections throughout the world. I know it is a strange comment about a painter who works in an earlier style, but Cross somehow manages to remain a great original. Really an amazing accomplishment.

The whole experience of Salem is a very special one and it is only fitting that this distinguished gallery is part of it.

Pam Boynton
Pleasant Street
Groton, Mass. 01450
(617) 448-5031

Always open when home
Appointment advisable

Nothing in the world makes me feel more foolish than being unable to decide which door is the right entrance to a dealer's shop. I always have visions of being chased out of someone's kitchen by an irate spouse or animal. There are a million doors to Pam Boynton's house and you are welcome in all of them. Absolutely no one, including the animals, will do anything but give you a hearty greeting. Pam Boynton, boisterous of voice and spirit, is an old-time picker-dealer. On the surface there is a casual anarchy to the arrangement of the stock, which is a good selection of New England eighteenth-century country furniture and accessories. Mrs. Boynton is a very active picker, which means she turns up a lot of merchandise and moves it rapidly.

There are the occasional formal pieces as in a Chippendale four-drawer mahogany chest and Chippendale armchairs, but for the most part, what you will find in chairs is a large assortment of bow-back, birdcage, and fanback windsors; country Queen Anne, including some with Spanish feet; and banister-back armchairs. A very stylish piece was a Queen Anne corner chair with pad feet from Concord, New Hampshire. One of the sets of chairs, the birdcage windsors, had the label of their original maker, Daniel Stewart of Farmington, Maine.

Original paints seems to be a particular strong point with this dealer. There were many examples in chests, chairs, even a slant-front Chippendale chest, but I was especially charmed by a blanket chest whose yellow paint design was called sponge work. This is one of the few dealers who buys all the Shaker furniture and accessories she can find. The marvelous thing about picker-dealers is they do buy everything because their clients demand a wide range of material. Among the eighteenth- and early nineteenth-century accessories available were pipe boxes, burl bowls, dolls, mirrors, woodenware, English and American pewter, chalkware, and the early redware pottery produced by the colonists.

Pam Boynton will provide you with a most informal antiquing experience. I found it delightful, but this does not necessarily mean inexpensive. All good material demands its price today, and even the dealer's dealer charges accordingly. The experienced collector can do well with this dealer.

Robert Cleaves
Boston Road
Groton, Mass. 01450
(617) 448-5375

By appointment only

There is a mysterious underground in the antique business inhabited by some of the most knowledgeable people in the trade. Generally preferring to remain anonymous, they are known, to a chosen few, as the pickers who supply many dealers with some of their choicest objects. These shadowy figures maintain no shops, no stock, no signs. The antique collector who has the good fortune to find them usually does so by accident, rather than design. Robert Cleaves is one of the best of these pickers. In addition to enormous expertise in the field of American primitive painting and folk art, he is also a very, nice man. Mr. Cleaves who works out of his home is an extremely difficult man to find. He is constantly traveling in search of new material. I have always felt that pickers such as Bob Cleaves, who is tremendously respected in the trade, derive their greatest satisfaction in discovering their material and the least in selling the object. These men are the true treasure hunters.

There is no way to anticipate what you may find at the house. One day it could be a beautiful oriental rug, another a fine eighteenth-century American painted chest, or perhaps even a lovely piece of silver or porcelain. There is a good chance of finding an interesting painting. Mr. Cleaves's taste in art is wonderful and he does buy as many paintings as he is offered. Unfortunately for the collector, a good American painting usually is gone in a moment. Luck will play a large factor in determining the success of your visit to Bob Cleaves. Because there is so little material to be seen, many antiquers may wonder why I have suggested visiting this dealer. I think he has marvelous taste, great instinct, and for me there is a particular excitement in feeling I may be seeing an object that has never been on the market before.

Robert Cleaves is only interested in the collector who is capable of appreciating a marvelous object when it is shown without any razzle-dazzle!

Rolland Hammond
169 Andover Street
North Andover, Mass. 01845
(617) 682-9672

Monday–Friday 8–5
Saturday 8–12
Appointment suggested

Federal New England—few dealers are capable of evoking this period in American history as effectively as Rolland Hammond. Respected as a dealer of great culture and knowledge, Mr. Hammond's elegant shop specializes in the magnificent, formal, Hepplewhite, Sheraton, and Federal furniture produced in Boston and the North Shore (Newburyport-Salem) during the last quarter of the eighteenth century through the first quarter of the nineteenth. There are beautiful sofas, chairs, secretaries, plus a variety of tables and chests from this period. In addition, this dealer always has a small selection of Queen Anne, Chippendale and, on occasion, Pilgrim furniture. Chosen with exquisite care, a Queen Anne highboy blends harmoniously with a great Sheraton card table from Salem. The shop prides itself on its collection of American folk art which includes scrimshaw, primitive painting, painted furniture, decoys, et cetera. However, there is very little of this material on display because it is often bought for specific collectors and sold almost immediately. If you are interested in this field, call and explain your needs. Mr. Hammond also buys fine eighteenth-century English and American silver, again mainly for a particular collector's need. Very few dealers are willing to work so directly with their clients. The shop's decorative accessories—mirrors, glass, and porcelain—reflect the basic formality of this dealer's taste. Rolland Hammond has a special weakness for clocks and he has some wonderful ones, including a Willard clock with an alarm, which is very rare indeed. The antiquer of refined taste will thoroughly enjoy this splendid shop.

AUCTIONS

Robert W. Skinner Inc.
Route 117
Bolton, Mass. 01740
(617) 779-5528

Auctions held all year. Has good reputation in the business.

Museums and Historical Houses

Salem Historic Restoration Area
Essex Institute
132–134 Essex Street
Salem, Mass. 01970
(617) 744-3390

Tuesday–Saturday 9–4:30
Open Monday, June 1–October 15
Sunday and holidays 1–5
Closed Thanksgiving, December 25, January 1

The Essex Institute is comprised of a central building, containing the museum and library, housed in Plummer Hall, and the John Tucker Doland House, both fine examples of Victorian Italian Revival architecture, and six fantastically beautiful seventeenth-, eighteenth-, and nineteenth-century houses, fully restored and furnished, within walking distance of the Institute. The museum itself is a marvelous example of Victorian extravagance in display techniques, as opposed to the modern museum concept of cleanliness being next to godliness. Here all is clutter, but fabulous clutter, great furniture, paintings, ceramics, silver, dolls, toys, uniforms, documents—all pertaining to Essex county (Salem). Nothing could be more fascinating than the contrast between the late-Victorian taste of the museum organizers and the elegance displayed in the individual earlier homes. It is also interesting to note that by the mid-nineteenth century the Essex Institute was actively involved in the preservation of historic Salem. Tickets to visit the houses can be purchased at the Institute building.

SALEM INSTITUTE HOUSES

John Ward House

Tuesday–Saturday 10–4;
Sunday 1–4:30, June 1–October 15

Seventeenth-century house.

Gardner-Pingree House

Tuesday–Saturday 10–4 all year
Sunday 1–4:30, June 1–October 15

A Samuel McIntire house, in his most developed style.

Peirce-Nichols House

Tuesday–Saturday 2–4:30 all year

An early Samuel McIntire building.

Assembly House

Tuesday–Friday 2–4:30 all year
Saturday 2–4:30, June 1–October 15

Remodeled by Samuel McIntire.

Andrew-Safford House

Thursday 2–4:30 all year

One of the most important Federal houses in New England.

Crowninshield-Bentley House

Tuesday–Saturday 10–4;
Sunday 1–4:30, June 1–October 15

An elegant eighteenth-century house.

The Peabody Museum of Salem
161 Essex Street
Salem, Mass. 01970
(617) 745-1876

Monday–Saturday 9–5
Closed Thanksgiving, December 25, January 1.

The Peabody Museum is completely captivating. Filled with lore of the sea, you can practically hear the wind in the rigging. It is a museum dedicated to the great days of the sailing ships of

Salem and everything they may have encountered in their journeys to the east, including people, objects, and animal life. Endless numbers of ship paintings by Salmon, McFarlane, Walters, and their peers, plus ship models, logs, account books, navigating tools and, most exciting of all, a room with great figureheads from the ship's prows mounted on the walls. Chinese paintings of the shipping ports of Macao, Hong Kong, Canton, and Whampoa have exactly the same details as the great Hong Export bowls. The examples of China Export porcelains are wonderful, especially a huge pair of blanc de chine goose tureens given to the East India Marine Society in 1803. The Peabody, incidentally, is an outgrowth of this Society formed in 1799, which was made up of Salem ship captains. The second-floor galleries contain models and paintings of the great steamships. If you have ever sailed or dreamed of sailing on either the old *Queen Mary* or the old *Queen Elizabeth*, the giant-scale models of these two great ladies will make you weep with nostalgia. The Peabody's collections are divided into three major categories—marine history; ethnology, which consists of the material culture of non-European peoples with emphasis on the Pacific and Far East but including North American Indian specimens; and for all nature lovers, there is an amazing Essex county collection of birds and mammals of land and sea—fish, reptiles—and rocks and minerals. Never mind all this description, I expected this to be a museum for children but found I didn't want to leave.

Marblehead Historical Society
Jeremiah Lee Mansion
161 Washington Street
Marblehead, Mass. 01945

Monday–Saturday 9:30–4
May 15–October 12

The wealth of Marblehead merchants during the eighteenth century is personified by the sheer grandeur of the Lee Mansion. The house with its great architectural details, elaborate furniture, rugs, wallpaper is breathtaking.

Addison Gallery of American Art
Phillips Academy opposite Andover Inn
Andover, Mass. 01810

Monday–Saturday 10–5
Sunday 2:30–5
Closed weekends of July 4, Labor Day,
December 25, and January 1

American eighteenth-, nineteenth-, twentieth-century paintings,
drawings, prints, sculpture, glass, and furniture.

Museum of the American China Trade
215 Adams Street
Milton, Mass. 02186

Tuesday–Saturday 2–5
Closed holidays

Greek Revival House (1833). Porcelains, textiles, and other objects of the China trade. Export porcelain examples are unique.

Whaling Museum
18 Johnny Cake Hill
New Bedford, Mass. 02740

June–September, Monday–Saturday 9–5
October–March, Tuesday–Saturday 9–5
Sunday, all year, 1–5
Closed Thanksgiving, December 25, January 1

New Bedford was known as the original whaling city and became a ghost town after the whaling industry ceased during the nineteenth century. The Whaling Museum has a collection of scrimshaw, ship models, a half-scale reproduction of an authentic whaling bark, and replicas of old artisan's shops.

This is literary New England—home to Emerson, Thoreau, Hawthorne, Alcott. Walden Pond is here in this amazing village.

Concord Antiquarian Museum
Lexington Road and Cambridge Turnpike
Concord, Mass. 01742

Monday–Saturday 10–4:30
Sunday 2–4:30
Closed November–mid-March

Period rooms, dating from 1685 to 1870, filled with furniture and decorative art from the locality, including a replica of Emerson's study.

Inns and Restaurants

Longfellow's Wayside Inn
Wayside Inn Road, off Route 20
South Sudbury, Mass. 01776
(617) 443-8846

Open all year

Lunch and dinner. Dining room closed Christmas. Lodging available.
Yes, this is the inn that inspired the poems.

The Colonial Inn
Concord, Mass. 01742
(617) 369-9200

Open all year

Breakfast, lunch, dinner. Lodging available.

General Glover House
Off Route 1A, on Salem Street
Vinnin Square
Swampscott, Mass. 01907
(617) 595-5151

Open all year

Dinner Monday–Saturday, 5 P.M.; Sunday noon.

The Lyceum (in restoration area)
43 Church Street
Salem, Mass. 01970
(617) 745-7665

Open all year

Lunch and dinner daily.

Rosalie's
18 Sewall Street
Marblehead, Mass. 01945
(617) 631-9888

Open all year

Lunch and dinner daily.

CENTRAL MASSACHUSETTS

Museums and Historical Houses

Old Sturbridge Village
Sturbridge, Mass. 01566
On route 20 near intersection of 90 and 86

Daily April–October 9:30–5:30
March, November 9:30–4:30
December–February 10–4
Closed December 25, January 1

A recreated rural New England village, *circa* 1790–1840, contains more than forty buildings moved here from throughout New England.

Old Deerfield Village
Deerfield, Mass. 01342
Route I-91, junction route 5 North

Monday–Saturday 9:30–noon, 1–4:30
Sunday 1–4:30
Closed Thanksgiving, December 24–25, January 1

Thirty buildings over 150 years old; eleven, completely furnished with period antiques, are open to the public. The main street or Deerfield is considered by many to be the most beautiful in the United States. This village was the northeast frontier of New England in the seventeenth century. Life was by no means tranquil. Deerfield was destroyed twice by the Indians and, in 1675, the Bloody Brook Massacre completely emptied the town for seven years. Largely rebuilt in the eighteenth century, it has remained an unspoiled exquisite memory of another time.

Inns and Restaurants

Publick House
Sturbridge, Mass. 01566
(617) 347-3313
Open all year

Lunch and dinner. Lodging available. Reputation for very fine food.

Deerfield Inn
Deerfield, Mass. 01342
(413) 774-3147
Open all year, except December 23–25

Lodging available. Breakfast, lunch, dinner. Located on same street as historic houses.

WESTERN MASSACHUSETTS

Museums and Historical Houses

Sterling and Francine Clark Art Institute
Williamstown, Mass. 01267
(413) 458-8109

Tuesday–Sunday 10–5
Closed Mondays, January 1,
December 25, Thanksgiving
Admission Free

Tucked away in the Berkshires is one of the finest art museums
in the United States. Rural museums, even those situated in college towns, are more often than not horse-and-buggy affairs filled
with much enthusiasm and scholarship but very little art. Sterling
and Francine Clark, collectors with a strong point of view, were
determined to place their life's work in a sympathetic environment. Their final choice of the exquisite New England village of
Williamstown was inspired. It was far from accidental. The Clark
family's association with Williams College, which is located there,
went back several generations. The school felt, as did the Clarks,
that the collection should function as a training ground for young
art scholars in addition to serving the public. Once committed,
Mr. and Mrs. Clark spared no expense in creating what became
their gift to posterity. The buildings that house the paintings, silver, and porcelains are beautiful and serene. The scale of the museum makes the viewing experience delightfully intimate.

Mr. and Mrs. Clark as painting collectors cover a wide range of
material starting with the early Renaissance and climaxing with
an extraordinary group of Impressionists. The collection has a
consistency of taste and a very curious color myopia. These collectors love pretty paintings; fortunately, most of the time, they
managed to balance a preference for the sweet with a marvelous
sense of what is great art. The only group I had absolutely no
sympathy for were the French nineteenth-century pretty peasant
paintings. The fine Millets, Pissarros, and Courbets the Institute
owns only point up the triteness of most nineteenth-century
French genre painting. The color bias I noticed, especially in the
Impressionist collection, which is superb, was a preference for
blue. In an abstract way, the bulk of the collection is blue even
when it actually isn't. This is not meant to be a negative criticism;
it is merely an observation. There is an interesting game you
might play with yourself as you go through the institute. Bearing
in mind the collectors' preferences as to color and subject matter,

see if you can select which paintings are not part of the original collection but were either donated or additions bought after the Clarks's deaths. It is a fascinating exercise in perception.

The core of the collection is nineteenth-century French painting. A supremely gallant Géricault, "Trumpeter of the Hussars," is the epitome of romanticism. The selection of Barbizon and Academic painting is first-rate, though I personally find these particular schools somewhat innocuous. An interesting example of changing museum taste is the resurrection of a number of Bouguereau nudes from the storerooms. Frankly, I do not understand why. They are still perfectly awful paintings. The Institute owns the largest cow picture I've ever seen; it is by Troyon and really quite marvelous. These cows couldn't be more bovine. However, if cows don't excite you, don't despair; there are Troyon geese, dog, and sheep paintings.

The Impressionist collection is unique for the extraordinary number of great Renoirs, over thirty paintings. The Renoir gallery is smashing. It is Renoir at his best—human, lush, gorgeous— really paying attention, nothing mechanical. Particularly exquisite is a portrait of Mme. Claude Monet. Pattern on pattern on pattern, used lovingly and softly, all in blue. Renoir's feeling for the vocabulary of blue is astonishing in its expressiveness. There is a marvelous still life of apples in a bowl that is a small masterpiece. The blue bowl fairly leaps at you across the room. Renoir's flesh tones are always glorious, but there is a painting of onions that is as sensual as any nude. The color tones of the onionskin are luminous. All of the Renoirs are of amazing quality but my favorite nude is the blonde bather. I suspect this painting has haunted the dreams of many young college students, both male and female.

The other Impressionists are well represented, if not in the same quantity as Renoir, certainly in quality. The Degas ballet dancers are there as well as a number of superbly realized horse bronzes. A tiny Degas jewel is "Before the Race," with its mounted jockeys wearing their vivid jerseys. What marvelous shapes and colors! The Manets, Monets, Lautrecs, Sisleys hold their own beautifully. It is always fascinating to me how a particular painting will demand attention even when the competition is intense. There is a Berthe Morisot portrait of a girl combing her hair that is in a gallery with a number of small but marvelous Manets, yet this Morisot has a vibrancy that demands your attention. What is more mysterious than the excitement of a fine work of art?

John Singer Sargent and Winslow Homer are among the American painters on exhibit. Lovely as the Sargents are, the Winslow Homer canvases absolutely dominate the walls of their gallery. In one of the rooms there is a curious juxtaposition of a Rembrandt and a Goya. The male subjects in both paintings are wearing huge hats, which figure prominently in both portraits. It is interesting to see how two great artists treated the same problem. A fascinating Turner, "Rockets and Blue Lights," looks completely abstract. Eliminate the figures and it is a mid-twentieth-century work.

Among the Renaissance paintings is a beautiful humanist study by Piero della Francesca, "Madonna and Child" with four angels. There is nothing remotely religious about the painting. The fashion details are elegantly observed even to the opulent barefoot angels. Another gem is the "Journey of the Magi," *circa* 1440, Florentine School, which has the brilliance of an illuminated manuscript.

There is an odd sameness to the collection except for certain extraordinary works. It is safe, very important, but not surprising, obviously reflecting the taste of its owners which was very fine but limited. However, the exceptions are worth a trip from anywhere in the United States. Purchased out of their endowment is one of the world's great Fragonards. "The Warrior" is Fragonard's statement of life. Shattering all the pretty conventions of eighteenth-century French painting, it is a revealing human document. This painting is indeed a treasure. The other great exceptions are the paintings from the Lehman Collection, which were donated to the Institute in 1976. It is unfair to compare collectors, but the few paintings that comprise the Lehman group radically illustrate the difference between safety and genius. The Renaissance paintings and the three Jan Gossaert (called Mabuse) are marvelous. Do not miss them. If necessary spend an extra day; it is worth it.

The Institute has a fine collection of drawings, especially Degas. They are not always on exhibit; if you wish to see them, call ahead for an appointment. There are examples from Dürer to Picasso.

The Clark antique-silver collection is one of the finest in the United States. It is especially strong in pieces by the great eighteenth-century English silversmith Paul de Lamerie. There are thirty-two examples of this rare master. The small porcelain collection has pieces of eighteenth- and nineteenth-century Meissen, Vienna, Höchst, and Sèvres.

I have never met a person who was not delighted by their visit to this Art Institute. Whatever reservations I have are merely tiny pebbles in my search for perfection. It is a wonderful collection.

Hancock Shaker Village
Hancock, Mass. 01237
Junction routes 20 and 41, five miles west of downtown Pittsfield

June 1–November 1, daily 9:30–5

An original Shaker community, dating from 1780 with eighteen buildings, over 1,000 acres of gardens, fields, and woodlands. It is starkly beautiful.

Inns and Restaurants

Treadway Williams Inn
Main Street
Williamstown, Mass. 01267
(413) 458-9371
Toll free 800-631-0182

Open all year

Breakfast, lunch, dinner. Large, attractive commercial establishment.

The Village Inn
Lenox, Mass. 01240
(413) 637-0020

Open all year

Breakfast, lunch, dinner. Lodging available.

*The Barrows House
Dorset, Vt. 05251
Route 30, six miles from Manchester
(802) 867-4455

Open all year

Breakfast, lunch, dinner. Lodging available. Delightfully comfortable inn with excellent food.

*Arlington Inn
Route 7
Arlington, Vt. 05250
(802) 375-6532

Open all year, except for April and November.

Lunch and dinner daily, except Tuesday. Lodging available.

The British Maid
State Road, Route 2 East
Williamstown, Mass. 01267
(413) 458-4961

Open all year, closed Monday

Breakfast, lunch, dinner.

The Mill on the Floss
Route 7
New Ashford, Mass. 01267
(413) 458-9123

Open all year

Dinner daily; lunch June–October

* These two charming inns are located in Vermont but within an hour's drive of Williamstown, Massachusetts.

LeJardin
Route 7
Williamstown, Mass. 01267
(413) 458-8032

Open all year

Dinner daily, except Tuesday. Breakfast and lunch June–September.

III

Our Unblemished Past

Northern New England is a land where time moves to another rhythm. There is a sense of stillness, of privacy undisturbed for centuries. The sparkling white villages are more beautiful than can be imagined. Hancock and Dorset are figments of a perfect fantasy. The farms nestling among the rolling foothills of the Berkshires have always been there, or so it seems. Back roads are haunted with abandoned villages whose structures refuse to decay, though all life has gone. Its pine forests, astonishing mountains, bottomless lakes possess a resoluteness that is the very fiber of its people. The coastal cities of Portsmouth and Portland reflect their nautical past in the great captains houses that still grace their streets. As always, the seas that crash endlessly against the rocky coastline triumphantly shout their siren song: Come to me! Come to me!

VERMONT

Antique Dealers

Robert Avery Smith
Route 103
P.O. Bellows Falls
Rockingham, Vt. 05101
(802) 463-4296

By appointment only

Robert Avery Smith is one of the quality dealers in New England. He is a rare man in every sense of the word. Extremely diffident, the clues to this fine dealer lie in his stock. One quick glance about his lovely eighteenth-century house indicates the depth of knowledge and marvelous taste this specialist in oriental carpets and American primitive painting brings to all his purchases. His reputation among rug and painting dealers, who can be a very rough group indeed, is unique in the trade. He is a trade dealer in the sense that all antique dealers are trade dealers. No dealer in fine merchandise is ever too expensive for another dealer as long as the quality warrants the price and, of course, the dealer has the client to pay for it.

The inventory is not large and there is a good deal of turnover, especially in the rugs. What can make for complications in buying from Mr. Smith is a certain degree of hesitation about what he chooses to sell. Don't be distressed, just patient, if there is a painting or even a piece of furniture not available at the moment you want it; like many unrequited passions, they are that much more desirable when postponed. The rugs are predominately Caucasian, Turkish, Turkomand, and Mongolian, with an occasional example of the more formal Persian. There was the most terrific Kazak. This rug, as were all the other carpets, was a completely uncliché example in terms of color and pattern.

The furniture, again not a large selection, is fine eighteenth-century New England country, with the traditional ladder- and banister-back armchairs, small tables, wonderful painted chests such as a William and Mary, *circa* 1740, in the original eggplant color. The only piece of formal furniture available was a very dainty Connecticut cherry lowboy with elegant Spanish feet. This little beauty is a wonderful illustration of the refinement of craftsmanship to be found in the rural areas of New England during the eighteenth century.

Mr. Smith and his late wife were well known for their expertise in textiles, and the shop continues to carry fine eighteenth- and nineteenth-century examples of crewel, coverlets, quilts, and textiles. When Mr. Smith can find a piece of folk art that meets his exacting standards, be they wood carvings or weather vanes, he buys them.

However, I must return to the primitive paintings. Again, there are only a small number but that same consistency of taste prevails. This is a relatively expensive dealer who, I feel, is truly worth the price. The words "quality dealer" are bandied about so freely today that when you finally meet one like Robert Avery Smith, it seems an understatement.

Hillary Underwood
21 Pleasant Street
Route 4
Woodstock, Vt. 05091
(802) 457-1750

Appointment advised

Like fine wine, a vintage dealer improves with age. A New Englander born and bred, Mrs. Underwood, rather than softening around the edges, has remained as bright, tart, and delightful at eighty-odd years as she was twenty years ago. The more so called country dealers I've met, the more astonished I've become by their highly developed sense of sophistication. They know exactly what they're about and, I suspect, play their satisfied collectors like a violin.

There is literally something for every variety of American folk art enthusiast in this shop. Though originally a very active New England country furniture dealer, the stock in furniture is now minuscule, except for Mrs. Underwood's personal collection, and she will not sell any of this.

The material in the shop portion of her house is scattered about with a complete disregard for any kind of order. At first glance, it looks more like a jumble sale than an important dealer's inventory, but once your eye settles down you'll find a huge range of interesting folk art. These include wooden carvings of figures and animals, some wonderful signs, weather vancs, quilts, baskets, and pottery. There is a large assortment of painted hatboxes in all sorts of sizes. I found the primitive paintings of no particular quality, but if you enjoy collecting toys, this is definitely the dealer to visit. To the odd assortment of objects, add huge copper cooking pots, brass andirons, wooden architectural elements, old fire engines, and a goodly stock of old iron fireplace equipment.

A great deal of the material is as amusing and charming as Hillary Underwood herself.

Nimmo & Hart Antiques Inc.
Middletown Springs, Vt. 05757
(802) 235-2388

Appointment advised

The singular danger to the unwary traveler, using the back roads of Vermont to find Nimmo & Hart Antiques, is dodging the variety of animal life who use these thoroughfares as part of their natural landscape. I expected the cows because the Berkshires are dairy country, but the obstacles also included turkeys, goats, chickens and, finally, a big Irish Setter (who reminded me of Captain Ahab as he stood in the middle of the road, intently gazing from side to side, searching for whatever a Vermont Irish Setter searches for, but not moving a muscle to get out of the way). Frankly, I arrived at the shop wondering what to expect from dealers hidden in a corner of nowhere.

The answer was obvious as soon as I stepped into their charming home. Nimmo & Hart are dealers who brook no clichés in their taste. It is immediately evident that a very sophisticated sensibility prevails. The shop is delightful. It is filled with a fascinating combination of many different styles of predominately eighteenth-century American country furniture, which is their forte, and, incidentally, beautifully represented by a lovely set of bow-back windsors. It was an eighteenth-century Portuguese Queen Anne side table that completely took my fancy. These are dealers with a strong decorative sense who feel everything of a consistent quality is appropriate together. Their shop proves this point decisively. The country furniture is from England, the Continent, and America. The porcelains are English eighteenth-century soft paste such as Pratt ware, Astbury, Liverpool, Bow, Caughley. When they can find it, they love the European blanc de chine as in the Mennacy ware. There are three different varieties of early American redware available. It is always interesting to note the regional differences in pottery—in this case between Carolina, Pennsylvania, New England.

Though there is a small selection of French country chairs, tables, chests, and English eighteenth-century oak pieces, it is the American furniture that is the bulk of the collection—early ladder-back armchairs, Spanish-foot side chairs, a Queen Anne trestle table in pine and maple. I was especially taken with a New Hampshire button-foot tea table with original red paint and a scalloped apron. An interesting point was how natural the French directoire chairs placed on either side of this table appeared. The combination was perfectly harmonious. The same was true when a formal New York eighteenth-century Chippendale chest with bee's-wing mahogany graining was shown with a set of six painted, fancy Sheraton side chairs, *circa* 1840.

Nimmo & Hart love American primitive painting and folk art. There are always nineteenth-century portraits and even an occasional landscape. If they locate an eighteenth-century English painting which has the same naïve quality they find so appealing, of course they buy it. A great carved-wood whale made a sensational wall hanging.

Everything at these talented dealers' is chosen with a very personal and discriminating eye. The nicest part of the experience is discovering what lovely people they are to deal with.

Four Corners-East
802 Main Street, Route 9
Bennington, Vt. 05201
(802) 442-2612

Monday–Sunday 9–6
Closed holidays

Antique shops that directly reflect their owners' personal point of view rather than just being filled with good merchandise are few and far between. Russell Bagley and Ronald Cox hand-pick everything that goes into Four Corners-East as if it were going into their own home, and the result is a delightful mixture of material. Concentrating on eighteenth- and early nineteenth-century American furniture, primarily from New England, their stock ranges from formal pieces such as a fine Portsmouth secretary, which once belonged to a governor of New Hampshire, to simple country tables. There are lovely examples of Queen Anne and Chippendale furniture, including Chippendale chests, tables, and chairs and, if you are lucky enough to arrive at the right moment, Queen Anne highboys and lowboys. These are dealers whose inventory changes constantly. They are particularly strong in antique American andirons and, appropriately enough, Bennington pottery. The shop has all sorts of paintings, including American primitive portraits, Hudson Valley scenes and even, on occasion, English nineteenth-century landscape and marine paintings. There is no way to guarantee what you may find at any given time, but there is such a variety of material available, most antiquers will be sure to find something that is interesting to them.

Museums

Shelburne Museum
Route 7
Shelburne, Vt. 05482

May 15–October 15, 9–5 daily

Thirty-five seventeenth- and eighteenth-century buildings filled with three centuries of Americana, plus the side-wheeler *Ticonderoga.*

Sterling and Francine Clark Art Institute
Williamstown, Mass. 01267
(413) 458-8109

Open Tuesday–Sunday, 10–5
Closed Mondays, January 1, December 25, Thanksgiving

This great museum is just over the border in western Massachusetts and should be included in any trip to Vermont. Detailed description in western Massachusetts section.

Route 30 from Dorset to the hamlet of Pawlet is literally eighteenth-century Vermont, unbelievably beautiful and rural. Continue on Route 133 to Middletown Springs and you feel as if you've arrived in the middle of nowhere. For the adventurous, there is a tiny diner-coffee shop in Pawlet that is always filled with locals who look as if they were selected by central casting. It couldn't be more fun.

Inns and Restaurants

Arlington Inn
Route 7
Arlington, Vt. 05250
(802) 375-6532

Open all year, except April and November

Lunch and dinner daily, except Tuesday. Lodging available.

The Barrows House
Route 30, six miles from Manchester
Dorset, Vt. 05251
(802) 867-4455

Open all year.

Breakfast, lunch, dinner. Lodging available.

Inn at Sawmill Farm
Box 8
West Dover, Vt. 05356
Route 100, twenty-two miles from Bennington and Brattleboro
(802) 464-8131

Open all year, except for November 15–December 5

Breakfast and dinner. Lodging available.

Kedron Valley Inn
Route 106
South Woodstock, Vt. 05071
(802) 457-1473

Open all year, except for April

Breakfast, lunch, dinner. Lodging available.

Chester Inn
Route 11
Chester, Vt. 05143
(802) 875-2444

Open all year, except November and May

Lunch and dinner daily, except Monday. Lodging available.

Saxton's River Inn
Saxton's River, Vt. 05154
(802) 869-2110

Open all year

Lunch and dinner daily, except Tuesday. Lodging available.

Woodstock Inn, on village green
Woodstock, Vt. 05091
(802) 457-1100

Open all year

Large commercial establishment, but well done. Breakfast, lunch, dinner. Lodging available.

The Prince & The Pauper
Woodstock, Vt. 05091
(802) 457-1818

Lunch.

The Barnard Inn
Barnard, Vt. 05031
(802) 234-9961

Dinner.

NEW HAMPSHIRE

Antique Dealers

Roger Bacon
Route 1, Box 40
Brentwood
Exeter, N.H. 03833
(603) 772-2064

Appointment advised

Roger Bacon is one of the originals of the antique world. Probably the foremost dealer in Pilgrim furniture in this country, he has more seventeenth-century New England furniture than most museums, which are his biggest clients. This dealer provides the opportunity to literally step back in time almost three hundred years, when you enter his house. Built in 1705, it is filled to capacity with seventeenth- and early eighteenth-century New England furniture and magnificent oriental rugs that take on an entirely new decorative meaning when seen in this stark environment. The carpets function very much as tapestries did in an earlier era, to provide warmth, color, and pictorial richness to a room. The primitive American painting available is earlier than most of the examples you see on the market. The superb decorative accessories include the largest collection of seventeenth-cen-

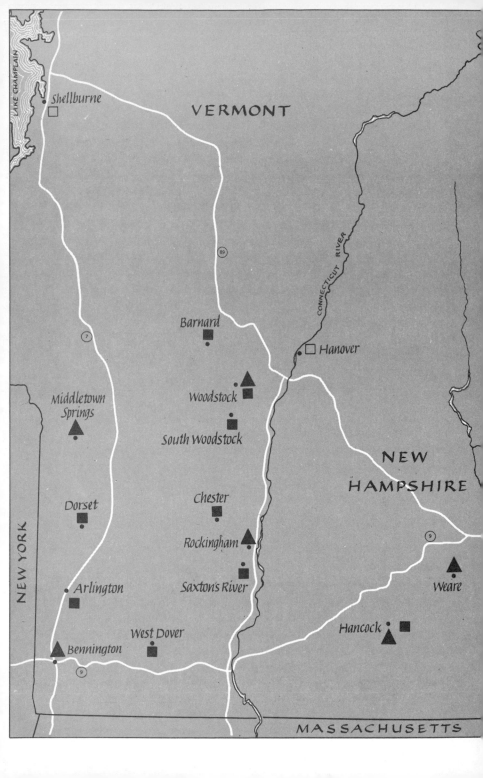

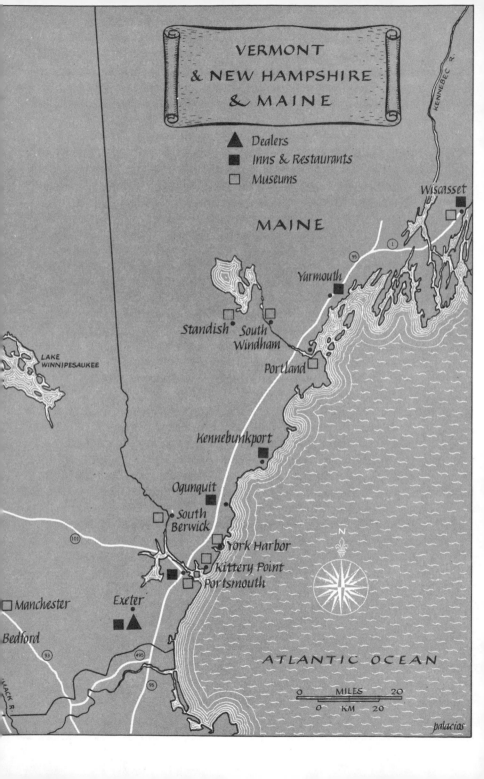

tury English comb ware—a form of early Staffordshire—to be found anywhere in the world. English and Dutch Delft bowls, brass candlesticks, tobacco boxes, and the classic early eighteenth-century Queen Anne mirrored lighting fixtures are just a smattering of the material to be seen. The huge hearths in the house provide its only source of heat. I don't know what it would be like to visit Ruth and Roger Bacon during the dead of winter, but I found October a perfect month and I'm inclined to believe a visit at any time to these knowledgeable, charming dealers would be wonderful for the collector interested in their period.

The amount of stock is simply overwhelming when you realize how old this material is and that many of the pieces, like the trestle, gateleg, and tavern tables, were probably used continuously for over 250 years. There are great examples of seventeenth-century chairs such as Carver and Brewster armchairs, to say nothing of the classic banister- and slat-backs. It is only proper that there is an equally large selection of William and Mary tables and chests, though most of these would date from 1700 to 1720 because of the time differential in periods. The craftsmen here were copying styles from a period that dated at least ten or twenty years earlier in England. Most Queen Anne pieces were constructed here, *circa* 1740–60, which is much later than the style in England. The smallest group of furniture is Queen Anne and the examples lovely, as in a lowboy with burl-fronted drawers and some fine Spanish-foot chairs, but this period is not a specialty of this dealer and he prefers concentrating on the earlier styles. There is no doubt the Bacons are true enthusiasts about their period, and when a particular rarity is uncovered, it is a joy to share their pleasure.

During my visit, Roger Bacon was literally bursting with pride over two recent acquisitions, both of which were going on loan to a museum. One was an American maple Cromwellian chair, an almost unheard of object in this country, and the other amazing find was a woodenware plate dated 1621, possibly the earliest recorded piece of this ware ever found in America. It was painted gray to simulate pewter. Incidentally, treenware is the English terminology for woodenware.

With a houseful of rarities, one might expect the prices to be equally rarefied but I found that, for the quality and uniqueness of the objects, the prices are eminently fair. This is expensive material, but such treasures are really beyond simple monetary determinations.

These dealers are treasures, have treasures, and will make you feel as if you've just gotten the bargain of a lifetime, which you may very well have.

The Cobbs
Old Dublin Road
Hancock, N.H. 03449
(603) 525-4053

Appointment advised

It was a very large dog, even for a great Dane. However, New Hampshire being the quirky kind of state it is, I thought perhaps my official receptionist at the Cobbs's might be a new variety of antique dealer or even collector for that matter. My enormous, gentle greeter turned out to be just one of an assortment of dogs, cats, and horses that are part of the very charming rural home of these young dealers in Americana. In their dining room, the original mural paintings by Rufus Porter, a local New Hampshire artist, have given their eighteenth-century house landmark status and will delight anyone interested in American painting. If you have ever wondered how a dealer starts, it is generally as a picker for other dealers. How quickly they establish themselves depends to a great extent on what kind of an eye they have, an ability to work twenty-six hours a day ferreting out antiques, and a lot of good humor. Dudley and Charles Cobb still function mainly as suppliers to the trade but are gradually beginning to acquire their own collectors.

The stock, which is eighteenth-, early nineteenth-, and occasionally seventeenth-century American country furniture, is not large and changes constantly. The best thing about picker-dealers like the Cobbs is that they do a great deal of buying and you never know what they may turn up. Since most New England dealers and collectors are purists about their furniture, when Charles Cobb finds a Pennsylvania, New York, or even a southern piece, their prices happily reflect a regional lack of interest. Most of the furniture consists of primitive versions of William and Mary, Queen Anne, and even Chippendale chairs, tables, and chests. Mrs. Cobb has her own loom and buys anything relevant to weaving. They also regularly have a small selection of China Export in the Rose Medallion, Canton, and Bird and Butterfly patterns. The Cobbs have always collected early American iron and have a special feeling for cooking, lighting, and fireplace equipment. In addition to the ubiquitous baskets, there is English soft paste, American pottery, American folk art, and even an oriental rug or two. I saw a magnificent pair of early English brass candlesticks that I know will make their way to Madison Avenue. What is most tantalizing about this kind of young dealer is the possibility of coming across a treasure before it makes its way through many hands.

There is another great plus to visiting the Cobbs; it is their close proximity to one of the most beautiful villages in New England—Hancock, New Hampshire. Between the fun of the shop and the marvelous local inn, you will have a super time.

Elizabeth Stokes
Sugar Hill Road South
Weare, N.H. 03281
(603) 529-2363

Appointment advised

Knowing what the antique business is today, it is difficult to believe the quality of some of the legendary dealers. Elizabeth Stokes is one of the great ladies of the antique world. At eighty-nine years of age, living alone in an extremely isolated area of New Hampshire, she remains as beautiful and charming as the day she arrived there over forty years ago. Regretfully, she is no longer as active as she has been in eighteenth-century New England furniture, though some of the finest New Hampshire, Maine, and Vermont pieces to ever appear on the market came through her auspices. She still does find an occasional chest or table, but these go immediately to other dealers who will shop her till the day she retires.

Mrs. Stokes, who was always a specialist in hooked rugs, still maintains an excellent stock of these items. Bright eyes sparkling with enthusiasm, she explains that finding a beautiful rug has always been like opening a Christmas present—gay and exciting. The best thing about hooked rugs is everybody can afford them, even the rarest. Mrs. Stokes has had many Frost-designed rugs over the years and still continues to find them.

Her own preference is for the earlier rugs, *circa* 1830–75, whose designs were usually much more spontaneous than later examples. These old rugs have a coarser surface but when done well are like enchanting paintings.

Perhaps if you aren't interested in hooked rugs, this is a dealer you could overlook. However, for me, sharing a little time with this remarkable woman was like finding a great treasure.

Museums and Historical Houses

Dartmouth College Museum
Hanover, N.H.

Open daily all year, with some special summer and vacation hours.

PORTSMOUTH

Strawbery Banke
Portsmouth, N.H. 03801

Original 1630 Portsmouth settlement site with thirty seventeenth-, eighteenth-, and nineteenth-century houses located at Hancock, Washington, Court, and Marcy streets. Open daily May 1–October 31, 9:30–5.

Well worth seeing; this is a relatively new restoration arca.

Governor John Langdon Mansion Memorial
143 Pleasant Street

June–September, Tuesday, Thursday, Saturday 1–5

Built in 1784 and described by Washington as "handsomest house in Portsmouth."

John Paul Jones House
Middle and State streets

May 15–October 1, Monday–Saturday 10–5

Captain Jones resided here when outfitting the *Ranger* in 1777 and the *America* in 1782. It has an interesting collection of furniture, china, silver, portraits, costumes, and documents on display.

Richard Jackson House
76 Northwest Street

June–September, Tuesday, Thursday, Saturday 1–5

Built in 1664, its exhibitions include seventeenth-century architectural details and furniture.

Rundlet-May House

June–September, Tuesday, Thursday, Saturday 1–5

The impressive three-story Federal mansion has been occupied continuously by the Rundlet-May family. It is complete right down to its original Federal furnishings and gardens.

Currier Gallery of Art
192 Orange Street
Manchester, N.H. 03104

Tuesday–Saturday 10–4
Sunday 2–5. Closed national holidays

Unusual collection of Renaissance to modern paintings, antique furniture, silver, glass, and other decorative arts. Definitely worth a visit if you are in New Hampshire.

Inns and Restaurants

John Hancock Inn
Hancock, N.H. 03449
Hancock is off 202 above Peterborough
(603) 525-3318

Open all year, except for one week early spring and fall.

Breakfast, lunch, dinner. Lodging available. Marvelously comfortable inn with a fine dining room and great bar. Village is enchanting.

Exeter Inn
90 Front Street
Exeter, N.H. 03833
(603) 772-5901

Open all year

Commercial motel. Breakfast, lunch, dinner. Lodging available.

*The Captain Lord Mansion
Box 527
Kennebunkport, Me. 04046
(207) 967-3141

Open all year

Breakfast and tea served daily. Lodging available.

* The Old Village Inn
30 Main Street
Ogunquit, Me. 03907
(207) 646-7088

Open all year.

Breakfast and dinner daily, except Monday and Tuesday during winter. Lodging available.

Daffodil's
Route 101 W.
Bedford, N.H. 03102
(603) 472-5188

Open all year

Lunch and dinner.

* These inns are located in Maine but within an hour of Exeter and Portsmouth, New Hampshire.

Red Lion
2470 Lafayette Road
Route 1, Portsmouth 03801; four miles south of traffic circle
(603) 436-6464

Open all year. Closed Monday, November–April

Lunch and dinner.

MAINE

Museums and Historical Houses

Lady Pepperrell House *c.* 1760
Kittery Point, Route 103
(Four miles east of Portsmouth)
(617) 227-3956

June 1–September 30
Tuesday, Thursday, Sunday 1–5

Superb mid-eighteenth-century example of northern colonial architecture. The house is beautifully furnished with period antiques.

Sayward House *c.* 1719
York Harbor, Barrell Lane
(Turn right off Route 1A after intersection of Route 103)

June 1–September 30
Tuesday, Thursday, Sunday 1–5

Fine eighteenth-century home, furnished with family pieces bought by Jonathan Sayward, a British sympathizer during the Revolution.

Hamilton House *c.* 1785
South Berwick, Vaughan's Lane
(Turn left off Route 236 opposite junction Route 91)

June 1–September 30
Tuesday, Thursday, Friday, Sunday 1–5

Magnificent Georgian mansion; completed, restored, and furnished. The author Sarah Orne Jewett, who visited Hamilton House as a child, used this romantic setting in her novel *The Tory Lover*.

Jewett House *c.* 1774
South Berwick, Route 236

June 1–September 30
Tuesday, Thursday, Sunday 1–5

Home of the author Sarah Orne Jewett. The New England Historical Society has preserved Miss Jewett's study just as she left it.

Marrett House *c.* 1789
Standish, Route 125

June 1–September 30
Tuesday, Thursday, Sunday 1–5

Original Georgian house, enlarged and remodeled in the Greek Revival style. Furnished with Marrett family pieces from the eighteenth and nineteenth centuries.

Parson Smith House *c.* 1764
South Windham, 89 River Road

Simple Georgian house, partially furnished with family antiques.

Nickels-Sortwell House *c.* 1807
Wiscasset
Corner of Main and Federal streets

June 1–September 30
Tuesday, Thursday, Sunday 1–5

Sumptuous Federal mansion with many exterior details copied from Asher Benjamin's *American Builder's Companion*, published in Boston in 1806.

PORTLAND

McLellan-Sweat House
111 High Street

Daily 10–5
Sunday 2–5
Closed Monday and holidays

Considered finest example of Federal architecture in Maine.
Furnished with period antiques.

Portland Museum of Art
111 High Street

Daily 10–5
Sunday 2–5
Closed Monday and holidays

Nineteenth- and twentieth-century American painting and
sculpture.

Tate House *c.* 1775
1270 Westbrook Street

July 1–September 15
Daily 11–5
Sunday 1:30–5

National historic landmark.

Victoria Mansion and Museum *c.* 1859
Park and Danforth streets

Mid-June–October
Tuesday–Saturday 10–4
Closed Sunday, Monday, and holidays

Perhaps the finest example of Victorian architecture in the
United States.

Inns and Restaurants

Squire Tarbox House
R.D. #2, Box 318
Wiscasset, Me. 04578
(207) 882-7693

Open June 1–October 1

Lunch and dinner by reservation only.

Homewood Inn
Drinkwater Point
Yarmouth, Me. 04096
(207) 846–3351

Open May 30–October 13

(Some rooms available from May 10 and after October 13)
Breakfast, lunch, dinner. Lodging available.

Captain Lord Mansion
Box 527
Kennebunkport, Me. 04046
(207) 967-3141

Open all year

Breakfast and tea daily. Lodging available.

IV

Center of the Universe

Welcome to Mecca. No other name does justice to the riches of material and experience available in New York City. It offers, if anything, an overabundance of whatever you are seeking. Its famous antique dealers, ever acquisitive museums, gourmet restaurants, luxurious hotels, and international auction houses continually solidify its position as the center of the art world. For all of us who are disciples, this is a pilgrimage that cannot be missed.

New York reveals itself to the walker. Walk Murray Hill, Yorkville, the Village, SoHo. Walk the Bronx Zoo. Fifth Avenue from Thirty-fourth Street to Eighty-sixth Street has an unbeatable combination of beautiful bookstores and strolling young musicians. Even Lincoln Center is not overrated. Try the little antique shops on Bleecker and Hudson streets; what the objects lack in age, they make up for in charm. Besides, the restaurants and people in the neighborhood are great. Nothing surpasses the view from Brooklyn Heights, of the sun setting over Manhattan. If you are really adventurous, try walking back over the Brooklyn Bridge and refreshing yourself with a cappucino in Little Italy or supper in Chinatown. Macy's basement is great, so is Alexander's. For instant nostalgia, have a banana daiquiri at the Plaza Oak Room bar; it's all the glamorous movies of the thirties and forties come alive. New York City is neither little nor old, but it is one hell of a town.

NEW YORK CITY

Antique Dealers

Israel Sack, Inc.
15 East Fifty-seventh Street
New York, N.Y. 10022
(212) 753-6562

Monday–Friday 9:30–5
Saturday 10–3:30
Closed Saturday during summer

Antique collectors are prone to rather interesting fantasies. Having conducted a small survey among American furniture enthusiasts, I found they all seemed to have the same recurrent dream. Heaven to them was an opportunity to browse through the two large floors of Israel Sack, Inc. on East Fifty-seventh Street, selecting whatever caught their fancy . . . at 1935 prices. I am sure Harold Sack, who with his two brothers runs the establishment, would be delighted to sell at those prices. Alas, today's inflation makes this an impossible dream. The Sacks recently thought nothing of spending over $600,000 at auction to acquire a few important pieces of furniture.

Interest in the furniture of our early heritage seems as natural today as breathing, but this was not always the case. Those pioneer collectors at the beginning of this century such as Eugene Bolles, whose collection formed the foundation of the American Wing at the Metropolitan Museum, showed audacious taste in selecting what seemed, to the *cognoscente* of that time, primitive furniture. The knowledge of the material and the courage to back their personal taste belonged to the collectors. Mr. Sack would be the first to tell you that his father, Israel Sack, learned from his collectors, as did all the early dealers in Americana.

Like a number of fine dealers of his generation, Israel Sack was originally a cabinetmaker, working in Boston for a man named Anderson who specialized in repairing antiques and faking new ones. This was in 1903! I wonder how many of those fakes are being sold today, by unwary dealers, as period furniture. The fakery did not fit in with Mr. Sack's ethical standards, and in 1907 he opened his own cabinet shop, on Charles Street, repairing fine pieces for early collectors. Gradually, he began buying from families interested in disposing of their furniture. Today the Sack family feels that their in-depth knowledge of cabinetmaking gives them an enormous advantage in that never-never world of whether a piece is absolutely right or if someone has been playing games with it. When eighteenth-century American furniture was relatively inexpensive, this was not a pressing consideration, but now, as the prices become astronomical, a mistake can mean a loss of thousands of dollars.

Israel Sack's reputation for knowledge and taste grew over the years as more of the great collectors dealt with him. In the twenties, they were Ima Hogg, Du Pont, Henry Ford, Francis Gawen. Two years before Williamsburg opened, the firm received a commission from the Rockefellers to search for American and English pieces for the restoration. The roster of great names continued into the thirties with Charles K. Davis, Mitchel Taradash, and Karolik, whose collection is in the Boston Museum of Fine Arts.

I feel this shop is an absolute must for the serious collector of American eighteenth- and early nineteenth-century furniture. If it is the unique treasure you seek or simply first-class quality, here it is with impeccable provenance. But what of the young collector who has knowledge and taste but whose money is limited? You will find a surprising range of material under $5,000. You will also discover that the better the dealer, the less likely you are to be overcharged for the more prosaic pieces. What may just be another decent table or chest to Israel Sack could seem a treasure to a lesser dealer and be priced accordingly. Harold Sack tells the story of a Philadelphia couple who had been afraid to come to the shop, positive they couldn't afford anything. Finally, taking courage in hand, they appeared one day and found a lovely worktable for $1,700. This was the beginning. Working within a limited budget over the years, they have put together what they call their Sack Corner and have, of course, become fast friends of the Sacks themselves.

I love to describe pieces that particularly captured my interest, but I simply don't know where to begin at Israel Sack's. How about a Chippendale cherry block-front desk from the Davis collection that practically sings and dances, or a great Willard tall clock, a Queen Anne walnut bonnet-top highboy from Massachusetts, *circa* 1750–60, a Queen Anne maple porringer-top tea table with its original red paint, or a mahogany Chippendale bombé commode or two? There are endless choices of the finest-quality Queen Anne, Chippendale, Sheraton, Federal eighteenth- and nineteenth-century furniture available.

Early in 1977, there was an exhibition at the Kennedy Galleries, in New York City, called Age of the Revolution and early Republic in Fine and Decorative Arts 1750–1824, sponsored jointly by Kennedy Galleries and Israel Sack. It had, at least for me, two of the most beautiful examples of American cabinetmaking I have ever seen. They were a pair of Chippendale mahogany serpentine-shaped card tables given by George Washington to Judge Berrien of Princeton, New Jersey, in gratitude for the use of his home during the Revolution. The tables, made in New York *circa* 1760–70, can match the quality and workmanship of any to be found in the world. Small, exquisite jewels of cabinetwork, they are more than wood, they are works of art. Separated for over a hundred years the tables were brought together again by Israel Sack, Inc.

For the collector whose first love is American furniture, this shop is a revelation. There are literally only a handful of dealers in the entire country in this category. In the world of American furniture, Israel Sack is the ultimate name.

Benjamin Ginsburg Antiquary
815 Madison Avenue
New York, N.Y. 10021
(212) 744-1352

Monday–Friday 9–5
Open Saturday by appointment
Closed August

In very rare instances the name of a shop is its best description. This is certainly the case with Benjamin Ginsburg Antiquary because that is precisely what Mr. Ginsburg is. A dealer, whose father and grandfather were dealers before him, he was formerly a partner in that illustrious firm of American-furniture specialists Ginsburg & Levy.

The present business is still conducted in a beautiful old house on Madison Avenue at Sixty-eighth Street. It is a comfortably old-fashioned firm with very contemporary prices, as one would expect, considering the quality of objects and the reliability of the expertise. A quiet, diffident man, it is obviously more pleasurable for Mr. Ginsburg to be researching his pieces than selling them. Should you detect a note of caution and suspicion in Mr. Ginsburg's manner, remember he is not to the salesman born. However, the genuinely interested antiquer quickly becomes a welcome visitor. What you will find most unusual, in speaking with Mr. Ginsburg or his associate, Mr. Rockwell, is their remarkable enthusiasm for exchanging information with a knowledgeable collector.

The scope of material available is much wider than most people realize. Of course, there are seventeenth-, eighteenth-, and early nineteenth-century American furniture and accessories of great distinction. Quite unexpected at this dealer is a small but select group of English pieces and decorations of the seventeenth and eighteenth centuries. A marvelous collection of eighteenth-century European porcelains, predominately English and Dutch Delft, is unpretentiously displayed throughout the building.

Mr. Ginsburg is a great authority on early European Delft and the shop carries a large and varied selection of choice eighteenth-century examples of this ware. It is extremely helpful to the inex-

perienced collector to be able to handle the material. By viewing many examples, they can learn not only the stylistic differences
between the English and Dutch varieties but, equally important,
what eighteenth-century glazes really look and feel like. This is
tricky pottery and the number of fakes on the market is awe inspiring.

I cannot emphasize too often how important a role the expert
dealer plays in the education of a collector. I feel it is better to err
in paying too much for a piece that is absolutely right than to
delude oneself with bargains that may be cheap but fraudulent.
Remember, you cannot learn from a fake.

The firm's resident expert on textiles is Mrs. Cora Ginsburg,
who for many years has traveled around the world in search of
beautiful examples of seventeenth-, eighteenth-, and nineteenth-
century fabrics. The most important piece of American textile the
gallery believes it has ever owned is the crewel bedcover made for
John Hancock's foster father; it is now part of the Winterthur
collection.

The early American silver is geared to the specialized collector
and not shown unless requested. Though the amount of silver
available at this dealer's is limited, the quality is excellent.

There is not a major museum in this country whose collection
doesn't include pieces from this firm. A matching William and
Mary highboy and lowboy made in Flushing, New York, by Clem-
ent, in 1722, are just two out of the many objects sold to Mr. Du-
Pont for Winterthur. The White House numbers among its
pieces from this gallery a Philadelphia armchair and the spectacular New York empire sofa table by Launnier in the red room.
The earliest piece of English seventeenth-century Delft in the
Smithsonian is also from this dealer.

I found a lovely selection of case and seat furniture in the shop.
An excellent example of the quality of English furniture available
is a small delicately scaled William and Mary walnut highboy
(with its original etched brasses and beautiful burl-elm veneering
on the drawer fronts) standing between a pair of tall-backed side
chairs, also of the same period, with gracefully curved stretchers
and elegantly carved bun feet.

A distinctly New York walnut card table, *circa* 1750, is basically a Queen Anne piece, but its ball-and-claw feet show typical Dutch influence. The table belonged to the Schuyler family who lived in a place called New Barbadoes Neck. A mahogany chest-on-chest, thought to be by Frothingham, *circa* 1760, and only seven feet tall, was probably made for a seventeenth-century house. Later eighteenth-century furniture, going into earlier-built houses, was usually smaller in scale to accommodate the lower ceiling height of these buildings. In case you have never seen bilsted (gumwood), there is a New York highboy constructed in this rare wood, with the proverbial Dutch ball-and-claw feet and extremely fine leaf carving on the knees, made for the Schenck family of Fishkill, *circa* 1750–60.

There are many examples of eighteenth-century American tables, chests of every variety, armchairs, wing chairs, side chairs, all of first quality; but for me, the most extraordinary was the set of four Queen Anne chairs, *circa* 1730, known as the Apthorp chairs, with their center splat veneered in mahogany to make a flame pattern and crested with a carved shell that is almost in full relief. These exquisite chairs have made their way over the centuries from New York to Boston and finally down to Washington, D.C., where the last family survivor sold them to Mr. Ginsburg.

The sense of scholarship this firm exudes is its own special magic. The histories of many of their pieces have been carefully researched and are available to the interested collector.

Rosenberg & Stiebel, Inc.
32 East Fifty-seventh Street
New York, N.Y. 10022
(212) 753-4368

Monday–Friday 10–5
Appointments preferred, but not absolutely necessary

There really is a problem in having too formidable a reputation. When the name Rosenberg & Stiebel is mentioned almost anywhere in the world, it is synonymous with the finest quality French eighteenth-century furniture, the so-called 3 F's. They are the dealers famous for their connection with various branches of the Rothschild family, whose members have both bought and sold to them over the last one hundred years. There is probably not an important collector of eighteenth-century French or Renaissance furniture, either here or in Europe, who has not purchased a piece at one time or another from this firm.

How does a young collector approach this gallery? As directly as possible! Both Mr. Eric Stiebel and his son Gerald Stiebel are charming, cultivated people, knowledgeable beyond belief, absolutely passionate about what they sell. Yes, they are expensive dealers. No, they are not! If that sounds contradictory, it really isn't. What is too much to pay for furniture and accessories of museum quality? What is cheap? A number of years ago I saw a piece of magnificent Japanese porcelain in the shop. It was more than I could afford. (I knew its mate was in the Wickes collection in the Fine Arts in Boston.) However, I couldn't imagine asking them for terms (paying for a purchase over a period of time, a common practice with almost every major dealer). By the time I made up my mind, the piece was gone. Of course, a few years later the same form sold in London for almost five times the price this expensive dealer was asking for it.

The range of material the gallery has sold and continues to sell is stunning. One room has four smashing Louis XV black-lacquer chinoiserie commodes; these ladies are the battleships of eighteenth-century furniture. They simply do not take no for an answer. Incidentally, if you are in a position to afford one of these beauties and think the auction houses will save you a fortune, think again. Very frequently a dealer like Rosenberg & Stiebel will be no more expensive at this level than the auctions and not infrequently somewhat less expensive, depending on when they bought their piece. Most important, the authenticity and provenance will be unimpeachable, very essential details when buying at this level. In addition, the same room contained a pair of black-lacquer Louis XV encoignures and a fine eighteenth-century Savonnerie rug. Another room contained a selection of seat furniture, pairs of Louis XV bergères and fauteuils in their natural woods, to say nothing of a small Louis XV marquetry desk. The objets d'art are the same quality as the furniture, be it a pair of eighteenth-century Meissen birds by Kändler mounted in bronze doré, a German carved-wood madonna from the upper Rhine, *circa* 1430, or an extraordinarily rare set of Limoges panels of the Lord's Prayer, done in 1540 by Colin Nouhallier. The only other set known in existence is illustrated in the Walters Gallery catalogue. The gilt mirrors, wall sconces, small tables, petit commodes are of the same uniform quality, and curiously enough, none of the objects suffer from being too fancy. They have all been chosen with great restraint.

Relatively few people realize the vast number of important paintings and sculpture Rosenberg & Stiebel has sold—Clouet's Diane de Poiters in the National Gallery, the Mérode altarpiece by Robert Campin in the Cloisters, the pair of Rembrandt life-size portraits in the Boston Musem of Fine Arts. Interestingly, a few years ago the Metropolitan had a loan exhibition entitled the "100 Best Paintings from the Boston Museum"; ten were originally from Rosenberg & Stiebel. Gerald Stiebel has fond memories of his first meeting with Perry Rathbone, then director of the Fine Arts; it was on his hands and knees as they were both crawling over the great Hunt carpet the museum eventually bought.

Mr. Stiebel feels for the young collector who is interested in art; there are still buys to be found in old masters drawings and even in sixteenth-century Renaissance bronzes. The gallery has a beautiful selection of sixteenth-, seventeenth-, eighteenth-, and nineteenth-century drawings which cover a large price range, depending on whether you prefer an Ingres nude, Tiepolo head, or simply a very decorative eighteenth-century sanguine of a large urn with wonderful dragon handles.

If you have admired the furnishings in the Wrightsman rooms at the Metropolitan, the superb red-lacquer desk, the bronze doré chandeliers, come to where they first were found. Yes, Rosenberg & Stiebel, unique dealers, unique people.

Doris Leslie Blau Inc.
15 East Fifty-seventh Street
New York, N.Y. 10022
(212) 759-3715

Monday–Friday
By appointment preferably

The joy of owning an oriental carpet can be one of the most pleasurable and intense experiences open to a collector. However, there are peculiar problems which can arise when one attempts to purchase an old carpet. These jewels of the East are guarded with something approaching paranoia by many rug dealers. Perhaps it is natural that the greatest art form of the Middle East should carry with it characteristics endemic to the area.

Doris Leslie Blau is a resounding exception to the classically suspicious nature of rug merchants. Possessing an open, spontaneous personality, she is quite irresistible. Whether you are the definitive collector, searching out a Hereke silk masterpiece, or, like most of us, simply trying to find an interesting little antique carpet for your home, you are in for a treat. Mrs. Blau, who is considered one of the most important rug dealers in the United States, is recognized for both her expertise and extraordinary flair. Taste is an intangible quality—some dealers have it, others do not. Doris Leslie Blau has smashing taste in rugs. If that sounds like a highly subjective statement, it is. For years I have anticipated the pleasure of buying a carpet from this dealer. Unfortunately, as a collector who must husband her resources, rugs were a secondary choice to Chinese porcelains. But I must admit, I am tempted to reconsider my priorities.

Fine antique carpets are very expensive today, but there is a range of affordable material open to young collectors if they allow themselves to be guided by a knowledgeable dealer. It is the wise person who starts building a collection modestly. It takes years to develop an appreciation of the subtleties of design and color that distinguish, for example, a serviceable Caucasian from a superb Caucasian. A Tabriz is not a Tabriz is not a Tabriz. As with any kind of collecting, there is no substitute for seeing as many examples of the finest quality pieces as possible. Furniture and porcelains can be viewed in quantity at museums. This is not true of carpets, and the photographs that appear in reference books have nothing to do with seeing a rug itself. It is equivalent to viewing a painting on television; unless you are in scale relationship to the object it is something other than what the artist created.

No dealer can tell you which is the right carpet for you. The choice is subjective. There is really no single greatest example as in furniture or porcelain, where the same form is used repeatedly. To the beginner, there are seemingly endless subdivisions of oriental carpets. This is not quite true; there are main categories everyone recognizes. They are Persian, Turkish, Caucasian, Indian, Chinese, and Turkoman. These delineations are practically the only thing carpet aficionados do agree on. The design motifs in very simple terms describe Russian and Indian carpets as floral; Turkish as both geometric and floral, with geometric predominating; Caucasian and Turkoman as geometric; and the Chinese as being distinguishable by their flat use of single-color fields such as blue or tan, with either dragon or cloud-band designs. Now that you have this information, I must admit it is largely useless to anyone but the most experienced collector because of the endless number of variations in design and color. Weavers moved so frequently that even experts disagree as to the place of origin of many carpets. In another instance, it is almost an exercise in esoterica to try to judge whether a carpet is a Shirvan, Kuba, Dagestan or Kabistan, so similar in execution are these Caucasian rugs to each other. There are Persian carpets with geometric design and Turkish with combinations of everything, including the Persian knot. What is important is that you find what particular quality of design and color you enjoy and buy the best example you can afford.

An interesting rug, even if not really very valuable, is a tradable commodity. There is no better way to define one's taste than by living with a piece for a while and then trading up to another. Every good dealer encourages this arrangement, especially for young collectors. Mrs. Blau is convinced that in some mysterious way a carpet directly reflects all the good feelings which surround it.

Carpets are considered antique if they are pre-1900, semiantique if they are at least forty years old. The great divide in rugmaking is the period from 1900 through 1914 which marked the gradual changeover to synthetic rather than vegetable dyes for color. There are still some fine rugs being produced, but on the whole there has been an enormous deterioration in quality and, of course, the former colors are impossible to duplicate. If it is possible, buy only a vegetable-dye rug; if not, at least try to see as many of them as you can.

The variety of beautiful carpets at Doris Leslie Blau Inc. will make your head spin. If your pleasure is a seventeenth-century Persian Isfahan court carpet, be relieved; there is one. Another seventeenth-century rarity is a Quenca carpet from Spain of such subtlety of color it will drive you mad, as will the prices for these treasures. There are perfectly splendid examples of Indian rugs such as Agras, fine Caucasians such as Kazaks, Kubas, and classic examples of Turkish, Chinese, Persian, and Turkoman. Not overlooked at all, though in much smaller supply, are the European carpets such as a very fine French Directoire Aubusson and a delightful French Victorian needlework carpet with wonderful colors. This dealer carries what she feels are the most interesting examples of the many varieties of both antique and semiantique carpets. It is a one-on-one experience with Doris Leslie Blau. She will not sell you a carpet unless you love it and are sure you will be happy living with it. She is a very special lady and so are her gorgeous carpets.

D. M. & P. Manheim
46 East Fifty-seventh Street
New York, N.Y. 10022
(212) 758-2986

Monday–Saturday 9:30–5:30
June–October, Monday–Friday 9:30–5:30

Many dealers who own two pieces of Staffordshire and a patch box of enamel consider themselves English-porcelain experts. The truth is, in this complicated field of study, there are very few recognized authorities. Miss Manheim, of D. M. & P. Manheim, specialists in early English porcelain, is renowned for her expertise in this area. Don't let the rather drab, cold look of the shop deter you from seeing its treasures. Almost nothing has been done to enhance the display of seventeenth-, eighteenth-, and early nineteenth-century Delft, Chelsea, Bow, Bristol, Swansea, Derby, Worcester, Coalport, Caughley, Whieldon, to name but a few of its soft- and hard-paste porcelain examples. What makes the experience unforgettable is Miss Manheim's great knowledge and love for her field. This unusual dealer communicates a sense of passionate intelligence as she explains the fine points of English porcelain and the intricacy of determining whether a mark necessarily dates a piece correctly. If you think white is simply white in eighteenth-century pottery, you have not even begun to look at the subtle differences in that color produced by individual factories during this period. There are collectors who do not realize that Staffordshire is the name of a county in England that had dozens of kilns producing different wares. It does not signify one particular kind of pottery.

Miss Manheim's personal preference is for the spontaneity of the soft-paste pottery with its exquisite flower painting derived from botanical studies of the seventeenth and eighteenth centuries. However, this dealer reminds us that the very formal, ornately decorated services, which are not to contemporary taste, were ordered for large rooms lit by candlelight, creating a much softer effect.

For the thousands of collectors in this country who think they have been buying eighteenth-century Battersea enamels, I have some startling information. Sir Stephen Janssen, who manufactured at York House, Battersea, the enamel on copper, which was decorated by transfer from engraved plates, remained in business for barely three years, 1753–56. In 1756 he went bankrupt and that was the end of Battersea enamels. There were, however, other small factories in England which did continue to produce enamel trinkets. They were not comparable in quality to the real Battersea. Most of the examples on the market today are either late nineteenth-century Bilston or French copies which were produced by Samson in Paris during the nineteenth and twentieth centuries. The latter is, unfortunately, the bulk of most collectors' "Battersea."

This dealer is a must for the serious English porcelain collector. There is no substitute for quality and knowledge. It is only after meeting a dealer like Miss Manheim that a collector realizes how much genuine study goes into becoming an expert.

J. J. Wolff Antiques Ltd.
825 Madison Avenue
New York, N.Y. 10021
(212) 879-3344

Monday–Friday 9:30–5:30
Saturday 11–4
Summer, Monday–Friday 9:30–5

Once upon a time, there existed a quite different world of antiquarians—a world of scholars and gentlemen. Alas, that breed is now an endangered species, down to a handful of dealers. Unquestionably, among the last is J. J. Wolff, a dealer in fine English furniture. The quality of the furniture in this shop cannot be duplicated anywhere in this country, other than in museums or the private collections he was instrumental in forming. If you have any feeling at all for superb eighteenth-century English furniture, the kind frequently illustrated in reference books, you will find this shop an absolute knockout.

I did not know what really first-class cabinetwork meant until Mr. Wolff himself lovingly pointed out the kinds of detail that differentiate a commercial piece of eighteenth-century furniture from one produced by an important workshop. I think the average collector of English furniture in this country feels eighteenth century is eighteenth century. Nothing could be further from the truth. Frankly, it is not to everyone's taste; some may find it too formal. But I feel that the only way to establish one's own judgment is by seeing the best, and this dealer unquestionably has the best.

Mr. Wolff's greatest source is his own clients reselling him a piece after twenty-five or thirty-five years. Furniture of this caliber rarely leaves England now. Like many another dealer, his father was a cabinetmaker, who numbered among his patrons Buckingham Palace! Mr. Wolff has been selling to Americans since 1928. His clients include Judge Untermeyer (Metropolitan Museum), John D. Rockefeller (Williamsburg), Mrs. Joseph Regenstein, whose collection is going to the Chicago Art Institute, to name but a few. The Nelson Gallery in Cleveland bought the finest pair of carved and painted Chippendale consoles, with their original pier mirrors, that Mr. Wolff feels he has ever handled. The pair is attributed to the workshop of Luke Lightfoot and were made for Sir Henry Blount in the eighteenth century.

Prices are expensive on furniture such as a great Chippendale mahogany commode, *circa* 1760, with ormolu mounts and exquisite carving on the sides. A highboy with ivory inlay on the drawers, illustrated in an English furniture reference book, matches a lowboy the shop owns with the same unusual detail. A rather unusual English piece is a George II walnut chest on stand made for the American market. There are sets of Queen Anne, Chippendale, and Regency side chairs, some with settees. Marvelous pairs of armchairs are tucked away in corners. I am sure two superb wing chairs I saw—one Queen Anne, the other Chippendale—were sold immediately. An interesting fact about English furniture is that, generally, the finest English chairs were made only by chairmakers, not cabinetmakers.

Of course, no English dealer worth his salt would be complete without a good Carlton House desk, but I doubt if there is another dealer with a pair of Heppelwhite serpentine mahogany commodes, one of which is fitted with drawers and the other is sans traverse. Though relatively large, they could not be more delicate in feeling. In addition to these amazing commodes there are chests of every variety, including a marvelous George I red chinoiserie one, with its matching stand. Mr. Wolff feels its decoration may be Dutch.

The gallery does not have a great many accessories, but the selection of gilt mirrors, ranging from Queen Anne to Adam, is glorious. There is some eighteenth-century English porcelain, and if you are lucky, you may find a tall clock or two.

A relevant question: Is there a place for the young collector in this shop? Yes, yes, yes. After sixty years in the business, Mr. Wolff and his associate Mr. Craig Williams understand and sympathize with the problems that face an inexperienced collector. There is a basement which is well stocked with eighteenth-century English furniture that is simpler and less expensive. More to the point, what you do get in this shop is quality and expertise not to be found anywhere else. And, I must add, Mr. Wolff, at eighty-odd years, is the most enchanting of men.

Vernay & Jussel Inc. (Formerly Arthur S. Vernay Inc.)
825 Madison Avenue
New York, N.Y. 10021
(212) 879-3344

Monday–Friday 9–5:30
Saturday by appointment
Summer, Monday–Friday 9–5

If you have ever wondered what the antiquing experience was like sixty years ago, Vernay & Jussel will do much to re-create that ambiance for you. Mr. Vernay, who was the first important English dealer in this country, started the firm in 1906. Mr. Jussel joined him in 1926 and bought him out in 1940. The starting auspices of the business are rather interesting. In 1906, Mrs. John Ravensky, who was then married to another gentleman, gave Mr. Vernay a helping hand, to the tune of a $2 million contract to decorate her house with eighteenth-century English furniture and accessories. Needless to say, this is an excellent way to start a business. The rich lived with great style in those pretax days and this dealer fulfilled a real function for them. He had fabulous taste, not only in English antiques but also as a decorator, and could be relied upon to turn newly rich Americans into English landed gentry, provided Duveen hadn't turned them into Renaissance princes. There is no doubt Mr. Vernay was responsible for starting the vogue among the wealthy for collecting fine English furniture. A house done by Vernay became one of the ultimate status symbols. A non-convert was Francis P. Garven, who returned $60,000 worth of English furniture because of his growing interest in American objects. Perhaps to compensate the firm for this loss, he recommended Mr. Vernay to Nicholas G. Brady, his brother-in-law, who managed to spend $4 million with the gallery. The sums are quite staggering if you translate the value of the money into today's terms.

However, that world no longer exists and no one is more aware of this than Mr. Christian Jussel who is most interested in reaching the young collector, as he is one himself. Mr. Jussel's great love is clocks, fine seventeenth- and eighteenth-century English ones. If you happen to share this interest, you will have a wonderful time whether you buy anything or not. As with painting, the maker is very important in determining value, and the gallery has clocks by key names such as Thomas Tompion, Joseph Knible, and George Graham to name a few.

The firm feels very fortunate when it is able to buy back its own stock. Primarily, it carries eighteenth-century Georgian and Chippendale case and seat furniture; very little Queen Anne is available. For the most part, the furniture and decorations are standard, good formal pieces. Their prices are not out of line for what they are and the kind of provenance that buying from this gallery gives them. Do not expect to find the kind of furniture and objects like those the shop supplied to the English Gallery at the Columbus Museum of Fine Arts or a piece as marvelous as the English Chippendale bookcase that is in Independence Hall in Philadelphia. But there still are a number of exceptional pieces available. I felt the most beautiful furniture in the shop was a set of six fantastically carved side chairs, *circa* 1740 (and illustrated in the reference books), from the Sir George Donaldson collection. In the same category were four carved-wood girandoles, attributed to Johnson, that were of great delicacy and beauty.

The shop carries very little English porcelain now; however, it did have a Chelsea dessert service, *circa* 1780, with classical head decoration that was very attractive. Perhaps the most intangible thing the shop does retain from its past glories is its very definite sense of quality.

SPECIAL NOTE:

Vernay & Jussel, Inc., has combined with J. J. Wolff Antiques Ltd., to form a new firm known as:

Vernay & Jussel incorporating J. J. Wolff Antiques Ltd.
825 Madison Avenue
New York, N.Y. 10021
(212) 879-3344

Monday–Friday 9:30–5
Saturday 11–4
Summer, Monday–Friday 9:30–5

A la Vieille Russie
781 Fifth Avenue
New York, N.Y. 10022
(212) 752-1727

Monday–Friday 9:30–5
Saturday 10:30–5
Closed Saturday during July and August

Terrifyingly austere in its elegance, A la Vieille Russie is a fabulous jewel box filled with priceless objets d'art. Geared to answer the needs of the sophisticated collector, there is really not another shop quite like it in the United States. Dazzling is the only word that even begins to do justice to its inventory of exquisite treasures. As the name of the gallery indicates, its special area of interest has always been Russian works of art. It includes sixteenth- to nineteenth-century icons, those fascinating primitive religious paintings which directly reflect a Byzantine past; eighteenth- and nineteenth-century Russian silver, including wine cups and tankards; nineteenth-century enamels in brilliant colors and extravagant shapes that so strongly denote Russian taste; eighteenth- and nineteenth-century porcelains and glass, predominantly made for the royal families; nineteenth-century Russian genre painting, which is about as boring as most of this painting is and, of course, the rage of collectors today; the exquisite work of that master jeweler Fabergé, whose trinkets, created for the pleasure of the aristocracy, far surpassed their function and became true works of art.

For those of you who are mesmerized by tiny boxes, a weakness shared by many, it would be difficult to find a better selection of eighteenth- and nineteenth-century French, English, German, and Russian gold, jeweled, silver, and enameled examples. The furniture is very fine, elaborate eighteenth-century French. There are also choice eighteenth-century French decorative accessories with marvelous seventeenth- and eighteenth-century Chinese porcelains mounted on eighteenth-century French bronze doré. Antique eighteenth- and nineteenth-century European jewelry of incredible beauty is another specialty of A la Vieille Russie.

Obviously this is not a shop for the casual collector. Paul and Peter Schaffer are serious dealers of taste and knowledge. They deal in objects of great rarity and cost. However, I have always been of the philosophy that the greater the dealer, the more likely you are to find a great buy. The challenge is being able to recognize it. Much of the price structure in the antique business is based on what is in fashion; for the antiquer of limited resources, the trick is to find what is not current. There is always something whose time has not yet come, even at a shop like A la Vieille Russie. I know, because it has happened to me.

Dalva Brothers, Inc.
44 East Fifty-seventh Street
New York, N.Y. 10022
(212) 758-2297

Monday–Saturday 10:30–5:30
Summer, Monday–Friday 10:30–5:30

There is no way to predict what your experience with Dalva Brothers Antiques will be. The current mood in the establishment will determine whether you are treated with great charm and courtesy or a certain degree of disdain, which in the halcyon days of the French dealers used to be standard procedure. Don't be disturbed; it's not personal and they usually get over it very quickly, especially if you are not too overawed by the furniture, accessories, and prices. If your taste is Parisian eighteenth- and nineteenth-century cabinetwork, this is the shop for you to visit. They have floor after floor of some of the best French furniture to be found anywhere in the world, and they are priced at the top of the market. As a matter of fact, I suspect their recurrent nightmare is to be found less expensive than some other dealer. There is no doubt that if you had bought certain fine pieces here ten years ago, they would be considered bargains according to today's prices, but to be honest, others would still be considered expensive for what they were. Now that you know you are not going to steal anything from this dealer, relax and enjoy the atmosphere. It is splendid. There is a marvelous array of marquetry furniture and extraordinary accessories that include literally one-of-a-kind objects such as a Louis XIV terra-cotta clock, now in the Getty Museum in California. The very rarest of Sèvres colors, namely the black, is found amid the collection of French eighteenth-century soft- and hard-paste porcelains and, of course, there is Meissen of the same period. The large Chinese temple jars are fantastic, but a good deal of the other K'ang Hsi porcelains are too damaged to justify their price.

There is a set of four huge Beauvais tapestries which were exhibited at the Victoria and Albert in London as part of "The Age of Neo-Classicism." Dalva Brothers was extremely proud to be the only dealer represented in the show. There is almost no provincial furniture, some Renaissance, and a group of Italian pieces best exemplified by a set of four completely Baroque seventeenth-century gilt stools, covered in the original tapestry, with great cherub heads carved in full relief emerging from the scroll legs. I found these stools so fabulous that I have to admit I felt the price was not too terrible. This is a very good example of the pricing formula —one doesn't necessarily faint over a high price for a very special object, but rather the real anger is directed at pricing just-good pieces the same way.

The gallery has a huge selection of marquetry commodes, tables, desks, console tables that cover every reign of the eighteenth- and early nineteenth-century French kings. Chairs, pairs of chairs, sets of chairs, even more sets of dining chairs also range from Régence to Directoire. The walls are covered with mirrors of every variety and paintings and drawings. If you happen to be looking for a Louis XIV floor, approximately 17 feet by 12 feet go no farther. The gallery has one that is sensational. It is German Baroque marquetry, all scrolls, cartouches, dragons, and so forth. Absolutely a beauty. I didn't have the courage to ask the price.

There is so much material spread over five floors that I heartily recommend doing no more than a floor or two at a time, otherwise you may come down with a severe case of that singular French disease known as marquetry fever. *Bonne chance!*

S. J. Shrubsole, Inc.
104 East Fifty-seventh Street
New York, N.Y. 10022
(212) 753-8920

Monday–Friday 9–5:30
Summer, Monday–Friday 9–5

Collecting with passion is not enough, it must be tempered by intelligence. This is especially true in certain areas of specialization such as silver. There are very definite criteria for judging a piece of antique silver which have nothing to do with age. Old is not enough. It is precisely this kind of information that is available at S. J. Shrubsole, Inc., the finest antique-silver dealer in New York City and one of the most important English-silver dealers in the world. Their stock consists of sixteenth- to nineteenth-century English, Scotch, and Irish silver and Sheffield plate, in addition to eighteenth- and nineteenth-century American silver plus a small quantity of early twentieth-century reproductions of excellent quality. It is only at a dealer like this one, with an extensive stock of superb material available, that the differences in price between similar objects, even by the same maker, can be illustrated and explained. A perfect example were two coffee pots of similar size and weight by the great eighteenth-century English silversmith Nelme. One was almost twice the price of the other. The reason: One had a full set of hallmarks in perfect condition; the other had only the maker's mark. There is a good possibility if you had found the unmarked pot at a dealer less experienced in fine silver, with its important distinctions, you might have paid too much for it. Condition is another vital factor. Damage devaluates even the greatest piece of silver. An unknowing dealer may charge you for age and maker, totally unaware of the true condition of his piece.

This is the type of information a silver collector must have in order to buy with discretion. It is also information that Mr. Shrubsole readily imparts along with delightful legends of the silver trade. The shop owns a marvelous covered bowl by James Fraillon, *circa* 1717, made for the Marquis of Annandale who pawned it with his bank in 1720 to settle his debts. Not exactly an extensive ownership! The bowl remained in the bank vault until 1966, when it was finally sold at auction. The amusing part of this story is that the bowl and cover were illustrated in the Dictionary of English Silver, where the author claimed the finial was of a later date. As Eric Shrubsole pointed out in a note of protest: How could a piece left in a bank vault for over 240 years acquire a later finial? Yes there was a letter of apology.

The shop has choice examples by Paul de Lamerie, Paul Storr, Hester Bateman, to name just a few of the eighteenth-century masters. For the young collector who isn't quite up to a 1551 communion cup at $150,000, there are many, many lovely things such as early spoons, cream jugs, salt cellars that are affordable and, most important of all, quality examples. A piece of silver is a joy forever, provided it is absolutely right. You will not have a more pleasant learning experience than at S. J. Shrubsole.

Bernard & S. Dean Levy
981 Madison Avenue
New York, N.Y. 10021
(212) 628-7088

Winter, Tuesday–Saturday 10–5:30
Summer, Monday–Friday 10–5:30

Bernard Levy and his son Dean are the merchant princes of the fine American-furniture trade. They have a huge inventory of superior eighteenth- and early nineteenth-century American furniture supplemented by choice collections of eighteenth-century American silver, predominantly nineteenth-century American painting, and eighteenth-century China Trade porcelains, all of which they sell at an amazing rate, considering their substantial prices. Formerly partners in the firm of Ginsburg and Levy, they have now established themselves in beautiful quarters on the second floor of the Hotel Carlyle.

Bernard Levy, who is the expert on furniture and silver in the firm, enjoys describing himself as a glorified picker. He cannot resist buying anything of real quality and as a result the firm has handled some rather unexpected objects. The fine English furniture he buys is usually sold to English dealers unless a client is specifically looking for an English piece. Even some eighteenth-century European furniture and porcelains have passed through their hands. When offered a number of fine Chinese Ming bowls, Mr. Levy bought them for a solid price and sold them for an astronomical one at an English auction. The real excitement for the

Levys, as it is for all fine dealers, is finding the rare piece. Selling in today's market is almost anticlimactic.

Mr. Levy has no sympathy for people who buy antiques for investment. They are accumulators not collectors. The only reason to buy is because you love a piece. It is mainly to service the young collector that the galleries are open on Saturday. During that day anyone is free to wander about and be left to the pleasures of simple browsing. No one will disturb you unless you request some information. I can't think of a better introduction to fine American furniture. Because the stock is so large, collectors have the opportunity of discovering for themselves what particular pieces are truly to their own taste. There are many varieties of objects even as rare as lowboys and block-front chests. You will be able to compare a typical Philadelphia mahogany lowboy, with its elaborate decoration and rather heavy form, to a simple New England walnut one, or a Pennsylvania lowboy, *circa* 1720, with an elegant Spanish foot, to what is probably the ultimate of this form, a block-front lowboy from the Brownell family of Providence. There are simple New England chests, block-front chests, serpentine chests, even an oxbow or two, all with different characteristics which help to differentiate the area of origin. The plainest of slant-front desks can be as beautiful in its terms as the most extraordinary Salem block front. In addition to many highboys, there are chairs, both single, pairs, and sets of every style, including a few fine country pieces. This dealer has a minimum of country furniture, but it would be interesting to see if there really is that much difference in price between a piece you'd find here and one at a so-called country dealer, provided they are of comparable quality.

The Levys have expanded their painting collection to the point where they probably sell as much art as many picture dealers. Dean Levy does most of the buying of paintings. Among the painters they have sold are Salmon, Buttersworth, Kroll, Shinn, Glackens, Cropsey, Hart, Bierstadt, Wolleston, and various known and unknown members of the Hudson River School. I saw a few paintings of excellent quality but most of the others were, for me, those terribly overly romantic-looking genre pictures of people, animals, landscapes with cows, et cetera. Again, I must repeat, most collectors seem to enjoy them, so use your own judgment because, to be honest, I can't stand the School and find their prices ridiculous.

Mr. Bernard Levy has always collected for himself the eighteenth-century silver of Myer Myer. The stock of silver is not large but does include a number of important pieces that date as late as 1817, as in the silver soup tureen presented by the citizens of Baltimore to Commodore Decatur for saving their city during the War of 1812. The Export porcelain is almost all armorial and when it isn't, its unusual form is what gives it its distinction. Again, not a large selection, but what there is, is not remotely run of the mill.

If I have not mentioned all the other kinds of decorative accessories that are available, like mirrors, American and English, sconces, candlesticks, just as I didn't mention all the different kinds of furniture, I am assuming you understand that if it was made during the eighteenth century and has great quality, you will find it at this gallery.

These are strong-minded dealers who love their objects and enjoy their business. But do remember, a little paranoia is part of every dealer's personality. Don't be disturbed if you are assured there is no other dealer in America who knows antique furniture as well as they do. They are right insofar as only a handful of American dealers do share their expertise. The dealers who do are listed in this book.

Ralph M. Chait Galleries
12 East Fifty-sixth Street
New York, N.Y. 10022
(212) 758-0937

Monday–Saturday 10–5:30
June–August, Monday–Friday 10–5:30

This is a most unapproachable-looking gallery, however before you are completely intimidated by its huge glass door, remember that terrible old cliché about a cold exterior hiding a warm heart, etc., etc., etc. The Ralph M. Chait Galleries fits that description so well I cannot resist using it. Physically, it is a cool, beautifully austere, timelessly modern gallery. The plum walls are lined with glass-fronted cabinets behind which the porcelains glitter like vari-colored gems. The Chaits have one of the finest collections of pri-marily sixteenth-, seventeenth-, and eighteenth-century Chinese porcelains to be found in the world. You would have to go to a museum to find anything comparable, especially in the K'ang Hsi Famille Verte and Famille Noire material.

The simple phrase "May I help you?" can be interpreted in so many ways depending on the dealer. But when spoken by either Allan Chait, director of the gallery, or his sister and associate, Marion Howe, it has only one meaning. There is never any doubt that an appreciator of Chinese porcelains is always welcome to visit, admire, learn, exchange information, or just plain gossip. I don't know if it is true with other highly specialized collectors, but Chinese enthusiasts have an absolute compulsion to know ev-erything that is going on in their world and frequently do!

The traditions of great knowledge, taste, and warmth are all part of their inheritance from their father, the late Ralph M. Chait, who was one of the acknowledged authorities in his field.

There are always fine K'ang Hsi vases, bowls, cups, plates, and animals available, provided a museum or important collector hasn't snatched them away as soon as they came through the door. A huge pair of K'ang Hsi Famille Verte plates, measuring twenty-one inches in diameter and decorated with scenes of danc-ing girls and musicians entertaining a high official, were made to imperial order, bearing the royal seal mark and double circle, and may very well have been given as a gift by the Emperor. Another huge Famille Rose plate is particularly distinguished for the soft-ness of its reds. The artist was not only very skilled but had a de-lightful sense of humor, for the plate has a great pink horse that is obviously a busybody and very interested in all the action taking place. This combination of great technical skill and humor is basic to the Chinese decorative approach to porcelain painting and gives it its universal appeal. There is a good collection of Ming blue-and-white porcelains that like the K'ang Hsi, Ch'ien Lung ma-terial covers a wide price range, depending on rarity, condition, and when purchased.

An unusual sixteenth-century Ming double-gourd vase, which is a Persian-inspired form, and most frequently found in the blue and white, is painted in blue on a tomato-red ground, and if that isn't rare enough, the bottom section of the vase is squared rather than globular like the top. There is also a fine selection of K'ang Hsi powder blue and the so-called spinach-and-egg decoration of the same period in a large variety of forms.

A ware that is perfect for a young collector to start with is blanc de chine, the seventeenth- and eighteenth-century Fukien pottery. It is relatively inexpensive and there are many different shapes available. Blue-and-white eighteenth-century copies of Ming porcelains are also within an acceptable price range. The exceptions are those oversize blue-and-white Ch'ien Lung copies that are ridiculously expensive and unbelievably ugly.

No fine Chinese dealer could call his inventory complete without a good selection of jade. There are many superlative examples of this rare material in, of course, the ubiquitous snuff bottles, animals, brush holders, bowls, and those strange boulder carvings of figures on a mountain. The gallery does have some China Export but only the rarest examples such as a monster-sized Famille Rose footed tureen and stand, made for Sir Nathaniel Curzon, *circa* 1759–60, based on a silver form and inspired by French decoration.

The gallery's early material ranges from neolithic pots to fine T'ang animals and wonderful examples of T'ang and Sung wood sculpture. My favorite pieces in the shop are a collection of massive-size Famille Noire vases and a Famille Noire temple jar so breathtaking in size and color that it would be as exciting to own as a piece of large sculpture. Unfortunately, the price is just as exciting. But frankly, in terms of price, I would rather have the finest example of a Chinese object than a second- or third-rate painting which, if in vogue, would be the same price.

Mr. Chait suggests that no matter what level of Chinese collecting you reach, don't be mislead by marks. They are not necessarily a guide to the age of a piece. Most important of all, buy only the best you can afford, even if it means collecting very slowly. I envy you the experience of discovering this great dealer.

Fred Nadler
31 East Sixty-fourth Street
New York, N.Y. 10021
(212) 744-6165

Monday–Friday. Appointment suggested

The vagaries of taste and fashion have always played a fascinating role in the antique business. Until twenty years ago China Export ware was the stepchild of antique porcelain, its reputation tarnished by dealers and collectors alike who regarded it as little more than kitchen pottery. This attitude was a reflection of nineteenth- and early twentieth-century taste for the opulently decorated European porcelains. It was an ironic situation because the eighteenth-century gentry, whose lifestyle everyone was so busily emulating, were absolutely mad for all things *Chinois* and ordered Chinese porcelains by the shipload from the various trading companies. As a matter of fact, most of the eighteenth-century European factories copied the Export designs because of their enormous popularity. Yet even during the years this ware was out of fashion, it always had a small coterie of collectors and dealers who appreciated its unique charm. In this country, one dealer in particular has been responsible for the growth of interest in China Export as a porcelain of beauty and value. Fred Nadler's imagination and courage in promoting this marvelous ware helped focus the attention of many collectors on its special qualities.

As a young dealer fifteen years ago, with a love for the Fitzhugh pattern in green, orange, yellow, and brown, with or without American eagles, he changed its acceptance from minor pottery to museum treasure. Today, with the most adventurous Export stock in the United States, his latest passion is Tobacco Leaf, that interesting, wildly colorful floral pattern influenced by Japanese design, which was made in the eighteenth century for the Portuguese market. Fred Nadler, who never does anything by halves, has the largest selection of Tobacco Leaf to be found, including such unique forms as tureens, cachepots, ice pails, candlesticks and vases, in addition to the standard shapes. The particular joy of collecting China Export is that a novice antiquer and a serious scholar can visit Mr. Nadler and each find an object uniquely suited to their individual needs and pocketbook. The variety and size of the inventory is amazing. The rarest objects, such as the great soup tureens, come in the most delightful assortment of shapes and patterns—from large animal forms (goose, cow, fish) to such enchantments as a fantastic eighteenth-century purple-and-white footed tureen of Baroque silver that looks like something Cinderella went to the ball in. It is an irresistible piece with a hair-raising price. There are tureens, dinner services, teapots, salt cellars, and bowls in the early Famille Rose which is distinguishable from the later nineteenth-century copies by its fine decoration and the wet, clear translucent look of the enameling.

For the specialist interested in armorial crests, there are literally dozens of examples. Mr. Nadler and his partner, Richard Trotta, have always loved the eighteenth-century Export animals, especially the dogs, and there is usually an assortment of breeds with marvelous Chinese faces. Most of this dealer's porcelains date from 1750 to 1820, with a small number from the earlier K'ang Hsi period, usually in blue and white rather than colorful enamels. Many of his Ho Ho boy figures, those ubiquitous Chinese laughing children, date from this period. Another specialty of this dealer is his huge stock of cachepots and garden seats that unfortunately have risen in price from simple pleasure to sheer mania much to Mr. Nadler's own distress. These nineteenth-century planters and garden pieces provided a starting point for many collectors' interest in China Export. With everything now showing the impact of inflation, this dealer feels the only solution for the young antiquer is to buy the finest piece he or she can afford, no matter how small in size. A great tiny teapot, cup, or spoon tray is still a great piece of porcelain.

Fred Nadler, like many talented antique dealers, is a restless soul. Joy for him is the excitement of finding the rarest object; for you, it will be the pleasure of sharing his discoveries.

Matthew Schutz Antiques
1025 Park Avenue
New York, N.Y. 10028
(212) 876-4195

By appointment only

There is a particular pleasure in following the career of a young dealer, especially when it surpasses your expectations. I met Mr. Schutz many years ago when I had a pretty little Louis XV chair to sell. As with most young collectors, life was one continual uphill struggle, consisting of selling one piece to be able to afford another.

We had a nervous conversation over price as we were both relatively new to this kind of financial horse trading. It went well and I thought him a surprisingly knowledgeable young man. From time to time we would meet about town and he was definitely looking more and more prosperous. Finally, some years ago I heard of his coup which put him in another category entirely. He had arranged to buy, over a number of years, a large part of Mme. Consuelo Balsan's furniture and accessories collection. To the French collector, that name is as fine a provenance as Rothschild. Simultaneously, he was also buying from other famous estates both here and abroad. The result is an apartment full of wonderful eighteenth-century French furniture and predominately eighteenth-century French and Chinese accessories. Do not be put off by having to call for an appointment. Mr. Schutz is still as nice a person as the one I originally met and, of course, his expertise is no longer remotely astonishing. What is surprising is his delightful taste and the pricing of his material. Considering its quality, it is as fairly marked as anything its equivalent on the market. I always enjoy buying from a dealer who sells from his home. It makes the experience that much more personal. If you love French furniture that is not overly ornate but of excellent quality, this is a dealer you should see.

A black lacquer Louis XV chinoiserie commode is a lovely lady from the Marietta Tree sale. There is a Régence desk of ebonized pearwood, inlaid with brass stringers, which has bronze doré face masks mounted on the knees. It is a good example of its period, very authoritative and masculine, yet, strangely enough, basically simple. A crazy little circular Russian table, Louis XVI-style, but probably late nineteenth century, is of solid bronze doré. It really is exquisite and has that exuberant exaggeration that the best

Russian copies frequently have. If you ever have an opportunity to see any eighteenth-century Russian silver, don't miss it, it is so delightfully ugly. A very fine Louis XV marquetry commode by Garnier has the unusual detail of being sans traverse for all three drawers. You will find no gilt seat furniture at this dealer. He prefers the natural woods in both his Régence and Louis XV chairs and paint on the Louis XVI examples. Since that is very much my own preference, bear it in mind if I seem lavish in my praise. A pair of very important early Louis XVI Chinese red lacquer cabinets have short bronze doré legs and a marble top. The lacquer panels are K'ang Hsi and were undoubtedly removed from either a screen or chest. It is a terrific example of the elegance of Mme. Blasan's taste. Yes, the price is pretty terrific, too!

There is a wonderful selection of decorative accessories. The most important group is a large number of eighteenth-century Chinese animals and porcelains mounted in bronze doré.

There is a large mid-eighteenth-century Famille Rose China Export dinner service with a marbleized border. It is a bit too busy for me, but the design is very unusual. A fantastic pair of large candelabra are bronze doré with Grecian-draped ladies holding huge doré lilies and roses. It originally came from Mrs. Walter's sale in 1941. Equally spectacular, are a pair of girondoles, *circa* 1760, made by the Englishman William Vile in the French taste. The paintings and drawings available are seventeenth- and eighteenth-century Italian and French as are the bronzes to be seen.

This is a dealer with great flair, who really does enjoy hunting things down for his specialized collectors. So whatever your interest, be it clocks, mirrors, or what, don't hesitate to ask him. He'd love to find a beauty for you.

J. T. Tai & Co. Inc.
810 Madison Avenue
New York, N.Y. 10021
(212) 288-5253

Monday–Saturday 10–5

J. T. Tai & Co. is a veritable Chinese puzzle. Like all good puzzles, it presents a number of interesting quandaries for the collector of Chinese artifacts, as Mr. Tai is the foremost dealer in early Chinese wares in this country. First, will they let you in the shop? Second, if they do allow you in, do you know the right questions to ask? I realize this sounds a bit like Alice in Wonderland, but if you don't know the key words, you'll be out in the street in about three minutes flat. I am not exaggerating. Mr. Tai, who has sold great Shang and Chou bronzes, to say nothing of innumerable Han to Sung dynasty wood and stone sculptures, to all the major museums and collectors in the world, does not brook amateur antiquarians. This gallery is only interested in serious Sinophiles, who have the sophistication to appreciate their material and the vast amounts of money necessary to buy it. They are not remotely interested in having the shop function as a schoolroom. Now that I have painted the blackest possible picture, let me admit it is not all that bleak. Mr. Tai, himself, is a charming man, once he is convinced you know what you are about. In a field where probably 90 per cent of the material on the market is fake, Mr. Tai's reputation is sacrosanct.

The street floor of the gallery holds the shop's collection of Ming and K'ang Hsi porcelains. I have always felt, for my taste, they are the least interesting of Mr. Tai's objects and very expensive for what they are. There are also on view a number of large T'ang and Sung wood and stone sculptures. It is on the lower floor that the rarest of the gallery's wares are kept, hidden, whenever possible. Wonderful T'ang pottery, horses, camels, figures, bowls, both glazed and unglazed, and even, on occasion, a marble sculpture from that period, which is extremely rare to find. Mr. Tai has owned one of the most beautiful T'ang stone Buddha heads I have ever seen. A Hunan piece, its hair was carved entirely in tiny snail coils, its face unbelievably gentle. It is fascinating how a piece you have loved can stay with you forever. The earlier dynastic pottery such as Han figures, Wei, Six Dynasties horses, and the Shang and Chou bronzes are also kept on this level.

The open sesame to this dealer is, of course, a request to see a T'ang horse or, if you are really courageous, a Shang bronze of some specific form. Then you will receive all the courtesies of the gallery. But I give you warning: If you are not familiar with this material, you will receive very short shrift. The problem, of course, is that there are so few dealers in the world with the necessary knowledge and experience to handle these objects authoritatively. Mr. Tai is unquestionably one of these and therefore must be seen.

Kennedy Galleries, Inc.
40 West Fifty-seventh Street
New York, N.Y. 10019
(212) 541-9600

October 1–Memorial Day, Tuesday–Saturday 9:30–5:30
Memorial Day–October 1, Monday–Friday 9:30–5:30
Closed last two weeks in August

My first visit to the Kennedy Galleries occurred during an exhibition they organized in conjunction with Israel Sack, Inc., for the Bicentennial. I felt it was, if not the most beautiful show I had seen, certainly neck and neck with my favorite, the Yale exhibition that went to England. I had been aware of their reputation as the top American painting dealers in the United States, but what I was unprepared for was the extraordinary quality and range of their stock. The Wunderlich family, who established the gallery in 1874, selling old master prints, is as active as ever. But in addition to the fine old etchings by Dürer or Rembrandt, which still can be found there, they are now the great specialists in eighteenth- and nineteenth-century American painting. Mr. Rudolf Wunderlich, who is president of the gallery, is an authority on our Western artists such as Remington, Russell, Catlin, and Bierstadt. Another member of the family recently discovered a talented young contemporary painter of Indian life named Michael Coleman, who can best be described as similar to Andrew Wyeth in technique but with a beautiful, subtle color sense unlike Wyeth, who is essentially a black-and-white painter.

The surprise, however, even for collectors familiar with the gallery by reputation, is the extensive collection of twentieth-century American representational painters. Mr. Lawrence Fleishman, who joined Kennedy Galleries as a partner in 1966, is the gentleman responsible for this huge expansion. Wherever your interest lies, be it a wonderful early primitive, a John Singleton Copley, any member of the Peale family, Bingham, Eakins, Harnett, Winslow Homer, Inness, Sargent, Stuart, to name just a handful of the eighteenth- and nineteenth-century painters available, add Prendergast, Georgia O'Keeffe, Hopper, Feininger, Demuth, Sloan, Marino, again merely a sampling. Among the artists they exclusively represent are Ben Shahn, Walt Kuhn, Burchfield, Abraham Rattner, Evergood, Leonard Baskin, and the list goes on and on. If you are overwhelmed, so was I! I couldn't have been more intimidated by the look, importance, and seeming impersonalness of the gallery. But there is always a starting point for any collector, namely genuine interest. I love Benjamin West drawings, and that seemed as good a place to begin as any. I wandered around a bit and finally approached a man seated at a desk and asked if they had any. He assured me they did and that he would be delighted to show them to me. He had never seen me before and I certainly did not know him. I liked one of the drawings, asked the price, and found it fairly marked. However, I was disturbed by a signature on it. I felt it shouldn't have one; it just didn't make sense to me. Instead of raised eyebrows or any settling back on dignity and reputation, my concern was noted and not deemed unreasonable. The young man then suggested that, if I was not in a hurry, they would be glad to send a copy of the drawing to an expert on West and get an opinion. I could not have been more delighted with both the good sense and good manners. This unassuming young man turned out to be Gerald Wunderlich, the newest member of the family to join the firm.

Imposing as this establishment looks, there is no question that everyone works on a one-to-one basis with the clients, be they novices with no more than a hundred dollars in their pocket, which will buy them an original, limited-edition contemporary graphic published by Kennedy Galleries. Or, for the more experienced young collector, there is the world of drawings, which is a wonderful world indeed! It is really the perfect place to start buying quality for relatively little money. And, of course, with the enormous expertise available at this gallery, no matter what your taste is in American painting you are guaranteed something that simply does not occur at auction, namely a uniformity of quality that is constantly being guarded.

The Antique Porcelain Co.
48 East Fifty-seventh Street
New York, N.Y. 10022
(212) 758-2363

Winter, Monday–Friday 9–6, Saturday 9–5
Summer, closed Saturday

The late Mr. Weinburg's position in that small, furiously competitive enclave of museum directors, rich connoisseurs, and powerful rivals, otherwise known as the international antique world, was simply that of the ultimate dealer. His reputation was extraordinary as an authority in the areas of his gallery's specialization, namely eighteenth-century European porcelains, exceptional eighteenth-century French furniture and objets d'art of extreme value such as solid gold and jeweled snuffboxes and watches of the same period. The list continues with important paintings, silk rugs, Renaissance jewelry, to name just a few more odds and ends. Perhaps to other dealers his greatest talent was the seeming ease with which he was able to gain access to the fine private collections of Europe whose owners rarely parted with anything except under the most discreet of circumstances.

Now, innocent antiquer, where are we in this treasure trove that has more examples of specific rarities in porcelains housed under one roof than most museums? Unless you are among the rather well-to-do, you will find the prices are as rarified as the objects. Are they worth it? Absolutely yes, provided it is the exceptional piece you are looking for. For the new collectors, it is like a trip to the Metropolitan in New York or the Victoria and Albert in London. The serious collector of European porcelain, even of somewhat limited funds, may definitely feel it is worth while to try to buy a really exceptional piece, be it a Sèvres saucer made for Catherine the Great or the rarest in color and decoration in eighteenth-century Worcester, a scale-yellow plate. It may mean sacrificing other pieces that are nice but unexceptional, to gather the monies together. If you are knowledgeable, there is a certain amount of eighteenth-century European porcelain on the market which is excellent but not unusual. Do not go to the Antique Porcelain Company for this category of material, because you will pay absolutely top dollar for it there. But, how many porcelain lovers have ever seen a thirty-four-piece Dr. Wall dessert service or the only known pair of Bristol hoopoes, which, of course, are birds, or the Swan service made for Count Brühl who was director of the Meissen factory, *circa* 1737, in Germany. Endless numbers of Vincennes mocha cups and saucers, with their great diversity of decoration and color, due to the custom of giving each guest a different-pattern cup, are to be found.

Sèvres is available in every color and form made in the eighteenth century in both the soft and hard paste.

To go beyond porcelains for the moment, there is a Marie Antoinette ink stand, a tiny marquetry Lous XVI desk by Reisner, a classic Louis XIV black boule commode that can only be described as imperial in its grandeur. Another Louis XV marquetry commode by Cresson is similar to the one in the Wallace collection. There is a sensational chandelier of Venetian crystal and bronze doré that was made in Russia for Catherine. As to be expected, the price is as sensational as the piece.

Miss Weinburg, who is now director of the firm, worked closely with her father for many years. Her advice is extremely valuable. One of the things she reminds collectors to be alert about is the delightful Nymphenburg flower and butterfly pattern. Though originally made *circa* 1750, the factory has continued to produce this pattern right through the twentieth century and only an expert can determine by the paste, quality of the painting, and changes in small detail when the pieces were actually produced. The same problem can exist in nineteenth-century Minton, which copies the eighteenth-century French Sèvres, and the English factory Leeds, which reproduced the earlier white Berlin ware. As is obvious, none of this matters if what you have paid for is what you have received. Unfortunately, many a collector of the early soft-paste wares, such as Chantilly, St. Cloud, Mennecy, and even the English Bow and Chelsea, have ended up with nineteenth-century copies.

In marked contrast to the Baroque feeling of much of the great German porcelains, it is very interesting to see examples of the earliest porcelain made in Europe by J. F. Böttger, in 1714–15, who actually was looking for a way to create gold. The so-called

Böttger stoneware is true, white, hard-paste porcelain, simple in both form and feeling. The earliest examples of Meissen are not marked, but the Böttger porcelain is.

There is simply no end to the rarities available at this great dealer. Though they function primarily to service the collections of museums and private connoisseurs, I cannot imagine a more delightful challenge than trying to find that piece which is not only unique but affordable!

Gerald Kornblau
790 Madison Avenue
New York, N.Y. 10021
(212) 737-7433

Monday–Friday 10:30–5
Appointment suggested

Until fairly recently, folk art occupied the somewhat dubious position of being neither fish nor fowl in either the antique or art world. Serious dealers such as Gerald Kornblau, who was one of the earliest specialists in the field, waged an uphill battle for years before these marvelous objects gained the recognition they deserved. Jerry Kornblau remembers when you couldn't give away fine weather vanes, cigar-store figures, or primitive paintings unless they were by Field, Phillips, Prior, Brewster, or their like. Nineteenth-century genre painting simply went begging. Happily or unhappily, depending at what stage of collecting American folk art you are, times and prices have drastically changed.

Folk art lovers are a finicky breed and Mr. Kornblau has all the right qualifications for dealing with them. Highly individualistic, solidly knowledgeable, he is an expert in a field that can be quite hazardous for the uninitiated, especially as the latest cottage industry seems to be the faking of primitive paintings. A few years ago it was weather vanes that flooded the market.

The stock is not large but of excellent quality. Finding an Ammi Phillips or Feke is not unusual, but this dealer's particular love has always been the anonymous nineteenth-century painters who plied their trade, usually without any formal training, among the local farmers and merchants. His stock really shines with a good selection of portrait, landscape, animal, and still-life works. There are the proverbial weather vanes but only in the most unusual forms, early pottery, wood and stone carvings, signs, quilts, and a small number of simulated wood grain painted chests.

Quality is the key word with this dealer. It is what he buys and, just as important, it is what he wants his clients to be able to recognize. Always preferring to work on a one-to-one basis, Jerry Kornblau tries to search out particular objects for his individual collectors, allowing the development of their taste to guide him.

TRADE DEALERS

The following group is made up primarily of trade dealers except for Metro Antiques, who I have grouped with them because of his location. The lower Broadway area between Tenth and Thirteenth streets and west to University Place is now the hub of the wholesale market in antiques. I have recommended the dealers I feel to be the most knowledgeable and responsible. There are many shops in this area, but most of them are filled with junk.

The sad thing that has happened in New York City because of the economics of inflation is the loss of that marvelous middle-range dealer who can no longer afford to pay both the huge rents that are now demanded uptown and the higher prices on superior stock. The trade dealers have in a sense taken over that niche. The choice in New York City now is between the very finest dealers in the world and the trade shops. Both should be seen.

Hyde Park Antiques Ltd.
818 Broadway
New York, N.Y. 10003
(212) 477-0033

Monday–Friday 9–5:30
Saturday 9–1
Closed Saturday July and August

A good dealer must have a passion and Mr. Bernard Karr's is Chinese Export punch bowls, the bigger the better. His main business, though, is selling eighteenth- and nineteenth-century English furniture, primarily to the trade and decorators. He is easy and pleasant with his retail customers provided you know what you want. The shop has a huge inventory of period furniture covering a wide price range. There are some lovely quality pieces to be found, such as a marvelous pair of small Regency side tables in zebrawood, a fine mahogany partner's desk, a small-scale Georgian burl-walnut bureau bookcase with mirrored panels. Another rarity is a pair of George III carved eagle consoles with marble tops. The main shop has Mr. Karr's current favorites in furniture and Export bowls, but another building contains floor after floor of every variety of seat furniture, including sets of Regency, Queen Anne, and Chippendale dining chairs both eighteenth and nineteenth century. (Incidentally, Mr. Karr does not hesitate to tell you if a piece isn't period.) I never saw so many dining tables in one place. There are endless pieces of case furniture such as chests, desks, bookcases.

The furniture is primarily mahogany and walnut. There is very little of the so-called country furniture. There was an oak Welch dresser in stock, when I went, but the shop mainly carries the more formal pieces. I found the furniture here the equivalent of what most retail dealers carry and considerably less expensive. However, we are not talking about great English furniture. There isn't any here, but then, there are only a handful of dealers in the entire country who have any stock at all of fine-caliber English furniture, and the prices generally preclude collecting by any but the rich. This is a good solid trade dealer who the majority of English collectors will do very well to investigate.

George Subkoff Antiques
835 Broadway
New York, N.Y. 10003
(212) 673-7280

Monday–Saturday 10–5:30
Summer, Monday–Friday 10–5:30

It is always exciting to walk into George Subkoff's sprawling, overcrowded shop on lower Broadway. I don't know why some trade dealers have it and others don't, but this shop definitely exudes the promise of hidden treasure. Even if experience has taught you that these treasures are few and far between, the promise is as stimulating as the realization to most collectors. Mr. Subkoff, a third-generation antique dealer, is a pleasant young man to do business with. Solidly knowledgeable, he is essentially a dealer's dealer. But there is nothing he enjoys more than working with young collectors starting on their way.

It is almost impossible to describe the range of material the shop carries. There are eighteenth- and nineteenth-century American and European furniture and nineteenth-century painting of every description. Other accessories are European, Chinese porcelains, an occasional piece of eighteenth-century English silver, objets d'art of every conceivable variety. There are mirrors and more mirrors, both American and European, in singles and pairs. As a matter of fact, he just sold a pair of mirrors to Boscobel.

This shop is a marvelous place to test the keenness of your eye. It does require careful looking to differentiate the junk from the interesting objects. It is not difficult to spot an eighteenth-century American highboy or chest of the same period or even a fine English Chippendale breakfront that had been at Williamsburg. But the young collector who found a very delicate eighteenth-century English mahogany kettle-stand table with cluster legs deserves full marks.

For the Western painting enthusiast, the shop has 120 unframed paintings by Samuel Colman, the American artist whose "Westward Ho" is in the Metropolitan Museum. In addition to Indian, Japanese, and Tibetan art, there are chandeliers and wall decorations of every variety. It all adds up to an antique supermarket. The dealers cover this shop daily; as a result things go in and out very rapidly, which makes it even more exciting.

Experienced antiquers have a surprise in store for them if they are interested in very fine eighteenth- or nineteenth-century American pieces. These are the goodies that are hidden away and only shown on request. Over the last few years the shop has had a Townsend Goddard tea table, a signed Frothingham secretary, a labeled Launnier pier table, just to name a few of the treasures. This is very expensive furniture no matter who is selling it. There is a very nice service Mr. Subkoff offers, which is unusual in a trade shop. Tell him what you are specifically interested in and he will try to find it for you. I feel strongly this is an up-and-coming dealer who will one day be important in the antique world.

Maurice Sigal Antiques Inc.
841 Broadway
New York, N.Y. 10003
(212) 533-3555

Monday–Friday 9–5

Maurice Sigal is a mad, marvelous picker. You never know what will turn up in this shop. Even though mishmash rather than potpourri describes the range of material and quality, Mr. Sigal, a knowledgeable Frenchman, usually seems able to turn up that occasional piece of European furniture and decoration that has real style and humor. He has an instinct for the decorative. The best of the eighteenth-century or early nineteenth-century French furniture generally disappears overnight. This is no mystery, as Mr. Sigal functions primarily as a source for the European dealers. If your French is good, you may have the pleasure of overhearing a little transatlantic bartering on the telephone.

It is not unusual to find an ordinary nineteenth-century French armchair sitting right next to something as unique as a perfectly splendid set of Russian Charles X seat furniture comprising two bergères and a settee. The bronze doré mounts, which are exaggerated winged sphinx, cover the entire front legs. They are absolutely wonderful. It is true you can bearly lift a chair, but what dash. They are a delightful example of Russian adaptation of French taste. Pieces of this quality are, of course, expensive. However, when you find something very unique in what is essentially a trade dealer, you can be certain when it moves uptown or overseas the price will really soar.

The shop has bits-and-pieces of everything, eighteenth- and nineteenth-century English and Continental mirrors, French provincial commodes, with occasional Italian and German pieces. The chairs for the most part are nineteenth-century copies with an eighteenth-century one here and there. There is a good assortment of Chinese lacquer available, both in cabinets and low tables. The accessories include anything from gilt-wood wall brackets, some paintings of dubious quality, bouillotte lamps, terra-cotta figures to one of the most beautiful examples of Japanese lacquer work I've ever seen, namely a pair of large Karabitsu boxes that are breathtaking. I am told these were probably gift boxes which contained presents being given by one noble family to another. The stimulating thing about shopping trade dealers such as Mr. Sigal, who is perfectly delighted to sell private collectors, is the possibility of coming across a special treasure when you least expect it.

Metro Antiques
80 East Eleventh Street
New York, N.Y. 10003
(212) 673-3510

Monday–Friday 10–5
Appointment suggested

At first glance Eleventh Street between Broadway and University Place in Greenwich Village is a far cry from the Piazza Navona in Rome. In place of magnificent fountains and great stone buildings is a collection of tacky tenements, left over from an even uglier time. But strangely enough there is a connection sitting in the middle of the block, a first-class antique shop, specializing in Renaissance furniture and objects, with the unlikely name of Metro Antiques. Mr. Maurice Margules, who is a passionate lover of this period, does not encourage browsing. Like many dealers who have very specialized material that requires background to appreciate, the casual novice can cause small explosions of temper. But like all true antiquarians, if you show real interest even without knowledge, he will be delighted to share his pleasure in his objects with you.

Fifty, sixty years ago no fine home was complete without its collection of Renaissance pieces. Mr. Duveen kept a steady flow going between Europe and the United States. However, tastes change and gradually the lighter, more delicate eighteenth-century French, English, and American furniture began to supercede those vast baronial pieces. As recently as ten years ago, there were so few American collectors interested in this period that these pieces frequently couldn't be given away at auction. The situation has changed. The European dealers have been buying heavily in New York for the last five years. The smaller American museums are actively enlarging their collection of Renaissance works of art. And, finally, American collectors have begun again to recognize the extraordinary architectural quality of Renaissance objects. Many of the tables, cabinets, and chairs bear more resemblance to sculpture than furniture. This is not surprising as they were frequently designed by the leading artists of their day.

The shop specializes in Gothic and Renaissance furniture, sculpture, porcelains, ivories, bronzes. However, Mr. Margules, who has beautiful, very personal taste, can't resist anything first rate even if it is not his favorite period. There were as fine a pair of English Queen Anne armchairs as I've seen anywhere sitting on top of a terrific Baroque red lacquer commode decorated with a diamond pattern that might be either early eighteenth-century Italian or Spanish. There are so many objects in the shop, which is comparatively small in size, that it is difficult to see everything without getting confused. But do look carefully and slowly; you will find piece after piece of unique quality. Crowded to one side, one couldn't really call it a corner because the table is so large, is the Vasari table which dates *circa* 1550 and, if not carved in Vasari's own workshop, is certainly based on his designs. If you are interested in what must be the epitome of Rococo furniture, there is a large Venetian bombé commode in perfect condition. There is also an equally marvelous refractory table, believed to be by the Flemish designer DeVries, *circa* 1590–1610.

The selection of statuary is beautiful with French, German, and Italian madonnas and saints abounding. Quality Renaissance furniture and sculpture are not cheap but nothing of any distinction is anymore. If this is your period, I cannot recommend this shop too highly. This is a young dealer very respected in the trade and unique for having a delightful sense of humor, once he relaxes.

Old Versailles Antiques
152 East Fifty-third Street
New York, N.Y. 10022
(212) 753-4479

Winter, Monday–Friday 11–5
Closed July 1–August 15

A casual stroll through Old Versailles Antiques will remind most collectors of the joy of roaming the shops on the Left Bank of Paris. A bit dark, dusty but pleasurably seedy, this is undoubtedly one of the best trade dealers in French eighteenth-century furniture and decorations in the city. Happily, the only missing ingredient is the proverbial French rudeness. Charles Kriz, who has managed the shop for years, is a lovely man of infinite patience and solid knowledge in his field. Though their trade is mainly European dealers and American decorators, private collectors are made very welcome indeed.

Their stock is primarily eighteenth-century French furniture and accessories, with a few Dutch, German, and Italian pieces of the same period. The eighteenth-century Portuguese furniture that occasionally turns up goes immediately to South America. The shop is well represented by excellent quality provincial pieces such as Louis XV fruitwood commodes, walnut buffets, small Louis XV and Louis XVI tables, and those marvelous big armoires everyone has been using for either stereo equipment or books. There has been a great rise in the price of the more elegant provincial furniture, partially due perhaps to the feeling that the fine marquetry pieces may be too ostentatious. Whether it is changing tastes or inflation that has made the difference is a mute point. The size of the shop's decorator trade does determine to some extent what they are interested in stocking.

The gilt seat furniture, be it Louis XV or Louis XVI, and the good quality marquetry tables and commodes almost all return to Europe when the shop does get them.

Their selection of antique decorative accessories is large and varied. There are doré bouillotte lamps, candlesticks, girondoles, beautiful eighteenth-century gilt-wood mirrors of every size and style, in pairs as well as individual ones. If you enjoy blackamoors, the shop has a unique pair of eighteenth-century Italian ones that are six-foot-tall gilt-wood torchères. They could not be more amusing, a pair of large, carved gilt-wood swans and all sorts of nineteenth-century Chinese porcelain animals, are, indicative of Mr. Kriz's preference for buying the more unusual accessories.

The shop's pride and joy at the moment is a large French eighteenth-century black lacquer Régence *bureau plat* (desk) with its old repair label still inside. The cabinetmaker who restored the desk in 1847 was so proud of it, he practically tells his life story on the label. Good antique rock-crystal chandeliers are difficult to find, but the shop always has a goodly number in stock. Louis XV and XVI chairs are to be found in painted gilt, and natural wood. There were two very different pairs of chairs that I found particularly interesting. One pair was very delicately proportioned Régence winged bergères, the other, a most unusual pair of Louis XIV children's open armchairs; both sets, aside from being beautiful, were perfectly scaled for today's room sizes. There is here, as in all antique shops, a large price differentiation depending on demand and rarity. Obviously, a fine chinoiserie brown Lacquer Louis XV commode is going to be much more expensive than a very simple mahogany Louis XVI commode unless, of course, it happens to be by a great cabinetmaker such as Reisner.

Mr. Kriz has no objection to very attractive furniture that may have been reconstructed. There is a fine line here—the pieces are antique but were not originally what they became. A good example in French furniture would be a dressing table becoming a small desk or perhaps enclosing the arms of an open armchair. Because this is a reputable dealer, you will be told if this is the case with something you have selected. Though these are eighteenth-century objects, the advantage to the young collector is that they are relatively reasonable to buy. It is also wise to remember that reconstruction is a common occurrence in both European and American furniture. It doesn't matter as long as you get what you have paid for.

For me this shop is the best of combinations—tasteful, reasonable, reliable and, most important of all, fun to do business with.

AUCTION HOUSES

The following auction houses are of excellent reputation, whether you belong in them or not depends to a large extent on your own experience, expertise, or sporting instinct. Frankly, it's the latter that has gotten me into the most trouble. I have done all the classic things, from bidding against my own husband to buying a piece I had not examined at exhibition. I did that at the Guest Sale at Parke Bernet. I was very lucky in this instance, not just stupid, only because most of the Chinese porcelains had come from the Chait Galleries.

If you can match your knowledge against an expert dealer, then you certainly have as good a chance to buy well at auctions as he does. But if you are using the auction catalogue as your guide, or the auction house's expertise, you are asking for trouble. It does no good to remind anyone suffering from auction fever not to bid beyond his or her limit on an item; even the most hardened dealers get caught in that trap. But remember, they can sell their mistakes! If you can't control yourself, leave a bid and don't attend the auction. It will save you money and anguish. Another important point: If it is a quality piece, it is almost never put in without a reserve (the price below which it cannot be sold). This is not necessarily unfair as it does protect the seller from the dealers combinations and the various eccentricities that can occur at auctions. However, many dealers and collectors have been actively using auctions as a way of establishing new high prices to either enhance their stock or their collections. It is now standard procedure and difficult to beat. Don't despair! As long as there are auctions, there will be sleepers. Keep alert, and good hunting.

Christies of London
502 Park Avenue
New York, N.Y. 10022
(212) 826-2888

Weekly auctions

Absolutely top gallery. Prices to match.

Sotheby Parke Bernet
980 Madison Avenue
New York, N.Y. 10021
(212) 472-3400

Daily auctions
September–June

King of auction houses in New York. Loaded with staff and pretensions.

P. B. 84
171 East Eighty-fourth Street
New York, N.Y. 10028
(212) 472-3583

Weekly auctions

Fun, not serious prices. Less important material sold here.

Wm. Doyle Galleries
175 East Eighty-seventh Street
New York, N.Y. 10028
(212) 427-2730

* Weekly auctions

Nicest people work here. Large dealer trade. Very often good material to be found.

Plaza Art Galleries Inc.
406 East Seventy-ninth Street
New York, N.Y. 10021
(212) 472-1000

*Weekly auctions

Old firm under new management.

---

* Weekly auctions means anything from once a week to once a month depending on how much material the individual auction houses have accumulated.

Phillips of London
867 Madison Avenue
New York, N.Y. 10021
(212) 734-8330

*Weekly auctions

Good reputation in England. Not in same category as Christies or Sotheby.

Phillips of London
525 East Seventy-second Street
New York, N.Y. 10021
(212) 879-1415

Sales of larger items are held in Phillips' 72nd Street Galleries.

Astor Galleries
754 Broadway
New York, N.Y. 10003
(212) 473-1658

*Weekly auctions

Essentially dealer trade.

Manhattan Galleries
201 East Eightieth Street
New York, N.Y. 10021
(212) 744-2844

*Weekly auctions

Essentially dealer trade.

Museums

The Cloisters
Fort Tryon Park
New York, N.Y. 10040
(212) 923-3700

Tuesday–Saturday 10–4:45
Sunday 12–4:45
Summer, Sunday 1–4:45
Closed Monday

Take No. 4 bus on Madison Avenue to Fort Tryon Park.

This museum is physically one of the most extraordinary places you will ever visit. Usually it is the objects in a museum that give it its particular distinction. Not so here; from the moment you enter, this building thrusts you back in time almost a thousand years. As you walk up the long flights of worn stone stairs leading to the entrance hall, it is not difficult to imagine the clatter of horses hooves and armour about you. The light is dim and even the smells from the herb and flower gardens are medieval. Yes, it is filled with beautiful sculpture, paintings, tapestries, and architectural materials of that period, but unquestionably, it is the ambiance which has been created out of them that is its rarest treasure.

The emotional experience of the Cloisters directly captures for the modern visitor a sense of the all-prevailing Church as it existed in the everyday life of the Middle Ages. The building is constructed around the remains of four ancient monastery Cloisters. Notice, as you wander through the various levels of the museum, certain architectural details that vividly illustrate this particular relationship. I was startled by the smallness of a door, set in the wall of the modest-size Fuentidueña apse. How insignificant a man must have felt in the presence of this God, magnified, of course, a thousandfold by the great cathedrals of Notre Dame and Chartres whose authority humbled even the mightiest knight. The ultimate expression of the medieval experience for me is the Unicorn tapestries. That they are beautiful beyond belief is just part of their power; their true mystery lies in another realm entirely.

Whatever else you do in New York City, you must not miss a visit to the Cloisters. If you do nothing more than sit in its gardens or walk its rampart, I promise you a moment in another time.

New-York Historical Society
170 Central Park West
New York, N.Y. 10024
(212) 873-3400

Tuesday–Friday 1–5
Saturday 10–5
Sunday 1–5
Closed Monday

The New-York Historical Society is New York City's "unknown" major museum. It is just terrific. Filled with fascinating pieces of Americana, from great paintings, furniture, and silver to crazy old advertising posters, wonderfully nostalgic nineteenth-century photos of New York City and all sorts of early conveyances. If this historic society doesn't seem very typical, it was never meant to be just about New York. Established in 1804 by John Pintard, as New York's first museum, its original founders saw it functioning as a continually growing repository for all kinds of documents pertaining to the history of the United States. Over the years, members, in addition to building its vast reference library, left it all manner of marvelous bequests. The result today is as fine a collection of American silver, Hudson River School painting, American genre painting, and Folk Art as you are likely to find. What you are not going to find anywhere else in the world is the almost complete set of original water colors for the Elephant Folio of *Birds of America*, by Audubon, which the museum has owned since 1863. These original studies are technically so brilliant and such beautiful works of art that they alone make a visit to this lovely, spacious old building an absolute necessity.

The American silver collection dating from the seventeenth century to 1850 is presented in chronological order, making it very simple to understand the changing progression of style and taste, which is especially apparent in the change from the classicism of the late eighteenth century to the ornate decoration of nineteenth-century silver. I was interested to learn that the silversmiths of the eighteenth and early nineteenth centuries functioned in a certain sense as the bankers of their day, as it was easier for merchants to convert their wealth to silver plate than store the actual money. This is probably the reason there is so much early silver, serving as it did both an aesthetic as well as a utilitarian function.

Another rarity of this museum is the Bella C. Laudauer Collection of Business and Professional Literature. In a word, it is a history of American business through advertising, and the part which is on view is completely delightful and amusing. I'm for a return to early advertising art, enough of television. The society is also famous for its collection of early photographs of New York. They always have a group on display somewhere in the building; be sure to see them. The picture they give you of early New York cannot be duplicated in any other medium.

Now to the more traditional objects found in museums, namely, paintings and furniture. Because this is an intimate museum, it is most appropriate that its main furniture collection is shown in three small authentic New England colonial rooms known as the Prentis Rooms. The furniture is late seventeenth and early eighteenth century, the accessories, all of the same period, are mostly imported as was customary, the paintings, by American painters of the period. The rooms are particularly successful in giving one a sense of how the gentry of the time lived, obviously neither luxuriously nor grandly.

There are paintings all over the building, but if you tire easily, don't leave before you've had a look at the Bard (both brothers) paintings of side-wheelers, those great boats that proudly steamed up and down the Hudson. This is genre painting at its best. The American portrait gallery on the fourth floor has a remarkable collection of paintings of famous colonial families, many by unknown artists, others are superb examples of the work of John Singleton Copley, Benjamin West, Gilbert Stuart, and the various members of the Peale family, to name just a few. However, I found one particular painter quite astonishing. His name is John Durand. Rather than describe him as a primitive artist, I prefer to use the word stylized. The set of portraits he did of the Beekman children are among the most beautiful examples of eighteenth-century American painting I have ever seen. I had never been aware of his work before, and I found it compelling and original.

The other major group of paintings in the museum is exhibited in the fourth-floor landscape room. This is a new installation for the society and is extremely successful. It is a softly lit room, with beige linen walls, gleaming light parquetry floors, and lovely islands of greenery. Very attractive and comfortable, it is filled with the great nineteenth-century American landscape painters—Cole, Bierstadt, Inness, Cropsey, Asher Durand, Kensett, Hart, Morse, Trumbull. There is another gallery on the first floor which houses a selection of monumental-size landscapes which are the living end as examples of nineteenth-century taste. The absolute epitome is a group of five paintings by Thomas Cole, *circa* 1836, titled "The Course of Civilization," which are the height of romanticism.

In addition to what I've already described, there is a collection of old fire-engine carriages, landaus, even eighteenth-century sleds in the basement. Toys, tools, Pennsylvania pottery, a marvelous group of paperweights, both American and European, can be found on various other floors. There are all kinds of corridors to turn in the New-York Historical Society, and each will lead you to a delightful experience.

Metropolitan Museum of Art
"Nooks and Crannies"
Eighty-second Street and Fifth Avenue
New York, N.Y. 10028
(212) 736-2211

Tuesday 10–8:45
Wednesday–Saturday 10–4:45
Sunday 11–4:45
Closed Monday

The unfortunate result of an incredibly successful merchandising campaign is that everyone in the world seems to have heard of the Metropolitan Museum of Art. What is worse, everyone in the world seems to be there at the same time. Thomas Hoving, its former director, has managed almost singlehandedly to change the entire museum-going experience. For those of us with fond memories of the time when a visit to this great museum promised the most marvelous of personal adventures, namely, an opportunity to escape the numbing sensations of daily life, an opportunity to use our eyes to heighten our natural powers of observation, to use our own instincts to their fullest extent, an opportunity to hear the quiet of ourselves become one with the most precious thing man has, his creative genius—Forget it! The place is jammed to the rafters, the noise level when you enter the main hall is unbelievable. However, there are still a few nooks and crannies of quiet that haven't yet been destroyed. But with this institution, which seems to be in competition with both Con Edison and Tiffany, I can't guarantee how long they'll be left undisturbed. I do wish they'd stop endowing the Met before it becomes the New York City version of the Duomo in Milan, four hundred years of construction.

To find refuge from the crowds head to the nether regions, namely the basement area that contains the European porcelains, European silver, watches, and Chinese Export porcelains. Generally, people end up there by accident looking for rest rooms. It is reached by the staircase off the Medieval Hall behind the main stairs. Incidentally, the Romanesque Chapel in the Medieval Hall doesn't get too inundated; most people just pass through on their way to the Lehman galleries. It is fascinating to notice the difference between the earlier twelfth-century statues of the Virgin and Child in the tiny chapel, the virgin with her sad, knowing expression, the child with his old-man face, to the fourteenth-century French Madonnas, obviously court ladies of fashion, holding their little Christ Child who is now truly a baby. These are no longer suffering women foretelling the tragedy to come. Do look for the wonderfully regal French sixteenth-century St. Barbara in the large hall. Its drapery, hair, and border detail are handled effortlessly; the sculptor treats his limestone as if it were no more difficult a surface to work than clay.

The Wrightsman Rooms right off the Medieval Hall are neither a nook nor cranny but well worth a quick walk through, despite the people. I visit them to see a set of four Louis XVI coral-colored velvet armchairs by Jacob, in the Grand Salon of the Hotel de Tesse, that are hidden in each corner of the room. These chairs are Louis XVI at its best, and I've coveted them for years. The special bonus to these rooms is the comments· of the people who seem to go through them principally to pick up decorating hints. I do admire their style!

I must warn you that the European porcelain and silver rooms do not have the greatest ventilation in the world, so be sure not to visit them after a large lunch; you'll never make it. The French ceramics, sixteenth to eighteenth century, are from the R. Thornton Wilson and J. P. Morgan collections. There are many rare examples exhibited. I especially enjoyed the Faïence pieces which are insane takeoffs on Meissen designs. There is a fantastic rooster tureen, complete with feathers, from Sceux, *circa* 1755, which on second thought might be a hen, as it does have little chicks among the feathers. Do you suppose, with the French love of specialization, it was only used for chicken soup? The Wilson collection of eighteenth-century German and Austrian porcelains has a particularly interesting plateau decorated with a view of the estate of a Baron Küner, *circa* 1760, that looks like one of those early engravings of a town plan. Most of the German and French porcelains are a bit too Rococo for my taste, but it is peaceful is these galleries.

There are all kinds of corridors down here and it is easy to miss a section. One long room has Dutch ceramics and a particularly excellent display of early Italian Maiolica. If the French and German pieces are not for you, head straight to the Dutch examples; they are delightful and the forms shown are all unique. I found the fifteenth-, sixteenth-, and seventeenth-century Italian Maiolica collection just wonderful. It is well exhibited, with simple intelligent commentary. The McCann collection of China Trade porcelains is down here also. It is in an inner room, and if it is possible, it has even less ventilation than other areas of the basement. So if China Export is what you really want to see, may I suggest you go directly to this room and not wander? The French eighteenth-century silver is in the Wentworth gallery and is just beautiful, and there is even a place to sit. Hidden in the deepest recesses of this basement is the section called Goldsmith's Work and Horology. These pieces are as worthy of being termed treasures as any painting in the museum. The watches, snuffboxes, and other objets d'art are unbelievably exquisite, the skill of their craftsmen is fantastic. If you see nothing else down here, do visit these inner rooms where the gold work is displayed.

I suggest, to recover from the lack of air, you head briefly to the Islamic rooms on the second floor. They are a beautiful installation and well air-conditioned. My only complaint, other than too many people, is that after going through them I didn't know where anything came from. I think perhaps the museum has gotten rather obscure in its approach to place of origin.

Don't waste your energy in the new Egyptian wing. The installation succeeds only in being incredibly dull. Old Egypt, rather than looking mysterious or even slightly sinister, has about as much excitement as a Sears Roebuck catalogue. It is all beige and boring. I came away hoping I'd never see another pot again. However, the Temple of Dendur is really wonderful. There is a hidden treasure in the Met called the Andfe Mertens Galleries for Musical Instruments. If it was ever banged, plucked, or blown, it is in this marvelous new group of rooms on the second floor. You go through the Henry Payne Bingham Galleries to reach this exhibition. The instruments are from every corner of the world and they are superbly displayed. It is really an interesting group of rooms.

I found in my wanderings that, if you stay out of the main thoroughfares, the rooms are not too bad. Good examples are the inner Greek and Roman statuary rooms. Everyone is so busy either entering or leaving the dining room that these tend to be overlooked. I wish I could have found a painting gallery to recommend, but they are always filled. Despite the crowds, don't miss the Costume Institute. It is the museum at its most creative.

I realize one could hardly describe the Lehman Galleries as either a nook or cranny, but I do love the tiny rooms in that wing, and no matter how many people are about, they should not be missed. It is marvelous to be able to see this extraordinary collection of small fourteenth-, and fifteenth-century Sienese paintings shown in rooms that make them particularly accessible to the viewer. It would be difficult to find more original paintings than

Sassetta's "Temptation of St. Antony Abbot", *circa* 1444 "The Expulsion from Paradise" by Giovanni di Paolo, or the Lippo Vanni "Madonna and Child," with its fat, red-headed baby pulling at his mother's robe. A very human gesture in a painting that is still quite stylized. Another fascinating painting is the beautifully designed "Adoration of the Magi," *circa* 1380, by Bariolo di Fredi. For the viewer of its time, the iconography of this painting would be the equivalent of reading a novel today.

One final suggestion: If the weather is good, have a picnic in Central Park. Dumas, the best French bakery in New York, is located on Lexington and Eighty-eighth Street. Buy some fresh croissants there, a little pâté, cheese, a lovely fresh fruit tart, and you are set. If this is not to your taste, the Madison Delicatessen on Madison Avenue and Eighty-sixth Street has super sandwiches and babka. Either way, it's much more fun than the crowds in the Met dining room.

The Frick Collection
1 East Seventieth Street
New York, N.Y. 10021
(212) 288-0700

September–May, Tuesday–Saturday 10–6; Sunday 1–6. Closed Monday and holidays.
June, July, August, Wednesday–Saturday 10–6; Sunday 1–6. Closed Monday and holidays.

No children under ten are admitted and those under sixteen must be accompanied by adults.

There is a simple way to describe the Frick Collection. It is, simply, the most beautiful private museum in the world. The superlative quality of its paintings and objets d'art are surpassed by no other major institution. The Metropolitan may have more paintings but none are better. This is an extraordinary feat for a solitary collector to have achieved. There were many wealthy Americans building their personal monuments at the same time Henry Clay Frick was developing his collection, but it would be difficult to find one selected with a more discriminating eye. The atmosphere this exquisitely serene building creates for its treasures makes the experience incomparable. The sense of intimacy shared is so strong that one expects to find Mr. Frick sitting in front of a favorite painting, enjoying it as much as you are. Perhaps he is. Certainly his spirit permeates these galleries which were his home.

There are visits to this museum when I never get beyond the inner garden, which is built like a small Roman court. It is my favorite place in New York to settle down for a bit of reflection. What inevitably happens is that I become so mesmerized by its stillness that not a thought enters my mind.

I will make only the most limited attempt to select my special favorites, because each time I visit the collection I fall in love with a new discovery that has been there all the time. There is such a wealth of aesthetic experiences available that your mood will determine your own choices. During my last visit, it was the Fragonard room that suddenly revealed itself to me. I am generally not excited by French eighteenth-century paintings, but the sheer genius and delight of this series of huge wall panels called the "Progress of Love" are not to be denied. That may not be quite true for everyone; commissioned by Mme. DuBarry for her dining pavilion, she rejected them as too old fashioned! The painting galleries are furnished with unique examples of eighteenth-century French and Italian Renaissance furniture. Most of the Chinese porcelains are Mr. Frick's favorite K'ang Hsi Famille Noire, the so-called Black Hawthorn vases. There are Italian Renaissance bronzes exhibited in almost all the rooms. One small gallery, a treasure trove of sixteenth-century Limoges painted enamels, is made even more amazing by the presence of Van Eyck's "Virgin and Child." This painting and the Bellini "St. Francis in Ecstasy," which the Frick also owns, are two of the greatest religious paintings of the Renaissance. And what of the collection's Vermeers? They are more astonishing each time you see them. Imagine what it must have been like to live in a house that had a Living Hall which contained El Greco's "St. Jerome," Titian's "Man in a Red Cap" and Holbein's portrait of Sir Thomas More. What could possibly surpass them, the Goyas, the Turners, the Hals? Only one painter, only one painting, the Rembrandt self-portrait. This portrait of the painter as an old man is literally indescribable in its power and sense of tragedy. It is a miracle of the human spirit. If you have never visited the Frick, you are about to have your own personal miracle.

Morgan Library
Thirty-sixth Street and Madison Avenue
New York, N.Y. 10016
(212) 685-0008

Tuesday–Saturday 10:30–5
Sunday 1–5
Closed Monday and holidays

This beautiful small museum specializes in drawings and manuscripts of the greatest rarity. I have never seen an exhibition here that didn't reflect the ultimate of taste and scholarship.

Asia House
112 East Sixty-fourth Street
New York, N.Y. 10021
(212) 751-4210

Daily 10–5
Thursday 10–8:30
Sunday 1–5

Asia House is the gallery part of the Asia Society. It is open only during special exhibitions as it has no permanent exhibit on display. It specializes in art of every form from China, Japan, India, Southeast Asia, Iran, and Afghanistan. Its shows are consistently of superb quality and originality. Not to be missed.

China Institute
125 East Sixty-fifth Street
New York, N.Y. 10021
(212) 744-8181

Monday–Friday 10–5
Saturday 11–5
Sunday 2–5
Gallery closed during summer

Tiny gallery with excellent rotating exhibitions on Chinese art. No permanent collection.

Japan House Gallery
333 East Forty-seventh Street
New York, N.Y. 10017
(212) 832-1115

Daily 11–5
Friday 11–7:30

Does interesting exhibitions on ancient and contemporary Japanese arts. No permanent collection. Japanese garden always open to public.

*MUSICAL ADDENDA

Wall Street Walk

This is the most exciting area of the city to visit on a weekend. Its personality is transformed on Saturday and Sunday, when the people disappear and the narrow, shadowed streets reverberate with ghostly sounds. My favorite walk starts at Battery Park because I love to smell the sea and dream of bygone voyages. Stop and tour the Custom House; it's well worth the time. As you walk up Broadway, keep looking down the side streets to your right (east). This jumble of tiny streets is where New York began its journey north. Trinity Church is at Wall Street and Broadway. A beautiful old church, it has the most interesting graveyard. As a matter of fact, it is a lovely place to have a picnic, and the church does not object in the least. Walk east on Wall Street to Nassau; on one corner is the Stock Exchange and the other corner has a

* Many churches in New York City have concerts which are listed in the weekend edition of the New York *Times*. Specially noteworthy are the concerts arranged by Richard Westenburg, musical director of the Cathedral of St. John the Divine, 1047 Amsterdam Avenue, New York, N.Y. 10025, (212) 678-6888.

wonderful old Federal building. If you continue up Nassau to Pine Street, you come to Chase Manhattan Plaza with the great Dubuffet sculpture. My favorite view of the entire walk is the one looking west along Pine Street toward the Trinity graveyard. The buildings literally converge upon the sky. Don't just walk around the Dubuffet—be sure to stand under it. This sculpture succeeds in creating an environment that overshadows the monster-sized buildings surrounding it. Finally, walk the perimeter of the Plaza streets. The architecture is fascinating.

NEW YORK STATE

Museums and Historical Houses

Van Cortlandt Manor
Off Route 9
Croton-on-Hudson

Daily 10–5
Closed Thanksgiving, December 25, January 1

This beautiful late seventeenth-, early eighteenth-century stone house was occupied for almost 250 years by the Van Cortlandt family. Sold in the mid 1940s to John D. Rockefeller, Jr., it became part of the Sleepy Hollow Restorations which includes Washington Irving's Sunnyside and the Philipsburg Manor. Carefully restored and furnished, containing many objects that remained in the family since the eighteenth century, it retains a sense of intimacy rarely found in historic homes. The house, though built for a wealthy, politically powerful Dutch family, actively sympathetic to the Revolution, is scaled to human proportions. The rooms are relatively small and furnished mostly with eighteenth-century New York pieces. It is a most livable house and lends itself to pleasant antiquing fantasies.

The acres of gardens are planted to resemble as closely as possible their eighteenth-century counterpart.

Within walking distance of the Manor House is the Ferry House, another restored eighteenth-century structure, which functioned as both tavern and inn for the ferry across the Croton River; used by Albany Post Road travelers between Albany and New York City. The Van Cortlandt family leased this property to various tenants who ran the tavern and operated the ferry crossing. It is furnished with pieces made by local eighteenth-century joiners of the Hudson Valley.

There may be grander restorations than Van Cortlandt Manor, but none lovelier.

Washington Irving's Sunnyside
Off Route 9
Tarrytown

Daily 10–5
Closed Thanksgiving, December 25, January 1

Washington Irving, America's first internationally recognized author, restored this seventeenth-century house in 1835 to suit his personal taste. It is a delightful combination of Dutch, Gothic, and Romanesque architectural detail, reflecting his many years of residence abroad. The house today looks very much as it did during the later years of Irving's life. It contains most of his original furnishings, paintings, and books. Sunnyside is a completely appropriate setting for the writer of "The Legend of Sleepy Hollow."

Lyndhurst
635 South Broadway
Tarrytown

May–October Daily 10–5
November–April 10–4

Gothic Revival mansion-home of Jay Gould. Large gardens.

Philipsburg Manor
Off Route 9
North Tarrytown

Open 10–5
Closed Thanksgiving, December 25, January 1

The Philipsburg family was given a land grant by the English Crown in 1693 that gave property rights to 90,000 acres, which were equivalent to those of the feudal lords in the Middle Ages. Choosing the wrong side during the American Revolution put an end to this ownership. The enormous estate was auctioned off into hundreds of individual parcels. The Manor House which is now part of this splendid restoration was bought by the Van Cortlandt family at the sale. In addition to the surprisingly unpretentious main house, the restoration includes, among other buildings, a working gristmill and granary. The property gives a fascinating insight into the complexities of these huge estates. It is also very beautiful.

Boscobel
Route 9D
Garrison

March 1–October 10, Wednesday–Monday 10–5;
November, December, March 10–4

One of the best restorations in New York State. Elegant, early nineteenth-century Adam-style mansion, magnificently furnished. Formal English gardens.

Olana
Intersection Routes 23 and 9G
Hudson, South

May 27–October 29, Wednesday–Sunday 10–5

Home of the great nineteenth-century American landscape painter Frederick Church. It is a thirty-five-room Persian-Moorish fantasy. Paintings by Church and other artists.

Shaker Museum
Off Route 66
Old Chatham

May–October 10–5:30

Shaker religious sect founded in New York State (1774). Four buildings with over 18,000 Shaker objects.

Albright-Knox Art Gallery
1285 Elmwood Avenue
Buffalo

Tuesday–Saturday 10–5
Sunday 12–5

A superb art museum, world-famous for its collection.

Inns and Restaurants

Bird & Bottle Inn
Route 9,
Garrison, N.Y. 10524
(914) 424-3006

Open all year·

Lunch and dinner. Closed Tuesday and January.

Old Drover's Inn
Old Drover's Inn Road
Dover Plains, N.Y. 12522
(914) 832-9311

Open all year

Lunch and dinner. Closed Tuesday and Wednesday, three weeks in December. Lodging available.

The Dutch Hearth Inn
Hillsdale, N.Y. 12529
(518) 325-3412

Open all year

Dinner only. Closed Mondays in summer and Monday and Tuesday rest of the year, and from March to mid-April. Lodging available.

V

Where It All Began

Philadelphia is a southern city. Its ambiance is quite startling, the feeling, one of a village, rather than a metropolis. In June, sit in the old churchyard along Pine Street and let the scent of the privet hedges wash over you. Stroll the little back alleyways of Society Hill with their hidden courtyards and lazy cats taking the morning sun. Admire the taste and restraint shown in combining eighteenth-century Philadelphia architecture with contemporary town houses in the sensitive restoration of the Pine Street, Society Hill, and Head House Square areas. Imagine a city that allows tiny pockets of green to exist instead of adding another house or two. Slowly but steadily, Philadelphia is reclaiming its eighteenth-century waterfront. Queen Anne Village, adjacent to the New Market and Old Swede's Church, is yet another area gradually making a physical recovery from over a hundred years of neglect. Lunch at the Philadelphia museum—food awful, conversation a delight. Astonishing things still happen in Philadelphia. A clerk at the local railroad station will rush to the platform to make certain you're getting on the right train. It is a city whose people envelop you gently with lovely manners. Weep a little as history overwhelms you in front of the small unpretentious building that housed our first Supreme Court. Walk Philadelphia today and sense the spirit of those extraordinary men who strode its streets and formed our world.

PHILADELPHIA

Antique Dealers

Alfred Bullard Inc.
1604 Pine Street
Philadelphia, Pa. 19103
(215) 735-1879

Monday–Friday 10–5
Saturday by appointment

Pennsylvania collectors are famous or infamous, if you prefer, for their insistence on regional purity. If it isn't Philadelphia, Lancaster, Chester, or what have you, the dealer might as well take his foreign wares, be they New England or Maryland, and depart. As with much antiquing lore, this too is exaggeration based loosely on some semblance of truth. Alfred Bullard Inc., English furniture specialists, has successfully maintained a shop in this city of purists for over fifty years. This enchanting shop, owned by William Bertelot and filled with lovely seventeenth- and eighteenth-century English furniture and accessories, is a haven of beautiful taste.

Bill Bertelot has chosen his pieces with an eye for lightness of scale and simple elegance. The furniture has an ease and understatement that marks good English country furniture, but it is the furniture of the gentleman squire rather than the yeoman farmer. There is a small quantity of seventeenth-century oak chests and tables, but these go very quickly. The great majority of pieces are well-made mahogany examples of George I, which is often mistaken for Queen Anne: the simpler Chippendale forms: Sheraton, Adam, and Hepplewhite, where line is more important than carving. There isn't a piece in the shop that wouldn't look perfectly correct in a room filled with great Americana.

This dealer's discernment shows itself again and again in such pieces as a Chippendale mahogany bookcase, *circa* 1760, with Gothic fretwork of amazing delicacy or a fine Adam serpentine side table with fluted legs, *circa* 1780, that had been in a Philadelphia family for generations. The shop, which always carries a large selection of chairs, had an exceptional set of Adam dining chairs, *circa* 1785, in the French taste (when I was last there). These chairs at first glance look unmistakably French, but careful investigation indicated the much finer construction that usually distinguishes English cabinetwork. I can hear the howls of protest erupting from French collectors. I am not discussing aesthetics, that is a matter of individual preference, merely construction. Aside from the very finest quality French pieces there is simply no contest between English and French woodwork. There is every variety of table, including dining, but one of the most charming was a tiny Sheraton satin woodwork table, *circa* 1785, which has such poise it literally speaks for itself.

It is interesting how consistent this dealer's taste is, even in Chippendale armchairs. Rather than the usual heavy, rather clumpy versions, his chairs are as graceful and beautifully proportioned as any Queen Anne or Regency piece. The stock also includes several sofas, again small-sized, and among the many chairs an exceptional pair of French Empire benches which Bill Bertelot couldn't resist buying even though it is almost impossible to sit on them.

The accessories include a large group of eighteenth-century mirrors; brass objects, such as boxes and candlesticks; porcelains with the emphasis on English and China Export; lighting fixtures, knife boxes. Really, all manner of decorative accessories you would expect to find in a well-furnished eighteenth- and early nineteenth-century home.

The particular pleasure of this shop, elegant as its wares are, is its lovely informal atmosphere. People kept dropping in just to chat, and no one seemed remotely disturbed or rushed. Definitely not New York, Philadelphia is closest in quality to Boston antiquing, but even more relaxed if that is possible.

Michael Fiorillo
1120 Pine Stree
Philadelphia, Pa. 19107
(215) 923-3173

Monday–Saturday 10–4

Michael Fiorillo is an antique dealer who collects stray animals. There is a certain appropriateness to this, for in a sense all antique dealers collect strays—stray furniture, paintings, porcelains—objects no longer wanted or needed by their owners. However, Mike Fiorillo, who is a grand old gentleman, has done it with great imagination, knowledge, and originality. His four-story shop, complete with dogs and a foundling cat, who spends all her time under an eighteenth-century pencil-post bed, is filled with an amazing diversity of material. This is a dealer's dealer whose range of stock includes Old Masters paintings and drawings, seventeenth- and eighteenth-century European and American furniture, African art, Italian Baroque wood statuary, early English Staffordshire animals, European and American eighteenth- and nineteenth-century silver and pewter, Chinese porcelains, Korean pottery, eighteenth-century English and Dutch Delft, Indian sculpture, oriental and Aubusson carpets, and enough decorative accessories to supply half the shops in New York City. This shop really does have something for everyone and in a wide range of prices. To give you a brief idea of the variety of furniture styles available, a seventeenth-century, red-and-gilt decorated Spanish-colonial side table was displayed in the window with a magnificent eighteenth-century Philadelphia Chippendale armchair and a New England pine drop-leaf dining table, *circa* 1700–15. Up-

stairs, the chairs, tables, chests of drawers and desks are arranged
with casual respect for either style or country of origin. There are
bits of brass and glass for very little money and paintings and furniture which cost thousands and are well worth it.

Mr. Fiorillo no longer expects to discover a Goya in a coalbin
nor any unrecognized Tiepolo's or Cranach's, as he has in the
past. But even in this time of enormous interest in art no one ever
agrees on pictures and the shop had a painting by the Italian old
master Guercino, hanging on the second floor for years, and
which no one believed in except Mr. Fiorillo and, finally, Chris-
tie's of London. It was sold recently as Guercino for a very
healthy price. This is a dealer whose only word of advice to the
novice art collector is, buy only what you love. Even for the expert, art as an investment is a very tricky affair.

There are very few dealers left of Michael Fiorillo's ilk. He is a
member of a fast-disappearing species, the dealer who possesses
enormous knowledge and great sensitivity as a human being.

Leon F. S. Stark
210 South Seventeenth Street
Philadelphia, Pa. 19103
(215) 735-2799
Monday–Friday 9:30–5

Unless you have the eye of a hawk, this impossible shop, which
is infinitesimal in size, will completely defeat you. Every square
centimeter, including the ceiling, is covered with the most amazing conglomeration of objects. At first glance it looks like a flea
market gone wild, what with the glass, brass, silver, porcelains,
pewter, bottle labels, corkscrews, tankards, sextons, compasses
and rulers, to give you even a scant summary. At second glance it
still looks like a flea market, but the glass decanters and stemware
turn out to be eighteenth- and nineteenth-century English, Irish,
and American, as are the brass candlesticks and pewter hollow
ware. The porcelains which sit in the shop with about as much
importance as a dime-store display are predominately eighteenth-

century English Delft, Staffordshire, Worcester, Caughley, and Liverpool, with a smattering of eighteenth- and nineteenth-century Continental porcelain, nineteenth-century American pottery, and a bit of China Export and Imari thrown in for good measure.

What can you say about a dealer who hangs his fine eighteenth-century American furniture from the rafters, hides his marvelous American quilts and oriental rugs on a balcony (which is only accessible to an antiquer with the instincts of a mountain goat), and exhibits great marine art and portraits by artists of the importance of Greenwood and Blackburn in the dark behind pillars? Leon F. S. Stark is certainly an original. He is also a major Philadelphia dealer, if quality of stock and importance of individual items count rather than size of inventory. There is nothing incongruous to Leon Stark in having a windowful of drinking bric-a-brac or piles of decorated Pennsylvania and Connecticut bellows heaped under a pair of mahogany card tables by Barry, one of Philadelphia's greatest cabinetmakers. A magnificent Bachman chest-on-chest which is another Philadelphia piece, a beautiful mahogany desk with ogee feet from Delaware, a Duncan Phyfe hanging cupboard are displayed as casually as a rare set of Struckland drawings, *circa* 1815, done for a naval chronical. Fine eighteenth-century American chairs, sofas, mirrors, tables, and innumerable paintings are there to be seen if you can find them.

The secret of this strange assortment of merchandise is very simple. Mr. and Mrs. Stark are inveterate collectors and will buy anything, no matter how seemingly insignificant if it pleases them. They are tart, delightful, gentle people of enormous knowledge in a wide range of areas. Philadelphia is a big city that isn't. These fine dealers reflect this unique quality.

Charles Sterling
1817 Delancey Place
Philadelphia, Pa. 19103
(215) 732-6466

By appointment only

If you have the persistence to find Charles Sterling you are well on your way to being a serious collector. I have known Mr. Sterling since he was fifteen going on fifty, a child dealer of great talent and assumed sophistication. The talent, now that he has reached the ripe old age of thirty, has grown even more impressive. He has an incredible eye for all manner of objects, especially paintings, and the sophistication fits like a second skin. The only thing that hasn't changed an iota is his amazing ability to disappear. Still basically preferring to function as a dealer to the trade, who incidentally find him just as difficult to locate as most of his collectors, Charles Sterling is a born treasure hunter and constantly travels in search of the next object. It is the quest not the sale that excites him most. Fortunately for dealer and collector alike, he does settle down now and then in one of the most beautiful houses in Philadelphia. If the call of the wild antique has lured Mr. Sterling off without a word of warning, don't despair: his enchanting wife, Kathy, makes a delightful substitute and has uncanny ability to soothe the most ruffled feathers.

What kind of stock will you find? There is simply no way to predict what this dealer will unearth or, if it is particularly choice, how long it will remain in the house. An exquisite Fabergé enamel case lasted a few hours, a fine Philadelphia chair, two days. However, a well-priced eighteenth-century Louis XVI chair has been there over a year only because there is relatively little interest in French furniture in Philadelphia. This does not discourage Mr. Sterling because he happens to love French furniture. Generally, the turnover of material is very rapid but there is usually a selection of eighteenth-century American, English, and French furniture, eighteenth- and nineteenth-century China Export porcelains, eighteenth- and nineteenth-century American painting, nineteenth-century European painting, oriental rugs, and odd pieces of nineteenth-century American and English silver, glass, and porcelain. It is not a large stock but it is invariably an interesting one.

Aside from the fun of never knowing what you may find there, and I must admit to a weakness for buying the unexpected, the prices are very fair and Mr. Sterling is really, despite my teasing, fun to do business with and as passionate an antiquer as any of his collectors.

Antony Stuempfig
2213 St. James Place
Philadelphia, Pa. 19103
(215) 561-7191

By appointment only

Scholarly old dealers are a rare breed in themselves; scholarly young dealers are an almost unheard-of species. Tony Stuempfig is young. His partially restored but still wonderfully dilapidated old house in Philadelphia may never be finished, but his excellent taste and quite extraordinary depth of knowledge concerning American Empire furniture assure his future as a dealer of substance. Dating from 1805 to 1825, this style of decoration has not exactly been a household word in the average collector's lexicon, though it has always had its own coterie of appreciators who valued the elegance of line and exquisite subtle workmanship of its finest examples. Unfortunately, the worst of American Empire is heavy, ugly, and ungraceful. If this has never been your period, you may be about to change your mind. This dealer's small stock consists of ravishingly beautiful examples from New York, Boston, Philadelphia, and Baltimore that will tantalize even the most dyed-in-the-wool eighteenth-century collector.

There are actually two different schools of American Empire furniture: The Francophile of Philadelphia, whose great cabinet-makers were Barry, White, and Quervelle, and its northern neighbor New York, with the incomparable Duncan Phyfe. Boston and Baltimore were the Anglophiles; as a matter of fact, there was such admiration for all things British at this time in Boston that some of the furniture is almost indistinguishable from the English. The key element to look for in fine Empire is always the extraordinary working of the woods, especially in the veneers. A dressing table that belonged to Rufus King is a classic Phyfe piece with its opulent veneering, secondary wood of mahogany, and fine French-made mounts. This furniture reflects as directly as any eighteenth-century piece the wealth and self-importance of its owner. In many cases Mr. Stuempfig not only knows the makers of the various chairs, tables, and sofas he has but also their original owners. Incidentally, ordering a table then was rather like buying a car today—most of the detailing was considered extra and priced accordingly.

Mr. Stuempfig does handle later periods of nineteenth-century American furniture such as the 1840 Gothic, the Egyptian revival of 1865–80, and even the American version of Louis-Phillipe made in New York and Philadelphia, *circa* 1870–80. As in the Empire, he trys to find the finest examples possible. The great advantage to these later periods is that they are readily affordable, while fine Empire has become quite costly. There are a number of American paintings and mirrors but these are definitely just adjuncts to the furniture at this point, although this is a dealer who does have the style to buy a painting that practically takes up an entire wall if he likes it.

Nineteenth-century furniture may not be for you, but this is such a talented dealer and his love and fascination for his objects make it a very interesting experience.

PHILADELPHIA AUCTION HOUSE

Samuel T. Freeman & Co.
1808 Chestnut Street
Philadelphia, Pa. 19103
(215) 563-9275

This old auction house is a Philadelphia institution. Good reputation. Sales held on a regular basis all year.

Museums and Historical Houses

Pennsylvania Academy of the Fine Arts
Broad and Cherry streets
Philadelphia, Pa.

Monday, Tuesday, Thursday–Saturday 10–5
Wednesday 10–9
Sunday 1–5
Closed January 1, December 25

Almost no one, outside of a small select group of Philadelphians and a few eccentric art historians, has ever visited the Pennsylvania Academy of the Fine Arts. It is the oldest museum and art school (1805) in the United States, and it also happens to have an absolutely marvelous collection of eighteenth-, nineteenth-, and twentieth-century American painting and sculpture housed in a fantastic Victorian building designed by Frank Furness, in 1876, specifically for the museum and school. A grand staircase leads up to the exhibition galleries with their huge skylights and astonishing architectural details. The sense of light and air in the individual rooms is intoxicating. A huge rotunda surmounts the staircase, its walls, a series of Gothic arches resting on polychrome and gilt iron columns. The only other Victorian building in this class is the National Portrait Gallery in Washington, D.C.

Conceived as a home for contemporary painting, the Academy reflects the strengths and weaknesses of the last two hundred years in American art. In addition to its fair share of standard Victoriana, there is fine work by such nineteenth-century painters as Kensett and Inman. The true strength of the collection lies in the eighteenth- and early nineteenth-century works by Gilbert Stuart, all the Peales and Thomas Sully, to name just a handful. The Stuarts are superb. One, a study of Mrs. Sarah Gatliff and her daughter, is as poignant as a Renaissance Virgin and Child. The handling of the sleeve fabric in a portrait of Rev. William White, D.D., is exquisitely suggested.

There is a gallery devoted entirely to the remarkable Peale family of artists. The Peales, carrying their home industry as far as it would go, even had their own museum, started by Charles Wilson Peale in 1786. It consisted of portraits of Revolutionary heroes and was expanded to include other great Americans and cases of zoological specimens. In the eighteenth century, science in any form fascinated everyone. Thomas Sully is shown at his romantic best in a series of portraits of the Kemble family. A pair of Claypool paintings of Mr. and Mrs. Pemberton are so elegant that Whistler would have entitled them "Studies in Gray." Lovely, sensitive portraits of the artist Benjamin West and his wife are by Matthew Pratt, a student of West's in London. West himself is represented by two monumental neoclassic paintings that are amazing examples of this school. I found one, "Death on the Pale Horse," very emotionally powerful, despite its enormous size.

The Academy's collection of the American Impressionists Childe Hassam, Mary Cassatt, John Twachtman, and George Inness is really first-rate, with two particularly lovely Inness paintings—"Apple Blossom Time" and "Woodland Scene." An ominous, exciting Winslow Homer is "The Fox Hunt." Take a moment to sit on the bench opposite the Homer, and look through the series of receding doorways to your left leading to other galleries. The view is an interesting study in perspective and design, obviously done by the architect to simulate a painter's sense of perspective.

A long, narrow gallery leading directly from the rotunda has examples of nineteenth-century sculptors such as Hiram Powers, Erastus Dow Palmer, Howard Roberts. There are busts of famous Americans done with varying degrees of skill. John Dixey's study of Alexander Hamilton is very successful. It is earlier than many of the other pieces and far more vigorous in execution.

Contemporary art is exhibited at all times, but the examples are changed frequently as is true with some of the other paintings. The Academy's inventory is so large that this is the only way to keep works from being buried indefinitely in their storage vaults.

This museum was a wonderful surprise. I expected to be in and out in less than an hour, instead a whole morning seemed to pass in just a few moments. Beautiful, exhilarating, devoid of people, the Academy is one of Philadelphia's hidden treasures.

Philadelphia Museum of Art
Twenty-sixth Street and Benjamin Franklin Parkway
Philadelphia, Pa. 19101
(215) 763-8100

Daily 9–5
Closed legal holidays

Before bicentennial fever set in, visiting the Philadelphia Museum was rather like spending a day with a favorite old aunt. She might be a bit stodgy, but the pleasures could always be depended upon. Unfortunately, someone, in a moment of madness, gave the museum millions of dollars to spend in order to make herself more enticing to the expected hoards of visitors. This surplus of funds has caused nothing but chaos. Most of the problem seems to be in the Near Eastern, Far Eastern, and South Asian wing, where the Chinese, Japanese, Cambodian, Indian paintings, porcelains, sculpture, and architectural examples are located. Intent on creating marvelous effects, the lighting is so obscure as to make it almost impossible to see anything. The organization of these galleries may have looked good on paper but there is no sense of unity or plan, either aesthetically or visually. This is particularly infuriating because there is so much excellent material that doesn't need to be enhanced by anything. The Crozier Collection of Chinese porcelains is all over the place, mostly hidden in dark corners, making study of any sort virtually impossible. The reconstructed Japanese and Chinese temples are unique and fascinating but so badly laid out that frequently you don't even know where you are. I quite understand the desire to create an authentic atmosphere but in the Indian Hindu temple, mystery simply degenerates into confusion. A curator may dream of re-creating the Orient but basically it is still, at best, simulation and stage sets. Obviously nothing will be done in the near future to improve the lighting, so perhaps the answer is to bring a pocket searchlight. Everything is well worth seeing.

The museum has a superb collection of decorative arts, both European and American. However, unless you are persistent, you'll never find the McFadden galleries which are a series of rooms off in their own little corner, containing glorious eighteenth-century English furniture and painting. The rooms themselves are from Sutton Scarsdale Hall, *circa* 1724. At the very end of this section is a tiny gallery whose walls are hung with beautiful Gainsborough portraits and landscapes. The paintings are few, but what quality! The museum's magnificent collection of eighteenth-century American furniture looks like a warehouse display, too crowded, with little or no air about the pieces. The section in the American Wing called Rural Pennsylvania is much more success-ful, enhanced by its show of red slipware pottery that is just charming. The Victorian pieces are wonderfully chosen examples.

Under my not-to-be-missed category is the smashing display of European arms and armor from the Kretzchman von Kienbusch Collection. The museum showed great taste and feeling putting this exhibition together. These objects are extraordinary works of art created by the most skilled craftsmen of their day and I can-not imagine any collector worth their salt not being fascinated by their beauty.

Two glittering painting collections form the cornerstone of the museum's art collection. The Renaissance paintings from the Johnson Collection are marvelous and none more so than Rogier van der Weyden's "Virgin and St. John, Christ on the Cross," *circa* 1460. An astonishing work both aesthetically and emo-tionally. Twentieth-century painting and sculpture, primarily dat-ing from 1910 to 1914, crucial years in the development of con-temporary art, form the basis of the renowned Arensberg Collection. Chosen with great originality, there is Klee after Klee after Klee, Picasso and Braque at their Cubist best and, most in-teresting of all, historically, a unique group of Marcel Duchamp paintings which clearly delineates his development as an artist from an admirer of Cézanne, through his subsequent preoccu-pation with movement, abstraction and, finally, a form of nihilist art. Duchamp is a fascinating genius. His career as an artist lasted barely six years, yet within that period, he produced works that have continued to influence artistic thought to this day. The mu-seum has many unique Cézannes and Manets, but they are part of different collections and must be sought out individually.

The Philadelphia Museum may be something of a maze to wander through but it has superb objects and, despite all the efforts of its directors to turn it into another Metropolitan Mu-seum of Art, it is still very Philadelphia and delightfully unpreten-tious.

Rodin Museum
Twenty-second Street and Benjamin Franklin Parkway
Philadelphia, Pa.

Daily 9–5
Closed legal holidays

This small museum, with the largest collection of Rodin sculpture outside of France, is completely enchanting. The classic marble building, surrounded by formal gardens and with its own reflecting pool, creates a totally French atmosphere. Such major works as the "Burghers of Calais" and that extraordinary colossal head of Balzac can be seen, in addition to many small bronzes and marble studies. Of particular interest are a number of Edward Steichen photos of Rodin. In them the sculptor looks like a piece of his own work. Steichen also did a series of the Balzac statues, photographing them by moonlight. The results are incredibly exciting.

University Museum
Thirty-third and Spruce streets
Philadelphia, Pa. 19104
(215) 386-7400

Tuesday–Saturday 10–5
Sunday 1–5
Closed Monday, Good Friday,
July 4, December 25

There is not a single painting or piece of furniture in the University Museum of the University of Pennsylvania, but it is one of the most fascinating places I have ever visited. The material, archeological and anthropological, was gathered from every corner of the world where man has left some traces of his existence. Subdivided into the Near East, which includes all the diverse ancient cultures of Mesopotamia and Persia; Egypt; the Mediterranean World, including Italy, Mycenae, Cyprus, Crete, and Classical Greece; North America, Middle America, and South America; Africa, Oceania, and Austronesia, and finally China and India.

The sculpture and artifacts are of great beauty and rarity. The Chinese galleries are visually the most exciting, as the space is huge and there are many oversize objects. A massive pair of cloisonné Foo dogs (possibly from the Imperial Palace in Peking) are over six feet tall. The selection of Shang and Chou bronzes is marvelous. In the classical-world galleries, you must see a Roman copy of the Greek marble statue Nike of Athena Parthenos, the original by Pheidias, *circa* 440 B.C. The flow of the fabric is all fluidity and elegance. The Benghasi Venus, *circa* 200 B.C., found at Benghasi in North Africa, which is in the same gallery as the Nike, is another dream of feminine beauty. No more than sixteen or eighteen inches high and carved in white marble, Venus, born from the sea, is shown wringing sea water from her hair. An extraordinary group of marble sculptures from Mexico are displayed among the treasures from Middle America. These carvings from Teotihuacan, *circa* 100 B.C.–A.D. 100, are extremely sophisticated and startlingly Egyptian in feeling.

This is a most intriguing museum. All the material, from Pueblo Indian artifacts to perfectly terrifying Melanesian totems and masks, is vividly and intelligently displayed, making the viewing both an aesthetic and learning experience.

Historical Society of Pennsylvania
1300 Locust Street
Philadelphia, Pa. 19107

Tuesday–Friday 9–5
Monday 1–9
Closed holidays

The Historical Society owns over eight hundred paintings, of which only about twenty are on permanent exhibition in their galleries. All of the paintings are wonderful, but if it is possible to select a favorite, then it must be John Singleton Copley's double portrait of Thomas Mifflin and his wife. Though reproduced in all the art books, there is simply no way to prepare you for the beauty of this work. Thomas Mifflin, a governor of Pennsylvania, was a man who really had an eye for painters. The Society has another painting of him as a young man by Benjamin West. There is also one, which the Society doesn't own, by Gilbert Stuart. Among the portraits by Charles Wilson Peale is a particularly effective one of John Dickinson. George Washington ends up looking more like a plump gentleman farmer than a great general, in the painting by Joseph Wright done in 1784. He has a rather gentle face despite the set of the mouth, which probably has more to do with false teeth than temperament. A group of early views of Philadelphia by Thomas Birch are quite fascinating as some of these buildings can still be seen today. The Society has more Benjamin West portraits than most museums.

The amount of eighteenth-century Pennsylvania furniture and silver on display is very limited, but it is of the same quality as the superb painting collection. The Society is most famous for its enormous library of printed material pertaining to Pennsylvania. Knowledge of the Society's collection is far too limited. It deserves to be seen by everyone interested in eighteenth-century Americana.

Barnes Foundation
300 North Latch's Lane
Merion Station
Philadelphia, Pa. 19066
(215) 667-0290

Open to public on limited basis
Friday, Saturday 9:30–4:30
Sunday 1–4:30
No children under twelve admitted
Phone or write for reservations

Private art collections that are transformed into museums by their owners usually fall into several distinct categories. The first I call the ego trip. A perpetuation of the owner's name with art that is usually a selection of second-, third-, and sometimes even fourth-rate examples by famous painters. These collections often find their way to less-knowledgeable communities who are grateful to have a museum of any sort. The second group, far more than being just rich collectors, are people of sensitivity and perception, who have the ability to select brilliant examples of paintings and objects but are limited in the sense that their choices are primarily formed by the fashionable taste of their time. The fabulous Frick Collection in New York City is the classic example of this genre of connoisseur. A great museum formed by a great collector. The final category consists of barely a handful of people, a unique breed of genius collectors who, via some mysterious instinct, have the ability to choose masterpieces with a radically different point of view, long before any vocabulary of acceptability has emerged. Dr. Albert C. Barnes was one of these giants. His collection is filled with what I call watershed works—individual paintings that mark the culmination of everything that has happened in the last four hundred years of painting and clearly predict what is coming in the future.

The first gallery you enter has three such works—a Cézanne, a Matisse, and a Picasso. Each artist, using his individual perception of historic art patterns, created new realms of visual thought. These three large canvases contain within them everything that was destined to develop over the next fifty years in Western art from Cubism to Abstract Expressionism. I must warn you, in passing, that there are over a thousand paintings at the Foundation, covering every square inch of wall space. Viewing is not an easy affair; there is simply too much to see. Labels are so discreet as to be almost nonexistent and the lighting is a disaster—there isn't any to speak of. All of which is totally unimportant as the paintings, which range from such Renaissance jewels as a portrait by Wolf Huber, the German fifteenth-century artist, to a veritable orgy of Impressionists and Post-Impressionists, are unbelievably beautiful. As a matter of fact, that is an understatement. The Cézannes, Matisses, Renoirs will floor you, as will a big Manet mother and child doing the family wash. A mundane subject transformed by Manet's genius for capturing the immediacy of the moment with all its tenderness and humor.

The little child wears a jaunty hat and an expression of absolute delight at being allowed to participate in this thrilling adventure. The painting is sheer enchantment and great Impressionist art.

There are hundreds of small paintings that are exquisite examples by Degas, Gauguin, Van Gogh, Glackens, Pascin, Soutine, Avery, and Rousseau, the French primitive, plus some of the finest Modiglianis to be seen anywhere in the world. Everywhere there are fascinating juxtapositions of paintings, as in one small gallery, between a somber-colored Rousseau, a vivid still-life arrangement by Matisse, and an austere Modigliani portrait of a girl wearing the loveliest shade of lavender skirt.

There are examples of old masters such as Titian, Tinteretto, and El Greco, but they have not been chosen with that sureness of touch that marks Dr. Barnes's selection of Impressionists and Post-Impressionists. One small Redon, "St. George and the Dragon," overwhelms everything around it, including a Veronese that suffers by comparison. The French, German, and Italian Renaissance paintings are much more personally felt. There are walls covered from floor to ceiling with Renoir nudes. Not since Rubens has any painter been as possessed by a passion for the flesh. The painting quality is so consistent that it is almost a relief to admit there are a number of not just bad paintings but real howlers. One, a Van Gogh nude on bed, is just possibly the worst painting ever done by this artist, as is a truly ghastly Leda and the Swan by Cézanne. Leda most resembles a bleached-blond man.

The upstairs galleries have very important Matisse paintings, many of them done in sequence. The arches on this floor contain the cut-paper series commissioned by Dr. Barnes from Matisse for that particular area. As always with Matisse, viewing is a consummate joy. However, for me, it is the Cézannes that command your attention. They are monumental symphonies of construction, emotion, and tension, riveting the eye, allowing it to go no farther than the volume of the canvas. Finally, as in the epic painting "The Card Players," you, the observer, become the fourth player.

Dr. Barnes never planned to open his collection to the public, even on the limited basis that exists today. It was meant to be, and continues to function as, a training ground for serious art scholars. The paintings are hung in a specific order that makes sense in terms of Dr. Barnes's teaching philosophy and the curriculum that was developed to use the paintings most effectively. Dr. Barnes felt the world was full of philistines with very little understanding or appreciation of what he was trying to do. We hope the gratitude felt by every art lover at being allowed to share the genius of this collection finally lays his angry spirit to rest.

Powel House
244 South Third Street

Tuesday–Saturday 10–5
Sunday 1–5
Winter till 4

One of the most magnificent Georgian houses in Philadelphia, built in 1765, it was the home of Samuel Powel, the last colonial mayor of Philadelphia. Mr. and Mrs. Powel lived a life of gracious elegance, entertaining lavishly such guests as Washington and Adams.

Hill-Physick-Keith House
321 South Fourth Street

Tuesday–Saturday 10–5
Sunday 1–5
Winter till 4

A fine house and garden built in 1786. Furnished primarily in the Federal-style appropriate to the time of its second owner, Dr. Physick, who was the most important surgeon in the United States and instrumental in saving the life of Chief Justice Marshall. Allow time to see its gardens; they are enchanting.

Old Pine Street Church
412 Pine Street

Monday–Friday 1–5
Concerts every Sunday at 4:30
during Winter.

Beautiful church built in 1767–68 with a wonderful graveyard for wandering.

Pennsylvania Hospital
Between Spruce and Pine streets, Eighth and Ninth streets
(215) 829-3251

Monday and Wednesday 9–4, by appointment only

The oldest hospital in the United States, founded in 1751 by
the ever-astonishing Ben Franklin and Dr. Thomas Bond. Pennsylvania Hospital is perhaps the finest example of an eighteenth-
century public building to be found in America. It also contains a
museum with a magnificent Benjamin West painting, in addition
to other art and medical memorabilia. The building and gardens
are not to be missed.

St. Peter's
Third and Pine streets
Parish House—313 Pine Street
(215) 925-5968

Monday–Friday 9–4
Visitors must be accompanied by the sexton.

Another colonial beauty with a fascinating graveyard for tomb-
stone enthusiasts.

Old City Hall
Southwest corner Fifth and Chestnut

Daily 9–5

Exquisite structure, built in 1790–91, was first home of the
United States Supreme Court. The completely human scale of
the building succeeds miraculously in conveying both a sense of
the era and the momentous decisions that took place in this
unpretentious structure.

Gloria Dei-Old Swedes Church
Swanson and Christian streets

Daily 9–5

The spell cast by this breathtaking old church, built in 1700, and its ancient graveyard can only be described as a passage to another world—a much simpler, more reflective one. A time when the church did, indeed, offer peace for the anguished soul.

Fairmount Park Historic Houses

A realization of William Penn's dream of Philadelphia as a "Greene Countrie Towne," Fairmount Park has been a very special enclave since the eighteenth century. The group of beautiful mansions constructed at that time were sold by their owners during the course of the nineteenth century to the city of Philadelphia, which was intent on preserving this magnificent area and creating a public parkland. Public transportation is available, from the Tourist Center at Sixteenth and J. F. Kennedy Boulevard, on a continuous schedule beginning at 9:30 A.M.

Historic Tour Houses
Daily 10–5
All houses open six days a week

Lemon Hill
Closed Friday

Hatfield House
Closed Wednesday

Mount Pleasant
Closed Wednesday

Laurel Hill
Closed Friday

Woodford
Closed Monday

Strawberry Mansion
Closed Monday

Cedar Grove
Closed Tuesday

Sweetbriar
Closed Tuesday

Solitude
Closed Thursday

Letitia Street House
Closed Thursday

Pine Street-Society Hill Walk

Center-city Philadelphia is a walker's paradise. No matter where you stroll, be it Independence Park, Rittenhouse Square, Queen Anne Village, or even Head House Square, there are beautiful things to see. I have selected the Pine Street-Society Hill area because it combines eighteenth-century Philadelphia and local antiquing. Pine Street above Sixteenth has some fine shops and lovely little side streets to wander about in, such as Camac, Panama, and Fawn, but I prefer to start my walk at 1300 Locust Street, home of the Historical Society and some terrific paintings. Walk along Thirteenth to Pine and head south. The antiquing below Thirteenth must be done at your own discretion, but nothing matches the restored buildings, old churches, Pennsylvania Hospital and finally, at the end of Pine at Second Street, Head House Square, a beautifully restored area that originally held the old market but now is filled with charming restaurants and shops. All the streets off Pine, but especially Third and Fourth between Pine and Locust, have houses that are a joy to see. If you are a bit footsore by the time you reach Third and Pine, sit in the tiny park called St. Peter's Way, just across from St. Peter's Church. Perhaps even more refreshing to the spirit would be a walk through the old graveyard. There are areas such as Rittenhouse Square which contain much grander houses than Pine Street, but nothing conveys the immediacy of eighteenth-century Philadelphia more than these enchanting simple buildings.

Inns and Restaurants

*Barclay Hotel
Rittenhouse Square, East
(215) 545-0300

*Latham Hotel
Seventeenth and Walnut streets
(215) 563-7474

Hilton Hotel
Civic Center Boulevard at 34th Street
(215) 387-8333

Holiday Inn-University City
Thirty-sixth and Chestnut streets
(215) 387-8000

Barclay Dining Room   (Lunch and dinner)
Barclay Hotel
Rittenhouse Square, East
(215) 545-0300

Le Bec-Fin   (Dinner only, 6 and 9 P.M.)
1312 Spruce Street
(215) 732-3000
Reservation required

Le Pavillon   (Lunch and dinner)
203 South Twelfth Street
(215) 922-1319

Charles   (Lunch and dinner)
1523 Walnut Street
(215) 567-5484

* Barclay and Latham within walking distance of Pine Street-Society Hill area.

Bogarts   (Lunch and dinner)
Latham Hotel
Seventeenth and Walnut streets

Bookbinders Sea Food House   (Lunch and dinner)
215 South 15th Street
(215) 545-1137

General Wayne Inn   (Lunch and dinner)
625 Montgomery Avenue
Merion Station
(215) 664-5125

In same town as Barnes Foundation.

There are a number of little restaurants in the immediate vicinity of Head House Square that are perfect for lunch.

PENNSYLVANIA

Antique Dealers

C. L. Prickett
Stony Hill Road
Yardley, Pa. 19067
(215) 493-4284

Monday–Saturday 10–5

When was the last time a dealer took apart a tall case clock for you and explained exactly the structural features to look for in a period piece? C. L. Prickett, a delightfully unassuming gentleman, who specializes in good quality American eighteenth-century furniture from New England, Pennsylvania, New Jersey, and Maryland, is both merchant and scholar. This combination is much rarer than most antiquers realize. Mr. Prickett believes it is essential for a collector to understand how to properly examine an antique. Very few dealers have the ability to explain their merchandise as explicitly as Clarence Prickett does. Whether he is showing you the fine points of a clock by Isaac Brokaw, *circa* 1788, of Elizabethtown, New Jersey, or a classic Massachusetts Queen Anne cherry highboy, *circa* 1760, or a superb Pennsylvania trifid armchair, with its original slipseat covered in the old leather and retaining much of the original finish, the intention is to share his pleasure and respect for these objects even more than to sell them. However, sell them, he does. The shop's turnover is very rapid because the stock is fairly priced for its distinction. Dealers, collectors, and museums cover this dealer regularly. The rarer the object, the faster it is sold. A tall case clock from the Norwich-New London area, with an eccentric base, was gone in a matter of days. Frequently, the detailing found in pieces from this region of Connecticut are quite individual in design and very sought after by certain collectors.

The look of the shop is marvelous. An old converted stone barn, with pegged floors and white-washed walls, creates a particularly attractive background for the furniture, mirrors, oriental carpets, and primitive paintings. The rooms are large and the furniture has space to breathe. The main floor contains the more formal pieces such as Queen Anne lowboys, Chippendale chests, sets of Queen Anne and Chippendale chairs, Hepplewhite sideboards and, even on occasion, a fine Queen Anne walnut dining table. This dealer has a special feeling for the ogee foot and many of his chests and slant-front desks have it. A marvelous New Hampshire desk, *circa* 1770, was constructed in flaming birch, with pine as its secondary wood. Secondary woods are frequently one of the methods used to determine the origin of a piece. A Chippendale chest, with ogee feet, fluted corners, and original bale handles, had cedar as its secondary wood, which means it might be either from Pennsylvania or New Jersey where this wood was found. However, certain styling details definitely marked the piece as Pennsylvania. It takes a tremendous amount of technical knowledge in addition to aesthetic instinct to pinpoint an object.

The country furniture is found on the second floor. It consists of sets of windsor chairs, including birdcage, bow and fan backs, tavern tables, gateleg tables, pencil-post beds, and blanket chests, to name just a small sampling.

C. L. Prickett is an excellent dealer who makes antiquing a pleasurable learning experience.

Matthew and Elisabeth Sharpe
The Spring Mill Antique Shop
Spring Mill
Conshohocken, Pa. 19428
(212) 828-0205

Monday–Saturday 10:30–5

Class is an intangible quality, difficult to describe, rarely encountered. To me it connotes graciousness, simplicity, and elegance without pretension; in a word, Matthew and Elisabeth Sharpe. These charming, erudite dealers have one of the most beautiful shops in the country. It is every antiquer's dream of home. I wanted to move in immediately. Room after room is filled with eighteenth-century American furniture, eighteenth-century China Export porcelains, oriental rugs and exquisite decorative accessories, all chosen with matchless taste. Nothing is ostentatious, everything is first-rate, the livability reflecting Betty Sharpe's irrepressible joie de vivre.

The shop, which was the original old barn of the property, has been divided into three levels. The lowest houses the simpler country furniture: windsor chairs, tavern tables, candle stands, blanket chests, walls full of eighteenth-century blue-and-white Delft, early English Staffordshire, blue-and-white China Export, predominately in the Fitzhugh pattern, and most of the small brass accessories such as tobacco boxes and candlesticks. Young collectors couldn't find a better place to start their joyful quest. The country pieces, which are a small part of the inventory, are beautiful examples, chosen by these very knowledgeable dealers and at prices that are competitive. What many young collectors don't realize is that a great deal of country furniture is fake or reconstructed, and they often mistake crudity of construction for age. At whatever level you begin buying, start with a dealer who really knows what they are about. An antique is always much less expensive than a fake.

The Sharpes, though barely half an hour from Philadelphia, do not specialize in Philadelphia pieces, although they have many fine examples on their main floor which is furnished as a series of living and dining rooms. All of the furniture, be it a Philadelphia mahogany bonnet-top highboy with a broken arch pediment, or a pair of Philadelphia Chippendale side chairs with ball-and-claw feet, or the elegant Queen Anne wing chairs from Massachusetts, or a beautiful New England walnut serpentine chest with ogee feet, or a cherry-and-tiger-maple Connecticut Queen Anne lowboy, has a consistent delicacy of proportion; nothing is gross, nothing too ornate. There are Queen Anne chairs, highboys, and lowboys, classic examples of Chippendale chests, desks, tables, chairs, and a number of Hepplewhite pieces that I thought were among the most beautiful furniture in the shop. One was a finely inlaid-mahogany sideboard; the other, a Philadelphia card table with a marvelously shaped front. A particularly attractive set of Sheraton dining chairs was also from Philadelphia. The most spectacular of the Famille Rose China Export tureens and punch bowls are displayed throughout these rooms, providing beautiful color accents to the furniture. Among the large selection of porcelains, two punch bowls were particularly distinctive; one, a superb hunt bowl, the design taken from an English sporting print, had a quality of painting that is unique to find in Export ware. (The Chinese usually reserved their finest artists for their domestic porcelains.) The other bowl, which truly lived up to its description as a punch bowl, was decorated with figures of Bacchus carrying on in a manner appropriate to the god of wine with the very amusing addition of nymphs cavorting around the bowl riding a Chinese version of a tiger. Really a wonderfully witty piece.

The third floor is where the bulk of the Export porcelains are kept as well as a very small selection of eighteenth-century English pottery. All of the material is exceptionally attractive, ranging from tiny spoon trays to magnificent tureens. The finest pieces would satisfy the most discriminating collector. The great advantage of buying from dealers with beautiful taste is that nothing is a throwaway. Even the less important pieces, which are perfect for the collector of either limited budget or knowledge, have distinct merit. You may only be able to afford a small plate, but you will be treated with all the courtesy and interest that these very special dealers reserve for a fellow collector.

In the eighteenth century, it was said all roads led to the town of Spring Mills. They still do, and it is a journey that will repay you in pleasure a hundredfold.

Trump & Company
Bethlehem Pike
Flourtown, Pa. 19031
(215) 233-1805

By appointment

Federal furniture had always left me completely cold. I found the shapes ponderous and generally wearying to the eye and the spirit. If prejudice is based on ignorance, then I was a classic victim of lack of knowledge. The moment of revelation for me was seeing Robert Trump's extraordinary collection of American Federal furniture at his galleries in Flourtown. There is nothing more exciting for a collector than meeting a dealer who is capable of opening one's eyes to what had been a completely closed area of interest.

As I walked through the shop, I realized there was much more to Federal furniture than the ugly, pretentious pieces I had always felt were typical of the period. I had mistaken the pebbles for the diamonds, and great Federal pieces are truly jewels of craftsmanship. Mr. Trump's selection of furniture reflects the sense of elegance and formality of its time. This was furniture made for the wealthy new Republicans.

The finest pieces are of great subtlety. Rather than the elaborate decoration of full-blown Chippendale or Queen Anne, it is the exquisite working of the woods, mahogany in most cases, that helps determine the quality of a piece. There is enormous consistency of taste at this dealer's. Bob Trump prizes delicacy of line above all else; even massive pieces like a pair of Philadelphia mahogany bow-front chests, *circa* 1820, with Egyptian figures carved in relief, by the great cabinetmaker Barry, seem to float effortlessly in space. All of the chairs and sofas have this lightness of scale. Every piece at this dealer's is of beautiful proportion; nothing appears oversize to the eye, even when the piece itself is actually very large. The detailing in this furniture is both fascinating and amusing. The motif of a sofa backrail was a long, coiled rope, and an enchanting footstool had human feet. All of the tables—from a spectacularly beautiful 1790 Newport Hepplewhite gaming table, with a large fan-shaped center motif, to a fine Pembroke table attributed to Duncan Phyfe—are of quality and style. There are sets of dining chairs, some with the classic saber legs; others, delightful examples of painted, cane-seated fancy chairs. One definitely has the feeling, with this dealer, that very few first-rate pieces of his period escape him. The stock is large, the prices relevant to the quality but not nearly as high as the equivalent quality in either Queen Anne or Chippendale.

Robert Trump's first passion was early hardware and brass, and as a very young dealer, still in college, he supplied this material to museums such as Winterthur, Mount Vernon, Kenmore, Cooperstown, and Williamsburg. The shop has a small selection of early iron, but because he collects it himself, Mr. Trump admits to competing with his clients for the best pieces. This scholarly, young dealer has decorative accessories, on a limited basis, that are of the same period as the furniture and would have been used with it. The European and American nineteenth-century porcelains, mirrors, paintings, brass, and silver may be small in number but are all fine examples.

I cannot recommend this dealer too strongly. Even if you have only the remotest interest in Federal furniture, Bob Trump's feeling for his period is so contagious that he makes converts out of non-collectors.

Elinor Gordon
Box 211
Villanova, Pa. 19085
(215) 525-0981

By appointment only

For many collectors Elinor Gordon is China Export porcelain and rightfully so. She has been a specialist in the field for over twenty-five years and has written a number of books on the subject. When Mrs. Gordon started her business in the early fifties, after having been a collector herself for many years, there was very little public recognition of these wares, either aesthetically or financially. They were generally considered the poor relations of European porcelain. Prices were very low and the amount of serious scholarship fairly negligible. As appreciation and knowledge have grown, so have the prices. Inconceivable a decade ago, rare Export pieces now bring as much at auction as Meissen and Sèvres. The Chinese have been exporting pottery in one form or another since at least the T'ang dynasty, but the pieces generally seen on the market today are those made for the European and American trade in the eighteenth and nineteenth centuries.

Mrs. Gordon is a solid, conservative dealer of very definite personal taste. Her advice to young collectors is excellent. Whenever possible think in terms of collecting one specific design, even if you buy only one or two pieces a year. It gives you a sense of focus and makes the search much more exciting. When I was putting together my green Fitzhugh dinner service many years ago, it became apparent to me that most dealers are stimulated by antiquers who seem to be collecting something unique. More frequently than not, I found no Fitzhugh but made friends with many interesting dealers. Mrs. Gordon's other suggestion is, Collect in terms of a specific color and stick to it.

There are many ways to collect China Export, but the most important advice anyone can give you is, buy the best you can afford and try to avoid repaired pieces unless they are of very rare form or decoration. Another detail to remember is that it is not unusual to find that decoration has been added at a later date. An armorial plate is worth much more than a plain one, and the temptation to add a crest was frequently irresistible. The Chinese never painted as many eagle platters as have appeared on the market. So, collector beware. Your best security is a fine reputable dealer like Elinor Gordon whose stock is varied enough for both the new collector and the connoisseur. She has examples of everything from complete dinner services, tea and coffee services, and magnificent bowls to tiny enchanting individual spoon trays and teapots that are a perfect starting point for the beginner. Mrs. Gordon makes it easy to enter this interesting world of porcelains.

Philip H. Bradley Co.
East Lancaster Avenue, Route 30
Downingtown, Pa. 19335
(215) 269-0427

Monday–Saturday 9–5

Categorizing Philip Bradley's vast establishment as an antique shop is a rather ludicrous understatement. What it most resembles in size and content is a collector's supermarket. When Mr. Bradley says he has an extensive stock of eighteenth- and early nineteenth-century American furniture and European and American decorative accessories of the same period, he is being modest. It is one of the largest and most varied inventories I have ever seen. Philip Bradley is first and foremost a merchant; he will buy anything he thinks he can sell rapidly. Basically a trade dealer, the shop reflects a personal point of view only insofar as three quarters of the furniture is Pennsylvania in origin, the balance primarily New England, with a small amount of English eighteenth-century furniture rounding out the quarter. The range of quality is as astonishing as the amount of merchandise. Dozens upon dozens of pieces of every imaginable style made in the eighteenth century are stacked on the floor with a total disregard for comparable quality. A simple, inexpensive country chest might have a magnificent Philadelphia mahogany highboy for its neighbor. At any given time, the shop has 100 to 150 pieces of case furniture (chests, secretaries, highboys, lowboys, desks) on hand; add to that, chairs and tables of every description, blanket chests, beds and clocks, and you begin to perceive the scope of this dealer's activity.

The amount of decorative material available is as large and catholic in taste as the furniture. There are American and European landscapes, ship and portrait paintings of excellent quality, in addition to dozens of nineteenth-century genre paintings that everyone seems to be collecting now, regardless of merit. Display is hardly a strong point of the shop; you really have to look for the paintings; even the very fine ones are frequently hidden behind a pile of odds and ends. Early American silver is a special interest of this dealer, as is eighteenth- and nineteenth-century fireplace equipment. The selection of andirons is huge. Almost anything in porcelains might show up here, including eighteenth-century English Staffordshire, Delft, Pennsylvania shipware, Bennington pottery, Gaudy Dutch, the Chinese wares of Canton, Nanking, Rose Medallion, and such rare China Export as the Fitzhugh pattern in brown.

What gives Philip Bradley his special position in the trade is not simply the amount of material he has but, rather, that a good percentage of the stock is of superior quality. This is very rare in a trade shop where price is usually the only determining factor in what the dealer will buy. The great majority of collectors, be they rank amateurs or knowledgeable specialists, are sure to find something at a fair price to suit their interests at this antiquer's emporium. A very small minority may find the experience exhausting rather than challenging.

Joseph Kindig
325 Market Street
York, Pa.
(717) 848-2760
(717) 252-2621

By appointment only

There are very few legendary figures in the antique business, as greed and envy have a way of tarnishing the greatest reputation. Even allowing for this, nothing has yet dimmed the luster of the late Joe Kindig, Jr., as dealer *extraordinaire!* Specializing in great eighteenth-century American furniture and priceless antique European and American arms and armour, he was unsurpassed in the antique world for knowledge, quality, price, and eccentricity of behavior. There is not a major dealer, starting with Sack and Walton, who does not have a favorite story concerning Mr. Kindig's foibles. Scourge of collector and museum curator alike, Joe Kindig, always in competition as a collector with his own clients, drove them to distraction by refusing to sell them pieces they desperately wanted.

Keeping with family tradition, his son Joe Kindig III is both a brilliantly stimulating and delightfully impossible dealer. Completely opinionated, he has the most highly developed aesthetic sense of any dealer I've met. He is the scholar his father was and just as difficult to do business with. For innocent collectors who believe a dealer is there to service their needs, Joe Kindig provides an alternative point of view. The Kindigs have always felt they were the custodians of their treasures. On the surface this seems a reasonable attitude, but in reality it means a collector must prove worthiness of ownership by being truly appreciative, in Mr. Kindig's terms, and willing to pay the astronomical prices asked, to protect the objects from the casual antiquer. This dealer will not sell to a collector who buys for investment; using the word is like waving the proverbial red flag. Difficult as this all sounds, it does make for a most challenging relationship. Joe Kindig, a passionate collector and great connoisseur, demands that his clients' interests match his. You may be a rank amateur as a collector, but if he feels the talent and potential are there, you will have a fantastic experience.

Located in the oldest area of York, the shop is magnificently shabby. Nothing has been done to destroy the honest integrity of its total disorder. This is only one of a number of buildings that house a huge inventory of the finest examples of Queen Anne and Chippendale furniture produced in New England, New York, and Pennsylvania. Half the stock is New England, largely Newport pieces, and the balance predominately Philadelphia. There is a small amount of so-called country furniture that has been chosen for its rarity. A good comb-back windsor with a writing arm is original throughout, as are all the country armchairs. There are lovely, unpretentious New England and Pennsylvania rural gate-leg table, chests, highboys, and desks, some of which Mr. Kindig describes as rather "pleasant." At another dealer's they would be considered treasures, but as this is not Joe Kindig's favorite material, that is about the highest compliment he is willing to pay this enchanting furniture.

Brilliant is the word used most often by this dealer to describe the great formal pieces made primarily in Philadelphia, Newport, New York, and Boston. Mr. Kindig has a restored eighteenth-century house filled with one great Newport piece after another, complete with shell carvings and blocked fronts. Two of his finest New York pieces are in this exquisite house. One, a superb Chippendale wing chair with opulently carved legs, is very similar in feeling to the Philadelphia variety. However, to the sensitive eye there is a certain restraint that marks it as a New York piece. A mahogany secretary with relief flower carving of incredible dimension is the other New York example. Scattered between all the buildings you will find piece after piece of extraordinary Philadelphia furniture, including a secretary that belonged to Wallace Nutting and a matching Philadelphia highboy and lowboy, which, of course, are shown in different rooms. It wouldn't occur to Joe Kindig to do anything as obvious as having a pair next to each other for quick observation. This is a dealer who insists you use your eyes. There are a number of Philadelphia highboys with their original finish. It is very interesting to realize how different the aesthetic taste of the eighteenth-century cabinetmaker was from our own. The surface of the mahogany in these pieces is flat and slightly opaque, making for a much subtler interplay between the grain of the drawer fronts and the very ornate carving. As perceived this way, the balance of the piece is restored and much of its seeming heaviness disappears. Again and again I felt this dealer was helping me to see great American furniture from a completely fresh point of view.

It seems like madness to use the term decorative accessories for the fantastic Queen Anne and Chippendale mirrors that are part of the stock. One particularly choice Chippendale mirror was by John Elliot of Philadelphia. The clocks, andirons, Pennsylvania pottery, great European brass candlesticks are equivalent in quality to the furniture. Willing to buy anything of great rarity, there is a complete room of nineteenth-century American scenic wallpaper.

The huge collection of literally priceless arms is beyond me except as objets d'art, which the early seventeenth-century German pistols obviously are. The craftsmanship is fantastic in terms of delicacy and skill. One room is filled with early rifles. If a gun lover finds I am using the wrong terminology, please forgive my ignorance. This is really a specialist's field and most of the clients for the arms are European. As with the furniture, it is only the rarest and costliest examples that interest this dealer.

Mr. Kindig is both a connoisseur and a connoisseur's dealer. There are so few of these in the world that he is to be valued as much as any of the objects he is occasionally willing to sell. He is a fascinating man, and for the right collector, unlike any other dealer you will ever meet.

Museums and Historical Houses

YORK

Museum of Historical Society of York County
250 East Market Street
(717) 848-1587

Monday–Saturday 9–5
Sunday 1–5

Closed January 1, Easter, Thanksgiving, December 25. Museum has library and research material, plus full-scale models of old village square.

Golden Plough Tavern
157 West Market Street

Half-timbered building of medieval-German design, built in 1741.

Bonham House
152 East Market Street

June–August Monday–Saturday 10–5
September–May Daily to 4

An 1840 house refurbished into period museum.

Inns and Restaurants

NEW HOPE

Logan's Inn
Ferry Street
New Hope, Pa. 18938
(215) 862-5134

Open all year

Lunch and dinner. Closed January 1, Thanksgiving, and December 25. Lodging available.

The Inn at Phillips Mill
North River Road
New Hope, Pa. 18938
(215) 862-9911

Open all year

Dinner only. Closed Tuesday. Lodging available.

1740 House
River Road
Lumberville, Pa. 18933
(215) 297-5661

Open all year

Breakfast for house guests only. Dinner only. Closed Sunday and Monday. Lodging available.

Washington Crossing
Routes 532 and 32
Washington Crossing, Pa. 18977
(215) 493-3634

Open all year

Lunch and dinner. Closed Monday and December 25. Lodging available.

LANCASTER AND YORK

General Sutter Inn
14 East Main Street
Lititz, Pa. 17543
(717) 626-2115

Open all year

Breakfast, lunch, dinner. Lodging available.

Accomac Inn
P.O. Box 126
Wrightsville, Pa. 17368
(717) 252-1521

Open all year

Lunch, May–September. Dinner all year.

DOWNINGTOWN

Coventry Forge Inn
Coventryville Road
Coventryville, Pa.
(Mailing address: R.D. 2, Pottstown, Pa. 19464)
(215) 469-6222

Open all year

Dinner only. Closed Sunday (November–April also closed Monday). Closed for month beginning December 24. Lodging available. Has fine reputation for French cuisine.

Chadds Ford Inn
Route 1
Chadds Ford, Pa. 19317
(215) 388-7361

Open all year

Lunch and dinner. Closed Sunday. Just down the road from the Brandywine Art Museum.

The Old Mill
Brinton Lake Road
Concordville, Pa. 19331
(215) 459-2140

Open all year

Dinner only. Closed Monday, Thanksgiving, December 25, and month of January.

Dilworthtown Inn
Old Wilmington Pike and Brittan Bridge Road
Dilworthtown, Pa. 19380
(215) 399-1390

Open all year

Lunch and dinner.

If you stay off the main roads in the vicinity of these Chester County restaurants, the landscape could not be more bucolic.

NOTE: Reservations must be made at all the inns and restaurants.

NEW JERSEY

Antique Dealers

Ardis Leigh
47 State Road
Princeton, N.J. 08540
(609) 924-9310

Monday–Saturday 10–5

Antiques for investment has been the keynote sounded in Ardis Leigh's advertisements for years, and, frankly, it was the reason I had never visited this dealer. The material in the ads looked beautiful, but I was convinced any dealer who thought in terms of collecting as a business investment must be overpriced. I couldn't have been more mistaken. Bill Leigh, who does the buying for his wife's shop, has a unique price policy for the antique world. The great majority of stock is sold at a straight 20 to 30 per cent markup over cost. The result is well-priced eighteenth-century American and English furniture. Needless to say, the shop does a large trade business. Mr. Leigh, whose father was the great Western illustrator W. R. Leigh, most enjoys the challenge of helping both the young collector and even the novice antique dealer build their collections. No matter what your budget, this dealer feels that, with proper guidance, there may be a fine highboy, of which he has many, in your future.

At least two thirds of the stock is American eighteenth-century Queen Anne, Chippendale, Hepplewhite, and Federal furniture

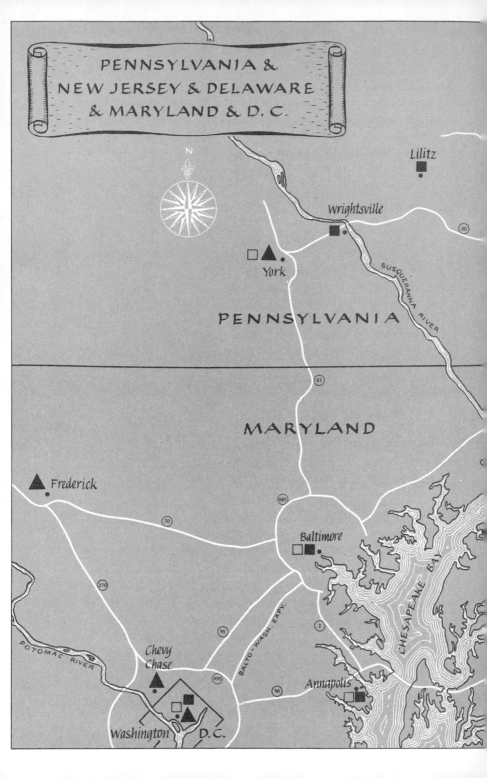

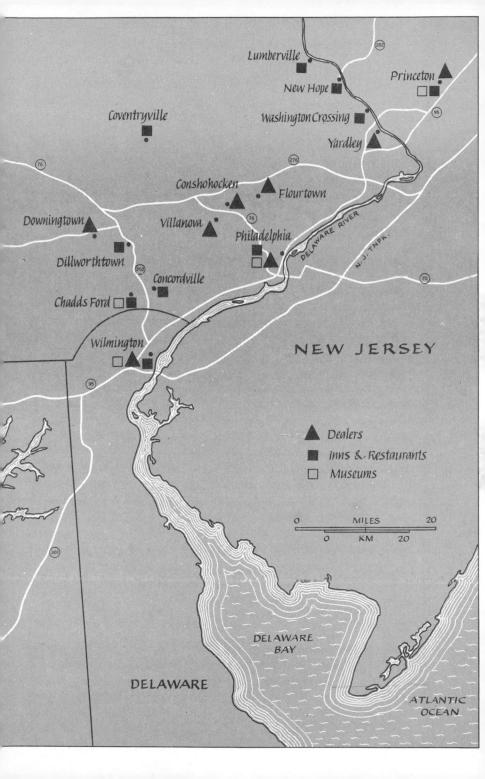

Lumberville

New Hope

Princeton

202

Washington Crossing

Coventryville

Yardley

95

76

276

Conshohocken

Flourtown

Downingtown

Villanova

76

Philadelphia

DELAWARE RIVER

Dillworthtown

202

Concordville

N. J. TNPK.

70

Chadds Ford

Wilmington

NEW JERSEY

95

301

▲ Dealers

■ Inns & Restaurants

□ Museums

0   MILES   20

0   KM   20

DELAWARE BAY

DELAWARE

ATLANTIC OCEAN

from New Hampshire to Virginia. It ranges from elaborate Philadelphia mahogany highboys, chairs, tables, and sideboards to the equally lovely but simpler lines of New England furniture and to such special delights as a New Jersey walnut Queen Anne, Spanish-foot lowboy. Ardis Leigh has a negligible selection of so-called country pieces. This dealer's true strength is in fine American furniture well priced and certainly competitive with the current auction market.

The English furniture, which comprises the remaining third of the stock, is especially strong in the more formal eighteenth-century mahogany and walnut pieces. There is always a large number of dining tables and chairs available. Most of the mirrors and other decorative accessories are also English. For the antiquer who would love to own a Queen Anne wing chair but cannot afford the costly American version, an English Georgian chair is a marvelously affordable alternative; the style is there but the price is less than half. English furniture of decent quality is still a good buy in this country.

Whatever the level of collecting, this dealer can supply you with excellent material at fair value. Mr. and Mrs. Leigh try to make the problems of choice as uncomplicated as possible by allowing their clients to live with a piece they may be considering, until they are sure it is right for them. As a matter of fact, you would be hard pressed to find a more co-operative antique shop.

The combination of good antiquing, a beautiful old town, and a marvelous University museum makes this dealer a choice selection for "the weekend connoisseur."

Museums and Historical Houses

The Art Museum
Princeton University
Princeton, N.J. 08540
(609) 452-3787

Tuesday–Saturday 10–4
Sunday 1–5 (Academic year)
Sunday 2–4 (Summer)

Every museum of consequence depends heavily on the generosity of benefactors for art objects and the funds to house them properly. In both instances, the Art Museum of Princeton University is batting one thousand. They have a terrific new building, which functions beautifully for the museum, and a really fine collection of Greek and Roman antiquities, Chinese art, medieval sculpture and objets d'art, European and American painting that encompasses Renaissance treasures, great impressionists, the Balken collection of American primitives, old master drawings, and modern sculpture by such illustrious names as Nevelson, Picasso, Smith, Noguchi, and Calder. The Boudinot Rooms contain the museum's eighteenth-century American furniture, with period painting and decorative accessories. The museum is just the right size. The individual collections are big enough to be impressive without resulting in museum fatigue.

The Italian and Flemish Renaissance paintings are of remarkable quality, not just for a university museum but for any major institution. A St. Anne, Virgin, and Child, attributed to Francesco Traini, *circa* fourteenth century, is very unusual in its design. The large figure of St. Anne fills the canvas; enclosed within her shape are the smaller figures of the Virgin and Child, creating a sense of unity and power that is modern in feeling. Another Madonna and Child attributed to Guido da Siena has much in common with the Expressionist Rouault. Both artists, four hundred years apart, were obviously influenced by early Byzantine painting. Don't overlook in the medieval sculpture gallery a painting called "St. Michael as Weigher of Souls" by the Villarroya master from Aragon, late fifteenth century. It is enchanting, and note the delightful way the artist designed the dozens of little angel heads as flowers. The same gallery contains an early sixteenth-century Flemish statue of St. Catherine of Alexandria, which is all elegance and grace until you see the feet which are shod in big clumpy shoes.

The Impressionist and Post-Impressionist group of Degas, Cézanne, Monet, Van Gogh, Soutine, Modigliani, in addition to a number of German Expressionists, is on permanent loan to the University from the Pearlman Collection. There is a particularly exciting painting called "The Red Horse" by Franz Marc. The

European seventeenth- and eighteenth-century canvases don't compare in quality with either the earlier or later examples.

Early Chinese bronzes and pottery form another superb group of objects. The diversity of shapes among the early bronzes is very well illustrated. There is an exceptionally large number of Six Dynasties (A.D. 220–589) tomb figures. For admirers of Matisse, do not miss the gallery containing Japanese screens. One of them called "Messenger of a New Year Letter," done in the ukiyo-e style, also known as "Painting of the Floating World," *circa* 1600–65, depicts non-perspective use of space and objects that influenced nineteenth- and twentieth-century French artists such as Manet and Matisse. This museum provides a first-rate collection for the interested viewer.

Bainbridge House
158 Nassau Street
Princeton, N.J. 08540
(609) 921-6748

Tuesday–Friday 10–4
Saturday and Sunday 2–4

Home of the Historical Society of Princeton, Bainbridge House was built in 1766. Restored as closely as possible to its original condition, the house now serves as a museum with period rooms and special changing exhibitions that pertain to local history.

Morven
55 Stockton Street
Princeton, N.J. 08540

Winter, Tuesday 1–3
Closed June, July, August

Probably the great historic house of New Jersey. Now the governor's official residence, it was built on a tract of land purchased from William Penn in 1701. A magnificent mansion, built in the Palladio style by Richard Stockton, whose grandson was a signer of the Declaration of Independence. It remained in the family's possession from 1701–1945.

Inns and Restaurants

Peacock Inn
20 Bayard Lane (Route 206)
Princeton, N.J. 08540
(609) 924-1707

Open all year

Lunch and dinner. Closed Sunday and month of July. Lodging available.

Nassau Inn
Palmer Square
Princeton, N.J. 08540
(609) 921-7500

Open all year

Breakfast, lunch, dinner. Lodging available.

Lahière's
11 Witherspoon Street
Princeton, N.J. 08540
(609) 921-2798

Open all year

Lunch and dinner. Closed Tuesday and first two weeks in August. Princeton landmark for food.

VI

A Taste of the Old South

Delaware, Maryland, Washington, D.C., contain within a narrow radius of each other a concentration of museums unmatched in the United States. Start with Winterthur, in Wilmington, Delaware, home to the foremost collection of seventeenth-, eighteenth-, and nineteenth-century American decorative arts to be found in this country. Continue down the Pike to Baltimore, where the Medieval and Renaissance objets d'art of the Walter's Art Gallery rival those of European museums. What original collectors Baltimore produced! The Cone sisters—two gentle ladies with an amazingly discerning eye—bought major Matisse paintings at the beginning of this century. The collection is now housed in a special wing of the Baltimore Museum of Art. Washington, D.C., in the last thirty years, has changed from an endless expanse of government buildings, interrupted occasionally by national monuments, into home for one museum after another. The treasures of the National Gallery, the Hirschhorn Museum, the Freer Gallery, the National Collection of Fine Arts, National

Portrait Gallery, and the Phillips Collection far surpass anything turned out by the United States mint.

DELAWARE

Antique Dealers

David Stockwell
3701 Kennett Pike
Box 3840
Wilmington, Del. 19807
(302) 655-4466

Monday–Friday 9:30–5
Appointment advisable

A short distance from the Winterthur museum, which has perhaps the single greatest collection of antique American decorative arts in the United States, is David Stockwell. It is a perfectly appropriate relationship, for Mr. Stockwell has been a respected name in fine American furniture for many years. Countless objects have been sold by him over the years not only to Winterthur but to many other important museums. What distinguishes David Stockwell as a dealer is not only his knowledge, taste, and beautiful manners, but an inventory that will knock your eye out. The shop is a big, beautiful, rambling country house filled with wonderful seventeenth- and eighteenth-century American furniture from the major regions, north and south; there are a small group of eighteenth-century English and Irish furniture; eighteenth-century American and European painting, mainly portraits and landscapes; rare examples of English and Dutch Delft and beautiful China Export porcelains.

A dealer such as David Stockwell makes it possible for the young collector to gain on-the-spot training. It is most unusual to find elsewhere the quantity of examples available for comparison between, for instance, eighteenth-century Irish furniture and the Philadelphia pieces for which it was obviously the prototype. This similarity is not mysterious if you are aware of the Irish influence in America. During the eighteenth century, Irish Quakers fleeing religious persecution settled in and about Philadelphia. They brought with them their great skills as cabinetmakers and the styling details with which they were familiar, namely, the trifid foot, which became typical of many Pennsylvania pieces, shell carving, and the so-called stocking leg. The irony is that these craftsmen, who created the very elaborate, ornately decorated Philadelphia furniture, were the simplest of people, living, themselves, only with objects that were completely functional and bare. This delightful dichotomy obviously disturbed no one!

There is a selection of costly, spendid pieces such as a Massachusetts mahogany black-front secretary with gilded shelves; the only known example of a piecrust-edge lowboy from Philadelphia; a tiny block-front chest by Benjamin Burnham whose inlay detail looks like crewel work and still has its original gilding. Among the many dining tables was a very interesting one from Baltimore, *circa* 1790, with a snake and eagle crest, the legend reading "Don't tread on me," an obvious reference to England's colonial policies. The collection of eighteenth-century English and American Queen Anne, Georgian, and Chippendale mirrors is marvelous. Though the vast majority of the stock is eighteenth century, there are also a number of nineteenth-century American Empire pieces.

David Stockwell has always loved clocks, the more splendid, the better, and has examples of Duncan Beard and Peter Stretch, the man who made the first clock for Independence Hall. There is a lovely story about Ben Franklin being responsible for the first public clock in Philadelphia. It seems Mr. Franklin brought back a watch from Europe and everyone stopped to ask him the time. Finally, dismayed by the constant interruptions, he requested that a public clock be built so he could go about his business undisturbed. The early William and Mary furniture and the more primitive country pieces are kept in the basement with appropriate decorative accessories. Another strong point of this dealer is his fine early brass candlesticks, boxes, and andirons.

Though an expensive dealer, in terms of pricing his large selection of truly outstanding pieces, there are many examples of simply first-class furniture that are no more costly than at any other shop handling this quality. It is always difficult to put a price on expertise, and in a sense, that is a large part of the cost when buying from a great dealer. Very often it is a price well worth paying. Any collector who has ever found it necessary to sell an object knows how important the provenance is to the quick and fair sale of the piece.

David Stockwell is an awesome name to many collectors. I guarantee the awe will turn to pleasure once you enter his marvelous shop.

Museums and Historical Houses

WILMINGTON

Winterthur Museum
Winterthur, Del. 19735

Advance reservations needed for main Museum
Tuesday–Saturday 10–4
Closed holidays

No reservations needed for South Wing
Tuesday–Saturday 10–4. Closed holidays
Write to Winterthur for reservations and rates.

Winterthur is the greatest collection of American antiques in the country. For scholar, collector, novice, this museum is the Bible of Americana. Henry Francis Du Pont, who is responsible for the development of Winterthur, planned the collection of exceptional woodwork, furniture, ceramics, glass, textiles, paintings, prints, and metal (silver, pewter, et cetera), spanning the years 1640–1840 to serve as a guide to the domestic history of our country. Over a hundred rooms were created, correct not only in every architectural detail but down to the smallest utensil.

The focal point, architecturally, of the William and Mary Parlor is the cedar-grained and marbleized paneled fireplace wall removed from a Lincoln, Massachusetts, house, built before 1700 by Thomas Goble II. The early Queen Anne and William and Mary furnishings are completely appropriate to the room, as is the European needlework imitation of a Turkey carpet, *circa* 1720–50, which is on a gateleg table, *circa* 1690–1710. (Oriental carpets were used in the seventeenth and eighteenth centuries as table coverings. Their brilliant colors and marvelous texture provided relief from the starkness of many of the rooms of this period.)

Every strata of society, from the simplest to the most elegant, is represented at Winterthur. One of the grandest rooms is the Readbourne Parlor, from Readbourne, built in 1733, Queen Annes County, Maryland. However, the furniture is primarily from Philadelphia, with the exception of the great japanned highboy made by John Pimm of Boston, *circa* 1740–50, for Commodore Joshua Loring. This extraordinary Queen Anne piece reflects the colonial taste for Chinese ornamentation. The colonies may have been three thousand miles away from the center of fashion, but it did not take long for new European trends to make their way over the ocean. A wonderful room known as the Chinese Parlor is composed of furniture, wallpaper, porcelains, and rugs that are either from China or reflect the Chinese influence on colonial craftsmen.

The richness of material available makes it almost impossible to select a favorite out of literally dozens of individual rooms, but certainly one of the most impressive is the Port Royal Parlor. The furniture is the so-called high-style Philadelphia mahogany of the Chippendale period. Opulent, magnificently covered in gold damask, it is shown to great advantage on a Persian carpet, *circa* 1900, woven in the Heriz region in a design often seen in earlier Kuba rugs. The effect of this room is smashing.

No antiquer should miss an opportunity to visit Winterthur not once but a hundred times.

Longwood Gardens
(302) 656-8591

Mid-April–October. Daily, except Monday, 10–4
Rest of year by appointment

These are the fabulous Winterthur gardens; more than sixty acres of formal plantings. Be sure to include it on any trip to Winterthur Museum.

Inns and Restaurants

Hotel DuPont
Eleventh and Market streets
Wilmington, Del. 19899
(302) 656-8121

Open all year

  Breakfast, lunch, dinner. Lodging available. Marvelously attractive, comfortable hotel.

Columbus Inn
2216 Pennsylvania Avenue
1½ miles west on Delaware 52
(302) 571-1492

Open all year

  Lunch and dinner. Closed Sunday, Easter, Labor Day, Thanksgiving, December 25.

MARYLAND

Antique Dealers

Webster Fine Art Inc.
4007 Bradley Lane
Chevy Chase, Md. 20015
(301) 654-8996

By appointment only

  Donald Webster is a fine painting dealer with whom very few collectors of American and European nineteenth-century art are familiar. Mr. Webster and his partner, Russell Burke, are what is known as private dealers. Experts in nineteenth-century American painting, they deal primarily with museums, major collectors, and other dealers. They keep no gallery, in the usual sense, because their inventory is often bought to order. By that I mean, a serious collector interested in acquiring a landscape by, let us say, Thomas Cole, Frederick Church, Jasper Cropsey, or Asher Durand would call and ask these dealers to find one. At this level of dealing, everyone knows where most of the major paintings are, especially those in private hands. Webster Fine Art, if they don't happen to own one at the time, will then proceed to try to find the desired artist. The same, incidentally, is true of eighteenth-century American furniture, but, again, it is only the rarities they are interested in dealing with. This is definitely not general collecting. Yet, if you are buying on this level, you could probably do well with these dealers because they are a primary source and the pieces have not yet passed through a number of hands, acquiring on the way an ever-higher price tag. They have had such eighteenth-century artists as Peale, Sully, and Stuart and recently sold a painting by the European artist Redon. At the moment they are delighted at having acquired an 1800 genre painting, by Jeremiah Paul, of George Washington bidding farewell to his family. Paul, incidentally, was a friend of the Peales.

These are extremely knowledgeable dealers of excellent reputation in a field infamous for slander.

Franklin Rappold
18 East Patrick Street
Frederick, Md. 21701
(301) 898-5533
(301) 663-6102

Thursday and Friday 11–3
Saturday 11–5

Franklin Rappold is an understated dealer who possesses great expertise in eighteenth-century American furniture. A dealer of conservative taste, with a background as a cabinetmaker and restorer, his furniture reflects a special feeling for the good woods and solid workmanship that distinguish fine country furniture.

An excellent example of the quality of material available at this dealer's is a mahogany Chippendale Pembroke table, *circa* 1790, with Marlborough feet. This table, though small in size, makes a very strong statement. Even a collector who has difficulty visualizing a wing chair in the frame would have little problem recognizing the graceful proportions of a New England Chippendale chair with elegantly carved ball-and-claw feet. A helpful key to the true dimensions of an unupholstered chair is the width of the back and the proportions of the legs. The smaller these elements are, the more delicate the scale of the chair. Another good wing chair, also from New England, still had its original linen upholstery. Interestingly, the upholstery on this Hepplewhite piece was hand sewn rather than tacked to the frame. A desk on frame, *circa* 1710–20, probably from Virginia, was a combination of walnut and yellow pine. The turnings on the legs of this early piece were exceptional. There are tables, chairs, and chests of all styles and sizes available, ranging from Queen Anne to Hepplewhite. A particularly beautiful Queen Anne maple tea table, *circa* 1740, had what is known as a scrub-top finish and pad feet. The shop generally has a piece or two of miniature furniture in stock. Though the debate continues, most knowledgeable dealers agree that these small pieces were produced for children and not as furniture samples.

Mr. Rappold has always enjoyed country furniture that still retains traces of its original paint. There is a good selection of these pieces in chests, tables, and corner cabinets in a variety of colors.

Among the decorative accessories are eighteenth-century English and American mirrors, oriental rugs, and a small group of Export China.

Franklin Rappold is a dealer of great dependability; well worth visiting again and again.

Museums and Historical Houses

BALTIMORE

The Walters Art Gallery
600 North Charles Street
Baltimore, Md. 21201
(301) 547-9000

Monday 1–5
Tuesday–Saturday 11–5
Sunday and holidays 2–5
Closed January 1, July 4, Thanksgiving,
December 24, December 25

The assemblage of rare treasures by William Walters
(1820–94) and his son Henry Walters (1848–1931) represents the
culmination of great nineteenth-century European collecting taste
in this country. The extraordinary objects in the Walters Art Gallery would be more familiar to a great German or French collection than one found in the United States. Very few collectors of
their time had the sensibility to appreciate Medieval and Renaissance objets d'art, which are the core of the collection. The enamels, ivories, bronzes, gold, jewels, statuary are literally priceless,
as the Von Hirsch sale in London in 1978 proved beyond doubt,
once and for all. But these objects are just the tip of the iceberg.
The Walters passion for beauty covered many areas such as the
classic world of Greek, Roman, Etruscan sculpture and pottery,
Egyptian art and artifacts, fantastic examples of Islamic pottery
and manuscripts, the rarest of Chinese porcelains, European
painting, spanning the early fifteenth to nineteenth centuries,
French eighteenth-century furniture, Sèvres porcelains. And this is
just a superficial listing of what these men were capable of gather-
ing together over two lifetimes of devoted collecting. The finest of
the objects represents a most rarefied aesthetic taste. This is not
casual museum-going. It is a demanding experience, as many of
the pieces are not familiar and easily assimilated. However, the·
Walters Art Gallery is literally a treasury one could return to
again and again, feeling as if you had barely scratched the surface.
It is a fascinating and rewarding museum.

Baltimore Museum of Art
Wyman Park, Art Museum Drive
Baltimore, Md. 21218

Tuesday–Friday 11–5, Saturday 10:30–5
Sunday 1–5
Closed Monday, January 1, Good Friday,
July 4, Thanksgiving, December 25

Yes, there is a Baltimore Museum of Art, and it is a wonderful museum. Many elements contribute to its success. It is large without being exhausting. Its collections are diverse but of excellent quality. The taste level is sophisticated, yet it is an informal museum. And, most important of all, it contains the Cone Collection of early Matisse paintings. These two unusual Baltimore sisters visited Leo and Gertrude Stein in Paris in the early 1900s and were introduced to Matisse and Picasso. They started to buy almost at once directly from Matisse, acquiring along the way paintings by other artists whose work they admired. It is a very special collection because it so directly reflects its owners' personal taste. This is early Matisse, of the small, intimate canvas —paintings that must have been a joy for the sisters to live with. The Cones had an eye; the Picasso, Cézanne, Vuillard, Cassatt, Boudin, Sisley, Gauguin paintings they selected have, for the most part, the same exquisite gentleness about them as the Matisse. Mary Cassatt's pastel "In the Garden" is one of her finest works, and the Bonnard family luncheon table, complete with dog waiting to be fed, is delightful. A great, lush Gauguin, "Woman with Mango" (1892), is a masterpiece of color, design, and femininity. The Cones deviated from their pattern by buying two of Matisse's large, bold nudes; the very famous "Blue Nude" is theirs, as well as his "Pink Nude." It is impossible to go through the Cone Wing without feeling you are directly sharing the sister's pleasure in their choices.

The American Wing, which houses the eighteenth- and early nineteenth-century furniture, paintings, and decorative accessories, has been designed as a series of complete room settings. This is a perfect way to display furniture and give a sense of its usage. Some of the pieces are local, as seen in the enchanting Oval Room from Willow Brook, Baltimore, 1799, whose furnishings are Sheraton fancy chairs, tables, and settees that were made in Baltimore, *circa* 1805, with painted views of the city on them for decoration. However, other rooms have examples of New England and Pennsylvania cabinetwork as well, the finest, perhaps, being a japanned highboy from Boston, *circa* 1730, which certainly ranks with either the one in the Boston Fine Arts or Winterthur. There are marvelous paintings by the Peales, Sully, Stuart, Wollaston, Earl, but good as they are, none of them holds a candle to the extraordinary John Singleton Copley portrait of Lumuel Cox (1770). The body gesture has a thrust and naturalness that defies description. It is as brilliant and dramatic as only a first-rate Copley can be.

In the European painting wing, the Jacob Epstein collection has superb examples of Titian, Rembrandt, Hals, and Gainsborough. A selection of lovely Dutch seventeenth-century painting forms part of the Mary Frick Jacobs Collection. Among this group is a Spanish painting of the Infanta Isabella (1600), which is exquisite. The child's face is as jewel-like as the great gems she is wearing.

The museum also has a large American folk art collection, European decorative arts, Far Eastern and African art, and the fascinating Antioch Mosaics. There is also contemporary art, which includes a huge Henry Moore sculpture that is rather badly placed for viewing. It is too large for the space it's in.

The predominate quality of the Baltimore Museum is its accessibility. There is no feeling of being roped off from objects; even many of the period rooms can be entered, rather than viewed from a distance. It is a most appealing characteristic to find in a museum; so few of them have it.

Carroll Mansion
800 East Lombard Street

Wednesday–Friday 10:30–4:30
Saturday and Sunday 1–5
Closed holidays

Home of Charles Carroll, who died here in 1832, and was a signer of the Declaration of Independence. House is furnished with period pieces.

Peale Museum
225 Holiday Street

Tuesday–Friday 10:30–4:30
Saturday and Sunday 1–5
Closed holidays

Built in 1814 for Rembrandt Peale's "Baltimore Museum," it later became Baltimore's first City Hall. It is now a municipal museum of Baltimore memorabilia and houses a collection of Peale portraits.

Mount Clare Museum
In Carroll Park at Monroe Street and
Washington Boulevard

Tuesday–Saturday 11–3:15
Sunday 1–3:15
Closed holidays

Oldest house in Baltimore (1754), now a museum with colonial furnishings.

ANNAPOLIS

Hammond-Harwood House
19 Maryland Avenue at King George Street

April–October, Tuesday–Saturday 10–5;
Sunday 2–5; November–March, Tuesday–Saturday
10–4; Sunday 1–4. Closed January 1, December 25

Magnificent Georgian house designed by William Buckland and built in 1774. Fine antique furnishings.

Restored Historic Sites

Tobacco Prize House
10 Pinkney Street

Revolutionary Soldier's Barracks
43 Pinkney Street

Customs House
99 Main Street

(All sites open Monday–Saturday 10–4:30, Closed January 1, Thanksgiving, December 25.

William Paca Garden
1 Martin Street

Monday–Saturday 10–4
Sunday 12–4
Closed December 25

Re-creation of elaborate landscaped gardens developed in 1765 by William Paca, a signer of the Declaration of Independence.

State House
State Circle, Center of Town

Daily 9–5
Closed Thanksgiving and December 25

Oldest state house in continuous use in the United States.

Inns and Restaurants

BALTIMORE-ANNAPOLIS

Maryland Inn
Church Circle
Annapolis, Md. 21401
(301) 263-2641

Open all year

Breakfast, lunch, dinner. Lodging available.

Danny's
1201 North Charles Street
Baltimore, Md. 21201
(301) 539-1393

Open all year

Lunch and dinner. Closed Sunday and last week in July.

Haussner's
3242 Eastern Avenue
Baltimore, Md. 21224
(301) 327-8365

Open all year

Lunch and dinner. Closed Sunday, Monday, December, 25.

Chesapeake
1701 North Charles Street
Baltimore, Md. 21201
(301) 837-7711

Open all year

Lunch and dinner.

WASHINGTON, D.C.

Antique Dealers

M. Darling Ltd.
3213 O Street, N.W.
Washington, D.C. 20007
(202) 337-0096

Winter, Tuesday–Saturday 11–6
Summer, Monday–Friday 11–6
Appointment advisable

For the connoisseur of great English furniture, waiting to discover the next treasure, may I recommend an exquisite gallery on a
tiny back street in Georgetown? The material handled by M. Darling Ltd. is comparable in quality to that of Mallard of London
and J. J. Wolff of New York. Macy Darling is a purist. No other
word does him justice. If an object is not the finest example of
seventeenth-, eighteenth-, or early nineteenth-century English fur-

niture, he will not purchase it. Is this rarefied taste? Absolutely yes, in the most exciting meaning of the word. Many of the pieces are bought directly from families that have owned them for generations. Mr. Darling feels nothing illustrates as vividly the social attitudes of a country as its great furniture. Seventeenth- and eighteenth-century England was the center of the universe to its citizens, and the furniture reflects this pride.

The stock is not excessively large, but it is exceedingly choice. A William and Mary ladies jewel cabinet, *circa* 1690, on a gilt-wood carved stand, was so delicate it almost floated away. Dutch influence was very evident in the design of the flower inlay on the cabinet itself. Another William and Mary piece was a Spanish-foot, high-back side chair with a strong sculptural feeling to the carving. As in all great examples, the carving was alive and flowing. If details of fine workmanship fascinate you, a superb early George II mahogany console table, *circa* 1740, will be irresistible. Very small in size, it has a gloriously carved apron, complete with eagle and foliated acanthus leaves. The best example of the Regency period, in the shop, was a set of mahogany dining chairs that were completely uncliché in terms of style and refinement of detail. An unusual dining table by Sheraton was designed in the shape of a hunt table. The table, which was very large, could be separated into four individual sections for more intimate dining. Perfectly proportioned for a modern room was a very shallow, but extremely elegant, veneered mulberry-knurlwood secretary bookcase, *circa* 1700.

All the pieces in the shop are selected with a discerning eye for perfection. Mr. Darling is a passionate collector who believes great furniture should evoke a moment of aesthetic and emotional recognition in the viewer. Whether it is a set of superb seventeenth-century William and Mary dining chairs or a restrained George II chest with exquisite veneering or any one of a number of distinguished small tables, the same demand for the ultimate in craftsmanship exists.

The decorative accessories in the shop are equally lovely and include fine Queen Anne and Georgian mirrors, candlesticks, wonderful seventeenth- and eighteenth-century clocks, Charles II stumpwork and, occasionally, European porcelains.

There is very little opportunity to see English furniture of this caliber in the United States except in museums. It is expensive only in terms of money, not for the quality offered.

AUCTION HOUSES

C. G. Sloan & Company Inc.
715 Thirteenth Street, N.W.
Washington, D.C. 20005
(202) 628-1468

Sales are conducted on a regular basis throughout the year. Good reputation.

Museums and Historical Houses

National Collection of Fine Arts
Eighth Street and G Street, N.W.
Washington, D.C. 20560
(202) 381-5180

Daily 10–5:30
Closed Christmas

Washington, D.C., has a monument to the Unknown Soldier. What you may not realize is that is also has an unknown museum. The National Collection of Fine Arts is not more than a ten-minute walk from the National Gallery of Art, but for all the attention it receives, it might as well be on Mars. The mysterious chemistry that fills one art museum and leaves empty another of comparable quality, in its own field, completely eludes me. This has been the undeserved fate of the National Collection, a fine museum specializing in American art from the eighteenth to twentieth century. It is a big museum packed with marvelous examples, imaginatively displayed, of some of the best work produced in this country. Among the rarities is a gallery devoted to Albert P. Ryder (1847–1917), a fascinatingly original painter with something of Redon's mysticism in his work. A group of sea-storm paintings were completely Expressionist in feeling. Beautiful examples of the American Impressionists—Twachtman, Cassatt, Hassam, Lawson, and Theodore Robinson, who painted at Giverny as did Monet—can be seen, as well as the works of Powers, Inness, Blakelock, Catlin, and Bierstadt. The eighteenth- and early nineteenth-century artists represented are Stuart, the Peales, Feke, and Earl, to name just a sampling. Look for the smashing self-portrait by Benjamin West, the American painter who became head of the English Royal Academy.

The museum contains the John Gellatly Collection, which is really a museum within a museum. A carry-over from the days before the National Collection specialized in American painting, the Gellatly Collection consists of European and Asiatic objects from the eleventh century B.C. to the eighteenth century. All of the pieces are of extraordinary quality. An exquisitely designed gallery held a display of Renaissance jewels, ivories, and metalwork, Greek and Roman jewelry, Chinese pottery and bronzes. The small selection of old masters paintings from this collection is equally outstanding.

Marvelous as this museum is in all the areas I've described, they are secondary to its modern American painting section. I have seldom seen large contemporary canvases treated with so much understanding of their spacial needs. The Klines are sensational; the artist's sense of mastery is all there. These are aggressive paintings that come right off the wall at you. Rauschenberg, Davis, Louis, Frankenthaler, Motherwell, Still, De Kooning have never looked more exciting.

There is always too much to see in Washington and never enough time, but the National Collection of Fine Arts is really worth discovering.

NOTE: The National Collection of Fine Arts and the National Portrait Gallery are in adjoining buildings.

National Portrait Gallery
Eighth Street and F Street, N.W.
Washington, D.C. 20560
(202) 381-5380

Daily 10–5:30
Closed Christmas

Almost all antiquers are history buffs, ever searching for information that might reveal the antecedents of their pieces. The only thing more exciting than finding out who may have owned your chest of drawers in the eighteenth century is discovering a picture of that person. Contact between you and the past is immediately established. That, in a nutshell, is how I feel about the National Portrait Gallery. It is filled with wonderful paintings of all the people you have ever read about in the history books. Yes, John Adams was a testy man and his portrait shows it quite plainly. If you want to know our founding fathers in a way words can never describe, visit this fascinating museum. It will certainly be an intimate experience because almost no one ever comes here. If you hate painting, have no interest in the men who influenced this nation over the last two hundred years, then come to see the glorious building that houses the National Portrait Gallery. It is the third oldest public building in Washington and undoubtedly one of the most spectacular Greek Revival structures in the country. The third floor contains The Great Hall, a triumph of American Victorian Renaissance style. It is also where President Lincoln's second inaugural ball was held. Visiting the Portrait Gallery may be a lonely experience, but it really is an interesting one.

Freer Gallery of Art
Twelfth Street and Independence Avenue, S.W.
Washington, D.C. 20560

Daily 10–5:30
Closed Christmas

The Freer offers the sensitive visitor a constant journey of discovery. Dedicated primarily to the art of the Orient—China, Japan, Korea and India—it also has examples of Persian, Egyptian and Syrian artifacts. The bibliophile would find their collection of Greek, Aramaic, and Armenian biblical manuscripts fascinating. Among the Western artists represented, the Gallery's most important exhibition is James McNeill Whistler's Peacock Room. Each time I've visited the Freer I've come away with a completely new set of impressions. It is a sophisticated museum that reveals itself subtly. At first, it was the fantastic early Chinese bronzes and Ming dynasty porcelains that completely captured my imagination. Perfectly displayed, they are totally accessible for study and reflection. Slight differences in color and decoration between Yung-lo (1403-24) and Hsüan-Te (1426-36) porcelains and the Ch'eng-Hua period (1465-87) (with its more painterly approach to design, fine control of the blue, and extreme delicacy of potting) suddenly become quite apparent even to a relatively unknowing observer.

For instant refreshment, if your spirit and feet are exhausted after one museum too many, sit in the gallery containing Japanese screens from the Edo period (seventeenth to nineteenth century). Let your eyes roam over their enchanted landscape of exquisitely drawn flowers, birds, and animals. Everything is vividly alive within their environment: The birds are playing with each other; an alert dog is ready to pounce at any moment on a wary crane who is very familiar with the ways of dogs. One particular screen, called "Flowers, Birds, and Animals of the Twelve Months" by Kokusai, has marvelous humor and understanding. What is most stimulating about the world of Japanese screens is the sense of entering a private landscape which exists only for you.

Each time you visit the Freer you will be astonished by its treasures; one day it may be the Persian gold, another the Japanese pottery, but you will never leave without a sense of renewal and discovery.

The Phillips Collection
1600-1621 Twenty-first Street, N.W.
Washington, D.C. 20009
(202) 387-0961

Tuesday–Saturday, 10–5
Sunday 2–7
Closed Monday, January 1, July 4,
Thanksgiving, December 25

Once a piece of art is institutionalized, a bit of the heart goes out of the viewing experience. Years ago, The Phillips Collection had a marvelously informal atmosphere. It was like dropping in for a visit with a friend who happened to own great paintings. Mr. and Mrs. Phillips had chosen their mainly French Impressionists, Post-Impressionists, and twentieth-century American works with impeccable taste and an unerring eye for the unique—the culmination point in the artist's work. Klees hung along the staircase with a nonchalance that added to their wit. The ornate music room had a Renoir and El Greco facing each other in a most exciting juxtaposition of genius. A small parlour was transformed by a large orange Degas dancer. Bonnard, Cézanne, Matisse, Braque, Marin, Dove, Goya, Daumier, Corot, to name but a few, were displayed with an unpretentiousness that made viewing a very special pleasure. There was definitely a rhyme and reason to the arrangement, but the choices were personal rather than academically correct.

Today the collection is as important as it ever was, but it is now a formalized museum in presentation. The pictures themselves are still a joy but it is no longer anyone's home. *C'est la vie!*

National Gallery of Art
Sixth Street and Constitution Avenue
Washington, D.C. 20565
(202) 737-4215

Monday–Saturday 10–5
Sunday 12–9
Summer, Daily 10–9
Closed Christmas and New Year's

The National Gallery is a fantastic museum worth a thousand visits and perfectly exhausting to cover, except in very small doses. Start by seeing the Titians: they are feast enough for anyone.

East Building, National Gallery of Art
Sixth Street and Constitution Avenue
Washington, D.C. 20565
(202) 737-4215

Monday–Saturday 10–5
Sunday 12–9
Summer, Daily 10–9
Closed Christmas and New Year's

Everything you have heard about this new building, which was constructed to handle special exhibitions organized by the National Gallery of Art, is true. It is beautiful and works like a dream for objects exhibited in it and the people seeing them. The exhibitions held in this building are changed regularly. Check closing dates of any exhibits you are particularly interested in viewing or you may miss them.

Hirschhorn Museum and Sculpture Garden
Eighth Street and Independence Avenue, S.W.

Daily 10–5:30
Closed Christmas

Joseph H. Hirschhorn's huge collection of mainly twentieth-century art is terrific. The museum, which was designed specifically for the collection, works most effectively. The Hirschhorn frequently organizes special exhibitions of great merit. Be sure to check for them when visiting. The only problem the museum has not solved is its sculpture garden. There is simply not enough space to show the individual pieces to their best advantage. It is a pity to see a big Moore desperately fighting for air. Perhaps Mr. Hirschhorn would consent to exhibiting fewer pieces on a revolving basis. It would greatly enhance the garden.

Georgetown Walk

Georgetown provides a delightful relief from the marble and granite of Washington, D.C. Located a few minutes' drive from the White House, it is easily accessible by taxi. An informal area of lovely old brick houses, tree-lined streets, restaurants, art galleries, antique shops, and boutiques, it has much the same atmosphere and charm as Greenwich Village in New York City.

M and Wisconsin streets are the heart of the shopping area and fun to stroll. I suggest starting the walk at a wonderful complex of buildings called Canal Square, off M and Thirty-first streets. These were originally factories that faced the C&O canal, which is the old towpath that runs through Georgetown. They have been imaginatively converted into a multilevel shopping center built around flowering gardens. Enter the towpath at Thirty-first Street. With its shaded cobblestone path and the sound of water passing through the locks, it is a pleasant respite for the weary traveler. Walk up Thirtieth Street from the canal toward O Street. This series of streets, with their combination of clapboard houses, Georgian mansions, and bright gardens is a remnant of nine-teenth-century Washington. N Street between Twenty-ninth and Thirty-first is also well worth seeing. No matter where you walk in this area you are within few moments of a restaurant. M Street itself, between Twenty-ninth and Thirty-first, has a number of particularly inviting-looking ones. Georgetown is the perfect antidote to one museum too many.

If you have any choice, do not visit Washington, D.C., during the summer months. The combination of heat, humidity and crowds makes it unbearable. The distances between museums in the Mall area are deceptive. On the maps they seem much closer than they actually are. I love to walk, but I'm convinced Washington, D.C., was designed for people traveling on horse rather than foot.

Inns and Restaurants

Madison Hotel
Fifteenth and M streets, N.W.
Washington, D.C. 20005
(202) 785-1000

Open all year

Breakfast, lunch, dinner. Lodging available.

Sheraton-Carlton Hotel
923 Sixteenth Street N.W. at K Street
Washington, D.C. 20006
(202) 638-2626

Open all year

Breakfast, lunch, dinner. Elegant old-fashioned hotel. Lodging available.

Hay Adams Hotel
800 Sixteenth Street N.W. at H Street
Washington, D.C. 20006
(202) 638-2260

Open all year

Breakfast, lunch, dinner. Lodging available.

The Jockey Club (Fairfax Hotel)
2100 Massachusetts Avenue
Washington, D.C. 20008
(202) 659-8000

Open all year

Lunch and dinner. Closed Sunday, legal holidays, and Saturday in summer. Charming for lunch. Right across the street from the Phillips Collection.

Montpelier (Madison Hotel)
Fifteenth and M streets, N.W.
Washington, D.C. 20005
(202) 785-1000

Open all year

Lunch and dinner. Has excellent reputation.

Cantina D'Italia
1214A Eighteenth Street, N.W.
Washington, D.C. 20036
(202) 659-1830

Open all year

Lunch and dinner. Closed Saturday, Sunday, major holidays.

My favorite place for lunch in Washington, when in the vicinity of the museums, is the cafeteria of the National Collection of Fine Arts. Everything is freshly and simply made, and there is even wine available. During mild weather, you can sit outside at a table in their beautiful garden and feed the birds.

APPENDIX

*Geographic Listing of Antique Dealers,
Museums, and Historical Houses*

CONNECTICUT

Colchester

Dealer   Liverant, Nathan, & Son

Essex

Dealer   Bealey, F.
                                Hastings House
                                Spencer, Robert

Farmington

Dealer   Cogan, Lillian Blankly

Museum   Farmington Museum
                                (Stanley-Whitman House)

Hartford

Museums   Connecticut Historical Society Museum
                                Wadsworth Atheneum

Jewett City

Dealer   Blum, Jerome
                                Walton, John

Litchfield

Dealer	Tillou, Peter
Museum	Litchfield Historical Society

New Haven

Museums	Peabody Museum Yale Center for British Art Yale University Art Gallery

Old Saybrook

Dealer	Wilson, Jane

Roxbury

Dealer	Wiese, I. M.

Stamford

Dealer	Gardiner, Avis, and Rockwell

Stonington

Dealer	Riordan, Marguerite

Wethersfield

Museum	Webb, Deane, Stevens Museum, The
Historical House	Bultolph-Williams House

DELAWARE

Wilmington

Dealer	Stockwell, David
Museum	Winterthur Museum

MAINE

Kittery Point

Historical House	Lady Pepperrell House

Portland

| Museums and Historical Houses | McLellan-Sweat House
Portland Museum of Art
Tate House
Victoria Mansion and Museum |

South Berwick

| Historical Houses | Hamilton House
Jewett House |

South Windham

| Historical House | Parson Smith House |

Standish

| Historical House | Marrett House |

Wiscasset

| Historical House | Nickels-Sortwell House |

York Harbor

| Historical House | Sayward House |

MARYLAND

Annapolis

| Museums | Hammond-Harwood House
Restored Historic Sites
State House
William Paca Garden |

Baltimore

| Museums | Baltimore Museum of Art
Carroll Mansion
Mount Clare Museum
Peale Museum
Walters Art Gallery |

Chevy Chase

Dealer   Webster Fine Art Inc.

Frederick

Dealer   Rappold, Franklin

MASSACHUSETTS

Andover

Museum   Addison Gallery of American Art

Boston

Dealers   Alberts-Langdon, Inc.
                                Bakker, James, Antiques Inc.
                                Childs Gallery
                                Firestone & Parsons
                                Gebelein Silversmiths
                                Gravert, George
                                Grossman, Hyman
                                Lowe, Samuel L., Jr., Inc.
                                Marika's Antiques
                                Moriarity, James
                                Shreve, Crump & Low & Co.
                                Vose Gallery

Museums and   American Meteorological Society
Historical   Boston Athenaeum
Houses   Boston Museum of Fine Arts, The
                                Boston Public Library
                                Harrison Gray Otis House
                                Isabella Stewart Gardner Museum
                                Women's City Club of Boston

Cambridge

Museum   Fogg Art Museum

Concord

Museum   Concord Antiquarian Museum

Deerfield

Museum   Old Deerfield Village

Groton

Dealers   Boynton, Pam
                                 Cleaves, Robert

Hancock

Museum   Hancock Shaker Village

Marblehead

Museums   Jeremiah Lee Mansion
                                 Marblehead Historical Society

Milton

Museum   Museum of the American China Trade

New Bedford

Museum   Whaling Museum

North Andover

Dealer   Hammond, Rolland

North Dartmouth

Dealer   Considine, George

Salem

Dealer   Marine Arts Gallery

Museums and   Andrew-Safford House
Historical   Assembly House
Houses   Crowninshield-Bentley House
                                 Essex Institute
                                 Gardner-Pingree House
                                 John Ward House
                                 Peabody Museum of Salem, The
                                 Peirce-Nichols House

Sturbridge

Museum   Old Sturbridge Village

Wellesley

Dealer   Den of Antiquity

Williamstown

Museum   Sterling and Francine Clark Art Institute

NEW HAMPSHIRE

Exeter

Dealer   Bacon, Roger

Hancock

Dealer   The Cobbs

Hanover

Museum   Dartmouth College Museum

Manchester

Museum   Currier Gallery of Art

Portsmouth

Museums and   Governor John Langdon Mansion Memo-
Historical   rial
Houses   John Paul Jones House
                                Richard Jackson House
                                Rundlet-May House
                                Strawbery Banke

Weare

Dealer   Stokes, Elizabeth

NEW JERSEY

Princeton

Dealer   Leigh, Ardis

Museums   Art Museum, (the), Princeton University
                                Bainbridge House
                                Morven

NEW YORK CITY

New York City

Dealers

Antique Porcelain Co., The
Blau, Doris Leslie, Inc.
Chait, Ralph M., Galleries
Dalva Brothers Inc.
Ginsburg, Benjamin, Antiquary
Hyde Park Antiques Ltd.
Kennedy Galleries, Inc.
Kornblau, Gerald
Levy, Bernard & S. Dean
Manheim, D. M. & P.
Metro Antiques
Nadler, Fred
Old Versailles Antiques
Rosenberg & Stiebel, Inc.
Russie, A la Vieille
Sack, Israel, Inc.
Shrubsole, S. J., Inc.
Schutz, Matthew, Antiques
Sigal, Maurice, Antiques Inc.
Subkoff, George Antiques
Tai, J. T., & Co. Inc.
Vernay & Jussell Inc.
Wolff, J. J., Antiques Ltd. (Incorporated
  into Vernay & Jussell Inc.)

Auction
Houses

Astor Galleries
Christies of London
Doyle, William Galleries
Manhattan Galleries
P. B. 84
Plaza Art Galleries Inc.
Phillips of London
Sotheby Parke Bernet

Museums

Asia House
China Institute
Cloisters, The
Frick Collection, The
Japan House Gallery
Metropolitan Museum of Art

Morgan Library
New-York Historical Society

New York State

Museums and   Albright-Knox Art Gallery
Historical   Boscobel
Houses   Lyndhurst
                               Olana
                               Philipsburg Manor
                               Shaker Museum
                               Van Cortlandt Manor
                               Washington Irving's Sunnyside

PENNSYLVANIA

Chadds Ford

Museum   Brandywine Art Museum

Conshohocken

Dealer   Sharpe, Matthew, and Elisabeth

Downingtown

Dealer   Bradley, Philip H., Co.

Fleurtown (Flourtown)

Dealer   Trump & Company

Philadelphia

Dealers   Bullard, Alfred Inc.
                               Fiorillo, Michael
                               Stark, Leon F. S.
                               Sterling, Charles
                               Stuempfig, Antony

Museums and   Barnes Foundation
Historical   Fairmount Park Historic Houses
Houses   Gloria Dei-Old Swedes Church
                               Hill-Physick-Keith House
                               Historical Society of Pennsylvania
                               Old City Hall
                               Old Pine Street Church

Powel House
Pennsylvania Academy of the Fine Arts
Pennsylvania Hospital
Philadelphia Museum of Art
Rodin Museum

Villanova

Dealer   Gordon, Elinor

Yardley

Dealer   Prickett, C. L.

York

Dealer   Kindig, Joseph

Museums and
Historical
Houses
     Bonham House
Golden Plough Tavern
Museum of Historical Society of York
     County

RHODE ISLAND

Newport

Museums and
Historical
Houses
     Breakers, The
Elms, The
Hunter House
Rosecliff
Sanford-Covell House

Providence

Museums and
Historical
Houses
     John Brown House, The
Museum of Art
Rhode Island Historical Society, The
Rhode Island School of Design

VERMONT

Bennington

Dealer   Four Corners-East

Middletown Springs

Dealer   Nimmo & Hart Antiques Inc.

Rockingham

Dealer   Smith, Robert Avery

Shelburne

Museum   Shelburne Museum

Woodstock

Dealer   Underwood, Hillary

WASHINGTON, D.C.

Dealer   M. Darling Ltd.

Museums   East Building, National Gallery of Art
                                    Freer Gallery of Art
                                    Hirschhorn Museum and Sculpture
                                       Garden
                                    National Collection of Fine Arts
                                    National Gallery of Art
                                    National Portrait Gallery
                                    Phillips Collection, The

INDEX OF ANTIQUE DEALERS